T0212729

Lecture Notes in Computer Science 9027

Commenced Publication in 1973
Founding and Former Series Editors:
Gerhard Goos, Juris Hartmanis, and Jan van Leeuwen

More information about this series at http://www.springer.com/series/7407

Colin Johnson · Adrian Carballal
João Correia (Eds.)

Evolutionary and Biologically Inspired Music, Sound, Art and Design

4th International Conference, EvoMUSART 2015
Copenhagen, Denmark, April 8–10, 2015
Proceedings

 Springer

Editors
Colin Johnson
University of Kent
Canterbury
UK

João Correia
University of Coimbra
Coimbra
Portugal

Adrian Carballal
University of A Coruña
A Coruña
Spain

ISSN 0302-9743   ISSN 1611-3349 (electronic)
Lecture Notes in Computer Science
ISBN 978-3-319-16497-7   ISBN 978-3-319-16498-4 (eBook)
DOI 10.1007/978-3-319-16498-4

Library of Congress Control Number: 2015933499

LNCS Sublibrary: SL1 – Theoretical Computer Science and General Issues

Springer Cham Heidelberg New York Dordrecht London

Cover illustration: Designed by Mauro Castelli, ISEGI, Universidade Nova de Lisboa, Portugal

Printed on acid-free paper

Springer International Publishing AG Switzerland is part of Springer Science+Business Media
(www.springer.com)

Preface

EvoMUSART 2015—the 4th International Conference and the 13th European event on Biologically Inspired Music, Sound, Art, and Design—took place during April 8–10, 2015 in Copenhagen, Denmark. It brought together researchers who use biologically inspired computer techniques for artistic, aesthetic, and design purposes. Researchers presented their latest work in the intersection of the fields of computer science, evolutionary systems, art, and aesthetics. As always, the atmosphere was fun, friendly, and constructive.

EvoMUSART has grown steadily since its first edition in 2003 in Essex, UK, when it was one of the Applications of Evolutionary Computing workshops. Since 2012 it has been a full conference as part of the evo* colocated events.

EvoMUSART 2015 received 43 submissions. The peer-review process was rigorous and double-blind. The international Programme Committee, listed below, was composed of 59 members from 21 countries. EvoMUSART continued to provide useful feedback to authors: among the papers sent for full review, there were on average 2.78 reviews per paper. It also continued to ensure quality by keeping acceptance rates low: 12 papers were accepted for oral presentation (27.9 % acceptance rate), and 11 for poster presentation (25.6 % acceptance rate).

This volume of proceedings collects the accepted papers. As always, the EvoMUSART proceedings cover a wide range of topics and application areas, including: generative approaches to music, graphics, game content, and narrative; music information retrieval; computational aesthetics; the mechanics of interactive evolutionary computation; and the art theory of evolutionary computation.

We thank all authors for submitting their work, including those whose work was not accepted for presentation. As always, the standard of submissions was high, and good papers had to be rejected.

The work of reviewing was done voluntarily and generally without official recognition from the institutions where reviewers are employed. Nevertheless, good reviewing is essential to a healthy conference. Therefore, we particularly thank the members of the Program Committee for their hard work and professionalism in providing constructive and fair reviews.

EvoMUSART 2015 was part of the evo* 2015 event, which included three additional conferences: EuroGP 2015, EvoCOP 2015, and EvoApplications 2015. Many people helped to make this event a success.

We thank the National Museum of Denmark at Copenhagen for offering its facilities for this event. We thank the local organizing team of Paolo Burelli (Aalborg University) and Sebastian Risi (IT University of Copenhagen).

We thank Marc Schoenauer (INRIA Saclay, Île-de-France) for continued assistance in providing MyReview conference management system. We thank Pablo García Sánchez (University of Granada) and Mauro Castelli, (ISEGI; Universidade Nova de Lisboa) for evo* publicity. We also thank Mauro for this year's logo design.

We want to especially acknowledge our invited speakers: Pierre-Yves Oudeyer (INRIA, Paris) and Paulien Hogeweg (Utrecht University).

Last but certainly not least, we especially want to express our heartfelt thanks to Jennifer Willies and the Institute for Informatics and Digital Innovation at Edinburgh Napier University. Ever since its inaugural meeting in 1998 this event has relied on her dedicated work and continued involvement and we do not exaggerate when we state that without her, evo* could not have achieved its current status.

April 2015

Colin Johnson
Adrian Carballal
João Correia

Organization

EvoMUSART 2015 was part of evo* 2015, Europe's premier colocated events in the field of evolutionary computing, which also included the conferences EuroGP 2015, EvoCOP 2015, EvoBIO 2015, and EvoApplications 2015.

Organizing Committee

Conference Chairs

Colin Johnson   University of Kent, UK
Adrian Carballal   University of A Coruña, Spain

Publication Chair

João Correia   University of Coimbra, Portugal

Programme Committee

Alain Lioret   Paris 8 University, France
Alan Dorin   Monash University, Australia
Alejandro Pazos   University of A Coruña, Spain
Amilcar Cardoso   University of Coimbra, Portugal
Amy K. Hoover   University of Central Florida, USA
Andrew Brown   Griffith University, Australia
Andrew Gildfind   Google, Inc., Australia
Andrew Horner   University of Science and Technology, Hong Kong
Anna Ursyn   University of Northern Colorado, USA
Antonino Santos   University of A Coruña, Spain
Antonios Liapis   IT University of Copenhagen, Denmark
Arne Eigenfeldt   Simon Fraser University, Canada
Benjamin Smith   Indianapolis University, Purdue University,
                         Indianapolis, USA
Bill Manaris   College of Charleston, USA
Brian Ross   Brock University, Canada
Carlos Grilo   Instituto Politécnico de Leiria, Portugal
Christian Jacob   University of Calgary, Canada
Dan Ashlock   University of Guelph, Canada
Dan Ventura   Brigham Young University, USA
Daniel Jones   Goldsmiths College, University of London, UK
Daniel Silva   University of Coimbra, Portugal
Douglas Repetto   Columbia University, USA
Eduardo Miranda   University of Plymouth, UK
Eleonora Bilotta   University of Calabria, Italy
Gary Greenfield   University of Richmond, USA

Contents

Generative Music with Stochastic Diffusion Search

Asmaa Majid Al-Rifaie[1]($\boxtimes$) and Mohammad Majid Al-Rifaie[2]

[1] Department of Computing, Goldsmiths University
of London International Programme, London, UK
as.majid.as@gmail.com
[2] Department of Computing, Goldsmiths University
of London, London SE14 6NW, UK
m.majid@gold.ac.uk

Abstract. This paper introduces an approach for using a swarm intelligence algorithm, Stochastic Diffusion Search (SDS) – inspired by one species of ants, *Leptothorax acervorum* – in order to generate music from plain text. In this approach, SDS is adapted in such a way to vocalise the agents, to hear their "chit-chat". While the generated music depends on the input text, the algorithm's search capability in locating the words in the input text is reflected in the duration and dynamic of the resulting musical notes. In other words, the generated music depends on the behaviour of the algorithm and the communication between its agents. This novel approach, while staying loyal to the original input text, when run each time, 'vocalises' the input text in varying 'flavours'.

Keywords: Swarm intelligence · Stochastic diffusion search · Generative music · Nature-inspired algorithm

1 Introduction

Nature inspired algorithms have been the source of many inspirations in arts and sciences. Swarm intelligence algorithms as one category of nature-inspired algorithms have been used increasingly to solve various optimisation problems. The behaviour exhibited by swarm intelligence techniques are inspired by the interaction of social animals and insects in nature: fish schooling, bugs swarming, birds flocking, ant colonies foraging, bacterial growth, animal herding, brood sorting by ants, etc. Examples of swarm intelligence algorithms are Particle Swarm Optimisation [1], Genetic Algorithm [2] and Ant Colony Optimistion [3].

Many techniques derived from swarm intelligence algorithms have been used to produce generative music. In the last several years, the development of compositional computer programs have been attracting several artists, musicians and researchers. While these approaches are mostly driven forward primarily from academic theory without the involvements of many composers, generative music has been a thriving field of research [4].

© Springer International Publishing Switzerland 2015
C. Johnson et al. (Eds.): EvoMUSART 2015, LNCS 9027, pp. 1–14, 2015.
DOI: 10.1007/978-3-319-16498-4_1

This work presents a novel approach utilising a swarm intelligence algorithm's optimisation capabilities in order to introduce a method for generating music.

In this paper, a swarm intelligence algorithm, Stochastic Diffusion Search, is explained, followed by details on how this algorithm is used to generate music based on an input text. Then a few examples of the generated music are presented and discussed. Conclusion and possible future research are included at the end of the paper.

2   Stochastic Diffusion Search

Stochastic Diffusion Search (SDS) [5,6], first introduced in 1989, belongs to the extended family of Swarm Intelligence algorithms to solve best-fit pattern recognition and matching problems. SDS has a strong mathematical framework, which describes the behaviour of the algorithm by investigating its resource allocation, convergence to global optimum, robustness and minimal convergence criteria and linear time complexity.

In order to introduce SDS, the Mining Game metaphor is presented (for more details please see [5]):

- At the start of the mining process each miner is randomly allocated a hill (his hill hypothesis, h).
- Then each miner selects a random region on his hill to mine.
- Whether the miner is happy or not depends on whether he finds gold.
- At the end of the day the miners congregate and over the evening each miner who is unhappy selects another miner at random to talk to. If the chosen miner is happy, he happily shares with his colleague the location of his hill (that is, he communicates his hill hypothesis, h, which thus both share and each picks a random region within the shared hill). Conversely, if the chosen miner is unhappy he says nothing and the selecting miner is once more reduced to selecting a new hill (or hypothesis) – identifying the hill he is to mine the next day – at random.

In any SDS search, each agent maintains a hypothesis, h, defining a possible problem solution. SDS has two phases:

- Test Phase (testing gold availability)
- Diffusion Phase (congregation and exchanging of information)

It is shown that using this algorithm, after few days, the miners will be able to find the hill where there is the maximum amount of gold available.

2.1   Method of Communication

Communication is important in all swarm intelligence algorithms, including SDS. In one species of ant, *Leptothorax acervorum*, a tandem calling mechanism (one-to-one) is used for communication. In this method, the ant that finds the resource location, recruits a single ant on its return to the nest, therefore the location of the resource is physically publicised [7]. In SDS, direct one-to-one communication (which is similar to tandem calling recruitment) is used. However the behaviour of the agents in SDS is simpler than the recruitment behavior of real ants.

2.2   SDS Search Example

In order to show how SDS works one search example will be discussed. The search example here shows how to find a set of letters within a larger string of letters. The goal is to find a 3-letter model (Table 1) in a 13-letter search space (Table 2). For simplicity purposes only three agents are assumed for this example.

Table 1. Model

Index	0	1	2
Model	N	O	T

Table 2. Search space

Index	0	1	2	3	4	5	6	7	8	9	10	11	12
Search Space	T	O	B	E	O	R	N	O	T	T	O	B	E

In this example, a hypothesis, which is a potential problem solution, identifies three adjacent letters in the search space (e.g. hypothesis '2' refers to B-E-O, hypothesis '10' refers to O-B-E). At first each agent initially randomly picks a hypothesis from the search space (Table 3)

- The first agent points to the 5th entry of the search space; in order to partially evaluate this entry, it randomly picks one of the letters (e.g. the first one, R) R N O
- The second agent points to the 9th entry and randomly picks the third letter (B): T O B
- The third agent refers to the 1st entry in the search space and randomly picks the third letter (E): O B E

Table 3. Iteration 1

Agent num:	1	2	3
Hypothesis:	$\underset{R-N-O}{5}$	$\underset{T-O-B}{9}$	$\underset{O-B-E}{1}$
Letter picked:	1st	3rd	3rd
Status:	X	X	X

The letters picked are compared to the corresponding letters in the model, which is N-O-T.

- First letter from the first agent (R) is compared with the first letter from the model (N), because they are not the same, the agent is set inactive.
- For the second and third agents, letters 'B' and 'E' are compared against 'T' from the model. Since none of the letters correspond to the letter in the model, the status of the agents are set inactive.

In the next step (diffusion phase), each inactive agent randomly selects another agent. If the selected agent is active, the inactive agent adopts the hypothesis of the active agent. If the selected agent is inactive, the selecting agent generates a random hypothesis. As hinted earlier, communications between agents occur during the diffusion phase. Assume that the first agent chooses the second one; since the second agent is inactive, the first agent must choose a new random hypothesis from the search space. Figure 1 shows the communications between agents. The process is repeated for the other two agents. As the agents are inactive, they all choose new random hypotheses (see Table 4).

Fig. 1. Agents communication

Table 4. Iteration 2

Agent num:	1	2	3
Hypothesis:	$\dfrac{6}{N-O-T}$	$\dfrac{10}{O-B-E}$	$\dfrac{0}{T-O-B}$
Letter picked:	2nd	3rd	1st
Statuse:	√	X	X

In Table 4, the second and third agents do not refer to their corresponding letter in the model, so they become inactive. The first agent, with hypothesis '6', chooses the 2nd letter (O) and compares it with the 2nd letter of the model (O). Since the letters are the same, the agent becomes active. The same process is repeated for the other two agents, and since the letters do not match the letters in the model, they are set inactive. This process is repeated until all agents are active. It is important to note that the number of agents is irrelevant to the number of letters in the model (e.g. it is possible to have 5 agents and a two-letter model).

3   Generative Music

In generative music, various computational techniques are used; some are closely related to swarm intelligence and some have been generated using other techniques. Generative music based on swarm intelligence uses the dynamic properties of the swarms; these properties are tightly linked to the communication and therefore movement of the swarms throughout the possible search space.

Using these properties, scientists and artists develop creative music. In one such paper, "Music Composition with Interactive Evolutionary Computation" [9] the authors describe a new approach to the music composition by means of interactive evolutionary computation (IEC) which discusses the interactive musical composition system. It is claimed that system can generate musical phrases by combining genetic algorithms and genetic programming.

Another attempt and more recently, "Experiments with Particle Swarm Optimization" [10] uses Particle Swarm Optimisation (PSO) [1] which is a swarm intelligence and evolutionary computation technique, developed in 1995, and is inspired by the social behaviour of bird flocking, to generate music. In particle swarms, members of the swarm neither have knowledge about the global behaviour of the swarm nor global information about the environment, the local interactions of the swarms result in a complex collective behaviour, such as flocking, herding, schooling, exploration and foraging. In this work, particles are made to follow a hypothetical point (focal point, fp); each agent selects a random point between A and B (fp) and moves to it until they reach the target. This example uses PSO to develop continuous music so swarms have to continue their movement; at the time that any agent's fitness is below a predefined threshold, focal point randomly moves to a new position in a search space and the particles search begins.

For a more detailed account of other related works in generative music using various computational techniques the readers are referred to "Evolutionary computer music" [4].

There are other works related to sonification of text. In one such work [11] a platform is proposed that allows the creation of user-generated mapping for the sonification of text messages and arbitrary clients to sonify text messages using a web-based API. While there are other works generating melodies from text input, SDS generated music is unique in its ability to generate non-identical musics from one input text.

4 Generating Music with SDS

A sentence is formed of few words and each word is comprised of letters. Each letter has its own tone and every word has its individual concept and meaning. With these concepts, humans aim to communicate with each other just like the agents in SDS algorithm. Humans, among other ways, communicate through text and the agents of SDS (as shown in the Sect. 2.2) communicate with each other through the words and letters.

The aim of this paper is to represent an input text as the sound they create; the output sound is based on letters, words and ultimately a longer string of characters. In other words, SDS is adapted in such a way to vocalise the agents, to hear their "chit-chat!" while communicating with each other throughout the search space.

The task of generating music is guided by taking the three below-mentioned parameters into account:

1. Pitch
2. Note Duration
3. Dynamic (or volume)

These values are determined by the input text as well as the behaviour of the algorithm while processing the input through its test and diffusion phases.

The next part explains the link between the above-mentioned parameters, the input text and SDS. Afterwards the process through which SDS is tasked to generate the music is explained.

The Relation Between Pitches and Letters. Each letter (or pair of letters) is mapped onto a musical note (an individual pitch which has its own MIDI number). In order to assign a MIDI number to a character or pair of characters, letter frequency will be used. Herbert S. Zim [12], in his classic introductory cryptography text "Codes and Secret Writing", gives the English letter frequency sequence as well as the most common pair of letters and the most common doubled letters (see Table 5).

Table 5. Letters frequency

Letter frequency	ETAON, RISHD, LFCMU, GYPWB, VKJXQ, Z
Pairs of letters	TH HE AN RE ER IN ON AT ND ST ES EN OF TE ED OR TI HI AS TO
Doubled letters	LL EE SS OO TT FF RR NN PP CC

Music is made of a set of 12 notes and each one of these notes has its individual MIDI numbers. The set of letters in Table 5 are divided into 12 separated sets where each will be associated with one of the 12 notes (see Table 6). One of the topics for future research is to conduct an investigation to find a better way in which letters are assigned to their possibly corresponding musical notes.

Using Table 6, an example is given on how to map a simple text (e.g. 'Hello World') into the corresponding MIDI numbers (see Table 7).

Note Duration and Dynamic. Duration refers to a certain amount of time or a particular time interval which may be described as short/long or with varying duration of time. This property plays a crucial role in forming one of the bases of rhythm within music. In music, dynamic refers to the volume of a sound or a note. Both of these parameters (i.e. duration and dynamic) will be defined using SDS parameters individually; more details are provided below in Sect. 4.2.

4.1 The Parameters of SDS

Each agent in SDS has a status which is a boolean value; this entails that an agent can be either active/inactive, true/false, or happy/unhappy. For SDS to generate music, three parameters are used. These parameters are based on the global number of agents (in all iterations) in each of the following categories:

Table 6. Frequencies and notes

Notes num	Notes	Sets Freq	MIDI Num
1	C	ETAON	72
2	C#	RISHD	73
3	D	LFCMU	74
4	D#	GYPWB	75
5	E	VKJXQ	76
6	F	Z	77
7	F#	TH TE TI TO RE	78
8	G	AN AT AS HE HI	79
9	G#	ON OF OR ND ST	80
10	A	ER ES EN ED IN	81
11	A#	LL EE SS OO TT	82
12	B	FF RR NN PP CC	83

Table 7. Example: Converting each letter or pair of letters to the corresponding musical note and MIDI number

Hello world		
Characters	Notes	MIDI
he	G	79
ll	A#	82
o	C	72
	F	space = 77
w	D#	75
or	G#	80
l	D	74
d	C#	73
	F	space = 77

1. Number of Lucky agents (l_g)
2. Number of Happy agents or (h_g)
3. Number of Unhappy agents or (u_g)

A lucky Agent is an unhappy agent randomly picking an agent whose status is true (i.e. happy). Deciding which agent is lucky happens during the Diffusion phase, whereas determining whether an agent is happy or unhappy occurs during the Test phase.

The following should hold regarding the above-mentioned parameters:

$$NP = h_g + u_g \tag{1}$$

$$l_g \leq u_g \tag{2}$$

where NP is the population size.

In this paper, the population size is set to 20. Given that SDS iterates 10 times, the maximum number of unhappy agents in each iteration is 20; therefore the maximum number of unhappy agents over the whole iterations is 200.

4.2 The Relation Between SDS and Music

In SDS, a model (or goal) is needed which can be one word. Initially the first word is set as a model, which is searched in the search space using SDS and the above mentioned three values are calculated and used subsequently to generate the duration and dynamic values.

Given that each character or pair of characters are to be converted into a musical note, each word is assigned as a model n times (where n is the length of the model according to Table 6; therefore a pair of letters will be considered as one). This process is repeated until reaching the end of the search space.

Searching for each model in the search space results in different values of SDS parameters. The number of lucky agents and unhappy agents will change from word to word. Additionally, even if each word is searched twice, due of the nature of the swarm intelligence algorithm, there is no guarantee that these figures stay the same in each run. In order to generate a musical note for each character in the search space, the mining process has to run as many times as the number of the corresponding musical notes (see Table 7 for an example).

Consider the model to be 'music'. The number of corresponding musical notes in this word is 5. Therefore, the mining process (i.e. test and diffusion phases) has to run five times, each time generating the necessary information (duration and dynamic) for that particular musical note (e.g. the first run will result in generating relevant values for the duration and dynamic of the musical note 'm'; the second run, for the musical note 'u' and so forth). This way, each character (or pair of characters) has separately generated values for the number of local unhappy agents (u_l) and the number of local lucky agents (l_l) which will be used to calculate the duration and dynamic at a later stage.

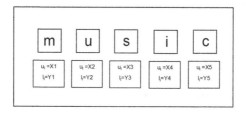

Fig. 2. SDS parameters for '*music*'

See Fig. 2 which shows that u_l, l_l values need to be generated for each character (or pair of characters) within the model. As shown in Fig. 2, each character of the word '*music*' is separated, this is because this word does not contain any of the pairs of letters shown in Table 6. However, when the word '*food*' becomes the model of the algorithm (see Fig. 3), the mining process has to run only three times. This is due to the presence of the pair '*oo*' which forms one musical note (see Table 6).

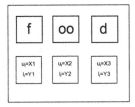

Fig. 3. SDS parameters for '*food*'

4.3   How SDS Generates Music

Algorithm 1 explains the process through which SDS processes the input text which will then get converted into music.

Algorithm 1. Generating music with SDS

```
FOR I = 1 TO N
  Choosing I'th word as model

  FOR J = 1 TO M
    Run SDS for T iterations
    Store the numbers of local unhappy and lucky agents
  END J

  Store the numbers of global unhappy and lucky agents

END I

- N is the number of words in the search space.
- M is the number of musical notes in the current model.
- T (the total number of iterations) is set to 10.
- SDS population size is set to 20 (NP = 20).
```

As mentioned earlier, the number of lucky agents impacts the duration of the corresponding note. In other words, a character (or pair of characters) with more lucky agents is "luckier" and plays for longer. The following formulas are used to calculate the duration and dynamic of each note:

$$l_n = \frac{l_g \times S_r}{n} \tag{3}$$

l_n is the normalised lucky agents; l_g is the number of global lucky agents in all iterations; S_r indicates that agents are averaged over 5 (i.e. $S_r = 5$); and n is the total number of notes in the input text.

After normalising the lucky agents, the following is used to determine the duration:

$$du = \frac{\alpha \times l_l}{l_n} \tag{4}$$

where du is the duration; l_l is the number of lucky agents for each note; and α is a constant value that adjusts the duration of the note and is set to 2.

On the other hand, the number of unhappy agents has effect on the volume of the note, which is calculated using the formulas below:

$$u_n = \frac{u_g \times S_r}{n} \tag{5}$$

$$dy = \frac{\beta \times u_l}{u_n} \tag{6}$$

where dy is the dynamic; u_n is the normalised unhappy agents; u_g is the total number of unhappy agents for all the notes; u_l is the number of unhappy agents for each note; and β is a constant value which adjusts the volume of the machine's speaker and is set to 10000.

4.4 Music Sheet

For each generated music in this paper a music sheet or score is presented. Therefore, the musical notes are placed on the staff according to Table 6. See Fig. 4 which illustrates where each note should be positioned on the staff.

Fig. 4. Staff-and-clef

Note Name (US name)	Note Shape	Time Duration
Whole Note	𝅝	2 (sec)
Half Note	𝅗𝅥	1 (sec)
Quarter Note	𝅘𝅥	1/2 (sec)
Eighth Note	𝅘𝅥𝅮	1/4 (sec)
Sixteenth Note	𝅘𝅥𝅯	1/8 (sec)
Thirty Second Note	𝅘𝅥𝅰	1/16 (sec)

Fig. 5. Note duration

Given each note has its corresponding duration (see Sect. 4.2), this needs to be reflected in the generated music as well as the score. Having used the time signature of 4:4 here, whenever the duration of a particular note towards the end of a bar exceeds this figure, a silent note is placed and the note is moved after the bar. The link between the notes and their corresponding time duration is shown in Fig. 5.

4.5 Sample Set of Generated Music

The scores in Fig. 6 illustrate two system runs, using a sample input text: "hello music sds welcome to the reality". The details of musical notes, the corresponding dynamics and durations and the algorithm's generated values are presented in Table 8. The recorded musics[1], correspond to the music sheets and the values in the table. The music library imported to generate the output is Sound Cipher [13], where piano and guitar effects are also added to the music.

Fig. 6. Music sheets showing two runs

Fig. 7. Music sheet for the third run

---

[1] Follow this link to listen to three runs of the music generated by the algorithm based on the input text 'hello music sds welcome to the reality': https://www.dropbox.com/s/bh4icqsdlpz04re/SDSMusic.zip?dl=0.

Table 8. Values generated by SDS while processing the input text

			First Run				Second Run				
			Before Normalization		After Normalization		Before Normalization		After Normalization		
			u_l	l_l	Dynamic	Duration	u_l	l_l	Dynamic	Duration	Pitch
1	Model :	hello	he	70	18	1261	0.387	48	19	905	0.431	79
2		hello	ll	111	24	2000	0.516	100	23	1886	0.522	82
3		hello	o	81	21	1459	0.451	126	32	2377	0.727	72
4		hello		89	30	1603	0.645	79	21	1490	0.477	77
5	Model :	music	m	47	18	846	0.387	148	18	2792	0.409	74
6		music	u	31	15	558	0.322	52	20	981	0.454	74
7		music	s	84	22	1513	0.473	86	19	1622	0.431	73
8		music	i	77	22	1387	0.473	82	24	1547	0.545	73
9		music	c	134	20	2414	0.430	99	20	1867	0.454	74
10		music		114	19	2054	0.408	43	14	811	0.318	77
11	Model :	sds	s	80	15	1441	0.322	75	20	1415	0.454	73
12		sds	d	143	21	2576	0.451	60	27	1132	0.613	73
13		sds	s	45	17	810	0.365	53	18	1000	0.409	73
14		sds		130	20	2342	0.430	44	18	830	0.409	77
15	Model :	welcome	w	62	21	1117	0.451	104	16	1962	0.363	75
16		welcome	e	124	24	2234	0.516	61	17	1150	0.386	72
17		welcome	l	47	15	846	0.322	80	24	1509	0.545	74
18		welcome	c	134	19	2414	0.408	50	17	943	0.386	74
19		welcome	o	58	25	1045	0.537	97	22	1830	0.5	72
20		welcome	m	50	19	900	0.408	143	20	2698	0.454	74
21		welcome	e	144	21	2594	0.451	99	23	1867	0.522	72
22		welcome		139	29	2504	0.623	68	22	1283	0.5	77
23	Model :	to	to	94	29	1693	0.623	148	26	2792	0.590	78
24		to		125	39	2252	0.838	88	21	1660	0.477	77
25	Model :	the	th	87	23	1567	0.494	85	20	1603	0.454	78
26		the	e	61	19	1099	0.408	109	19	2056	0.431	72
27		the		101	21	1819	0.451	75	22	1415	0.5	77
28	Model:	reality	re	187	10	3369	0.215	190	2	3584	0.045	78
29		reality	a	193	2	3477	0.043	188	8	3547	0.181	72
30		reality	l	181	10	3261	0.215	192	2	3622	0.0454	74
31		reality	i	189	8	3405	0.172	183	11	3452	0.25	73
32		reality	t	191	5	3441	0.107	184	7	3471	0.159	72
33		reality	y	188	6	3387	0.129	180	7	3396	0.159	75
34		reality		184	10	3315	0.215	185	5	3490	0.113	77
			Total:3775	Total:637			Total:3604	Total:604			

The generated musics shown here have a noticeable similarity[2] both while listening to the music or by looking at the music sheets. This is due to using the same seed (input text) for all three runs. These musics, while exhibiting loyalty towards the input text, have their own unique 'swarmic flavours' which distinguish them from one another; this is because each time SDS algorithm is run to process the input text, it returns varying dynamics and durations. This difference in dynamics and duration in each run is the reflection of the searching behaviour of the swarms.

In other words, the generated musics from different inputs have their own musical features; equally, those musics generated from the same seed, demonstrate 'loyalty' to the input text while at the same time exhibit their unique 'swarmic flavours'. Figure 7 shows three runs off the same text.

5   Conclusion

This paper introduced a music generating algorithm based on Stochastic Diffusion Search (SDS) which is a swarm intelligence algorithm mimicking the

---

[2] While different, the similarities between all three music sheets are evident. In every run, the differences in note values and rest values are noticeable (i.e. by comparing all the first bars of all the three runs with each other, you can see how the note values are different and also there is one rest value in the third run).

behaviour of one species of ants, *Leptothorax acervorum*. The input to the system is a plain text which also forms the search space for the swarm intelligence algorithm. Each letter or pair of letters are allocated a musical note; this process is based on the English letter frequency sequence as detailed by Herbert S. Zim [12], in his classic introductory cryptography text "Codes and Secret Writing" where each letter as well as the most common pair of letters and the most common doubled letters are highlighted. The swarm intelligence algorithm then generates the dynamic and duration of each note. This process leads to generating a music each time the system is run.

While the final generated musics from the same input have resemblance with each other (representing the original input text and the corresponding musical notes which are determined by the English letter frequency sequence), due to varying dynamic and duration, which are dependant on the searching behaviour of the swarm intelligence algorithm in each run, the output musics have a unique 'swarmic flavour'. In other words, while the musics generated from one input text are 'loyal' to their input, the behaviour of the swarms induces enough 'freedom' to ensure originality in the each resulting music.

Among the topics for future research is to investigate and find a better approach in which letters are assigned to their corresponding musical notes. Additionally rhythm is yet to be fully implemented in the system.

References

1. Eberhart, R., Kennedy, J.: A new optimizer using particle swarm theory. In: Proceedings of the Sixth International Symposium on Micro Machine and Human Science, vol. 43. IEEE, New York (1995)
2. Goldberg, D.E.: Genetic Algorithms in Search. Optimization and Machine Learning. Addison-Wesley Longman Publishing Co., Inc., Boston (1989)
3. Dorigo, M., Birattari, M., Stutzle, T.: Ant colony optimization. IEEE Comput. Intell. Mag. **1**(4), 28–39 (2006)
4. Miranda, E.R., Al Biles, J.: Evolutionary Computer Music. Springer, London (2007)
5. Al-Rifaie, M.M., Bishop, M.: Stochastic diffusion search review. Paladyn J. Behav. Rob. **4**, 155–173 (2013)
6. Bishop, J.: Stochastic searching networks. In: Proceedings of the 1st IEE Conference on Artificial Neural Networks, London, pp. 329–331 (1989)
7. Möglich, M., Maschwitz, U., Hölldobler, B.: Tandem calling: a new kind of signal in ant communication. Science **186**(4168), 1046–1047 (1974)
8. Blackwell, T.: Swarming and music. In: Miranda, E.R., Al-Biles, J. (eds.) Evolutionary Computer Music, pp. 194–217. Springer, London (2007)
9. Tokui, N., Iba, H.: Music composition with interactive evolutionary computation. In: Proceedings of the 3rd International Conference on Generative Art, vol. 17, pp. 215–226 (2000)
10. Herber., N.: Experiments with particle swarm optimization (2004–2011). http://www.x-tet.com/pf2004-10/pso.html

11. Alt, F., Pfleging, B., Schmidt, A.: Sonify-a platform for the sonification of text messages. In: Mensch & Computer, pp. 149–158 (2013)
12. Zim, H.S.: Codes and Secret Writing. W. Morrow, New York (1948)
13. Brown, A.R.: Sound Musicianship: Understanding the Crafts of Music, vol. 4. Cambridge Scholars Publishing, Newcastle upon Tyne (2012)

Music with Unconventional Computing: Towards a Step Sequencer from Plasmodium of *Physarum Polycephalum*

Edward Braund$^{(\boxtimes)}$ and Eduardo Miranda

Interdisciplinary Centre for Computer Music Research (ICCMR),
Plymouth University, Plymouth, UK
edward.braund@students.plymouth.ac.uk, eduardo.miranda@plymouth.ac.uk

Abstract. The field of computer music has evolved in tandem with advances made in computer science. We are interested in how the developing field of unconventional computation may provide new pathways for music and related technologies. In this paper, we outline our initial work into harnessing the behaviour of the biological computing substrate *Physarum polycephalum* for a musical step sequencer. The plasmodium of *Physarum polycephalum* is an amorphous unicellular organism, which moves like a giant amoeba as it navigates its environment for food. Our research manipulates the organism's route-efficient propagation characteristics in order to create a growth environment for musical/sound arrangement. We experiment with this device in two different scenarios: sample triggering and MIDI note triggering using sonification techniques.

Keywords: *Physarum polycephalum* · Sonification · Unconventional computing · Computer music · Future music · Biomusic · Step sequencer · Bionic engineering

1 Introduction

Computing technology has played a pivotal part in the development of music over the last 80 years. The field of computer music was conceived during the 1950s, where a computer scientist with a musical background manipulated the architecture of the CSIRAC machine to play a selection of popular melodies [1]. Since this early interdisciplinary endeavour, advances in computer science have had a significant impact on both the way audio media is consumed and produced. Therefore, it is likely that future computational advancements will impact the field of music. We are interested in researching how the developing field of unconventional computation may provide new pathways for music and related technologies.

During the past 70 years, what we consider to be conventional computation (Turing computation [2] and the von Neumann architecture [3]) has advanced at a rapid frequency. Amongst computer scientists, there is a growing consensus that we will one day reach the limit of today's conventional computing

© Springer International Publishing Switzerland 2015
C. Johnson et al. (Eds.): EvoMUSART 2015, LNCS 9027, pp. 15–26, 2015.
DOI: 10.1007/978-3-319-16498-4_2

paradigms, which is a result of our ever-growing need for faster and more efficient technology. As a result of this, research into new, unconventional, computing models is building in momentum and popularity. Defining what constitutes an unconventional computing scheme is a matter of personal orthodoxy. As an overview, words from Toffoli give a general definition of what an unconventional computing scheme is: *"a computing scheme that today is viewed as unconventional may well be so because its time hasn't come yet-or is already gone"* [4].

Research into new unconventional computing schemes develops new concept algorithms and computing architectures inspired by or physically implemented in chemical, biological and physical systems. Current unconventional computing paradigms include quantum computing, DNA computing, molecular computing and reaction-diffusion computing [5]. Researchers state that if the same level of development is mirrored in the advancement of new, unconventional, computation then the *"world of computation will be unrecognisably different from today"* [6].

In computer music, there is a tradition of experimenting with emerging technologies. Until recent years, developments put forward by the field of unconventional computation have been left unexploited, which is likely due to the field's heavy theoretical nature, complexity and lack of accessible prototypes. Lately, with research into unconventional modes of computation increasing, the accessibility of prototypes has been widening. This increased accessibility has enabled computer musicians to begin exploring the potential of emerging unconventional computing paradigms [7].

Although research into unconventional computing in music is in its infancy, there are a number of projects beginning to emerge. To the extent of our knowledge, these mainly adopt sonification approaches. One early example explored using chemical computing by way of a Cellular Automata model to control a granular synthesiser [8]. Another example investigated synthesising sounds with a hybrid wetware-silicon device using in vitro neuronal networks [9].

Regarding our research, there are many unconventional computing prototypes currently being developed that could hold potential for computer music. However, many of these require expensive laboratory equipment along with specialist knowledge to allow computational prototypes to be developed. At this stage of our research we needed a more accessible medium to begin conducting our experiments. Uniquely, the biological organism *Physarum polycephalum* (hence forth known as *P.polycephalum*) requires comparatively less resources than most other unconventional computing substrates: the organism is cheap, openly obtainable, considered safe to use and has a robustness that allows for ease of application. It is for these reasons we have selected *P.polycephalum* to begin investigating how new, biological, computing schemes may offer new pathways for music.

1.1 *P.polycephalum*

P.polycephalum (Fig. 1) is a unicellular organism of the order *Physarales*, subclass *Myxogastromycetidae*, class *Myxomycete*. From spore germination

P.polycephalum exhibits a complex thirteen-phase lifecycle, normally residing in cool, moist and dark environments. During its vegetative plasmodium phase, *P.polycephalum* exists as an amorphous single cell (visible via the human eye) with a myriad of diploid nuclei, which moves along gradients of chemical and light stimuli. The plasmodium propagates towards chemo-attractants and away from chemo-repellents, which have formed a gradient on a substrate. Propagation is achieved by extending pseudopods, which disperse forming a search front while building a route-efficient network of protoplasmic veins connecting foraging efforts and areas of colonisation (Fig. 1). Upon discovery of food, the plasmodium surrounds it with pseudopods and feeds through the process of phagocytosis, ingesting nutrients that are spread across the organism via shuttle streaming. Conversely, if matter is discovered which does not entice the appetite of the plasmodium, the area is avoided.

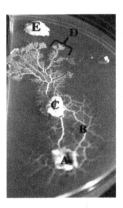

Fig. 1. A photograph of plasmodium of *P.polycephalum* showing: (A) inoculation of plasmodium into the environment, (B) protoplasmic network connecting areas of colonisation, (C) colonised food sources, and (D) extending pseudopods forming a search front along a gradient to food marked by (E).

The topology of plasmodium has been described as a network of biochemical oscillators: waves of contraction or relaxation which collide inducing shuttle streaming, distributing nutrients across the organism. This intracellular activity produces fluctuating levels of electrical potential as pressure within the cell changes. Typically this is in the range of $\pm 50\,mV$, displaying oscillations at periods of approximately 50–200 s with amplitudes of ± 5–10 mV [10], dependent on the organism's physiological state. When recorded in isolated zones of colonisation, patterns emerge in accordance with spatial activity and environmental conditions. Research has been put forward which highlights that such patterns can be used to accurately denote behaviour [11].

In regards to unconventional computing, *P.polycephalum* has been used for a wide variety of computations, such as execution of logic gate schemes [12], colour sensing [13] and robot manoeuvring [14] (see [15] for a collection of computing schemes harnessing *P.polycephalum* and directions for its use).

In this paper, we implement a step sequencer exploiting *P.polycephalum's* route-efficient foraging behaviour and fluctuating electrical potential. Our rationale for implementing such a device is derived from the organism's ability to solve mazes, find shortest paths and develop networks linking sources of nutrients. The idea of a *P.polycephalum* step sequencer was conceived when reviewing sets of time-lapse images with correlating electrical activities. We noticed how the organism oscillates protoplasm around a network of veins to colonised regions, and how this relates to the architecture of a musical step sequencer. We conceptualised a sequencer where *P.polycephalum* controlled step activation through propagation trajectories/colonisation, and sound event triggering with fluctuating levels of electrical activity.

2   The *P.polycephalum* Step Sequencer

A natural characteristic of plasmodium is the significant time it takes to span an environment: on average it takes several days to exhibit substantial growth. This creates an issue when harnessing its behaviour for real-time musical application. Currently, methods of exploiting *P.polycephalum's* behaviour for real-time computation is an active area of research in labs worldwide. As an interim solution, Jones has developed a computer approximation of the organism [16]. During the preliminary stages of our research into unconventional computing and music, we experimented with this approximation in sonification [17] and contemporary composition scenarios [18]. Although this approximation is useable, it is simple in its assumptions and implementation. To progress our research, it is beneficial for us to begin experimenting directly with the biological computing substrate. For us to achieve this, we record behaviour, which we then apply in our sequencer. The majority of computational prototypes with *P.polycephalum* record activities using time lapsed imagery of spatial progressions [15]. Although this gives a comprehensive record of movement, it lacks any information regarding intracellular activity and physiological states. As a result, for our experimentation we use a combination of time-lapse imagery and electrical potential data to record behaviour.

Step sequencers are software or hardware devices that loop through a defined quantity of steps at set time intervals. Each of these steps can normally exist in one of two states: active or inactive. When active, a predefined sound event will be triggered as the sequencer reaches its respective position in the loop. To implement the *P.polycephalum* step sequencer, we design an environment that represents a step sequencer's architecture. Shown in Fig. 2 is the design that we put together, which consists of six electrode zones (sequencer steps) $(S_1 \ldots S_6)$ arranged in a circular fashion with a central inoculation area (C). This 360° design mimics a sequencer loop, and gives each step equal weighting in the sequence. In order to entice propagation and promote colonisation in each zone (step activation), an attractant is positioned in the centre. This is also extended to the inoculation area to create an initial central node that can propagate in any of the six directions throughout the experiment, increasing the chance of steps becoming active in a non-sequential order.

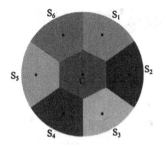

Fig. 2. Step sequencer growth environment design

2.1   Methods

In order for us to record the behaviour of *P.polycephalum* we use two forms of hardware: a USB manual focus camera and high-resolution data logger. Each experiment takes place in a plastic petri dish 90 mm in diameter with the camera centred above. To guarantee an environment that promotes growth, a black enclosure is placed over the experiment limiting the light intensity level imposed on the plasmodium. To illuminate the petri dish for image capture, an array of white LEDs turn on periodically.

Electrical potential levels are recorded using an ADC-20 high-resolution data logger manufactured by Pico Technology UK. Within each petri dish, bare wire electrodes are wired in place through small holes in the base with wiring underneath secured using adhesive tack. Electrodes are arranged with one reference and six measurements: the reference resides in the centre and gives a ground potential for each of the measurement electrodes.

Each step's electrode is coated in non-nutrient agar, which keeps humidity high and promotes growth/colonisation. Due to the agar substrate being liquid based and thus a conductor, a non-conductive plastic isolates each step, allowing electrical potentials to be recorded across the environment without interference. Shown in Fig. 3 is the electrode array layout before being coated in agar and after. Attractants (oat flakes) are placed on top of each step, maintaining an equal distance from the centre to entice the propagation and facilitate colonisation. To start each experiment, a piece of plasmodium is inoculated on the centre region. Inoculation sources are extracted from a small *P.polycephalum* farm (see [15] for farming techniques), and put through a period (approximately six-seven hours) of starvation before the experiment begins. This starvation process speeds up initial propagation speed.

Once the plasmodium has been inoculated into position, we begin to record behaviour. To achieve a uniform and coherent set of data we use our own developed software system, designed to record *P.polycephalum* behaviour [19,20]. Throughout the duration of the experiment, our software takes 100 data samples from each electrode at 1-s intervals, samples are then averaged to give a single reading for each second. This level of recording detail is necessary in order to

Fig. 3. Photographs showing the construction of the growth environment. Shown left is the bare wire electrode array wired into position. Right shows the completed growth environment with each electrode embedded within blocks of agar.

capture the natural gradients exhibited with various progressions, some of which are fairly prompt. Images are taken at intervals of 5 min with the LEDs turning on 5 s before and staying active for 10 s.

2.2 Results

The data collection process took just under five days to complete and was halted as the plasmodium entered its dormant Sclerotium phase. This occurred as a result of a drop in humidity as the agar substrate dried out in conjunction with a lack of nutrients as food sources within the environment became exhausted. The collection process generated an excessive quantity of electrical potential data: circa 330000 entries for each measurement electrode. Harnessing this quantity of information in our device would result in extremely long sequences of sounds. In order to circumvent this, we apply a compression algorithm. From our musical intention point of view, it is important while compressing this data that time based meaning and relevant gradients between behavioural patterns are maintained. Here, we view the data not as individual electrodes but as sets of entries for each second. First, we reduce quantity through combining blocks of 10 entries and averaging their measurements, leaving a single entry for $e_1 \ldots e_6$. We then process the subsequent data in the following manner: n entry is only withheld from removal if two measurements from $e_1 \ldots e_6$ present a change over a set threshold (b) from their counterpart within the previous entry stored (n^{-1}). This is expressed in the following where if $_x(\mathrm{S}) = 1$ the entry is withheld, otherwise it is lost:

$$\sum_{i=1}^{6} x(|e_i^n - e_i^{n-1}| \geq b) \geq 2 \tag{1}$$

This compression stage reduced the quantity of entries to circa 5500, while maintaining behaviour patterns and the voltage gradients between them.

Presented in Fig. 4 are graphs representing each measurement electrode's entries after compression.

It took the organism just under 12 h to propagate to a step. When the plasmodium arrives at an electrode's substrate, a fast change in voltage is registered, which in our results is an increase ranging from ±5–15 mV. Propagation to each step came equally from both the central node as well as neighbouring steps. Activities and conditions within colonised regions cause differing intracellular activity, which in turn can result in electrical impulses across the organism. Such impulses are typically registered in regions connected directly, but may spread a distance across the organism if the amplitude and conditions at other regions are favourable. This can be seen on electrodes 3, 4 and 5 in Fig. 4, marked by the rectangle. Also, regions that are propagated to simultaneously exhibit initial synchronised patterns in their electrical potential. In our experiment, this is the case for electrodes 1 and 2, as shown by the triangle in Fig. 4. The Sclerotium phase is characterised by a increase in voltage. This is marked by a circle on electrode one in Fig. 4.

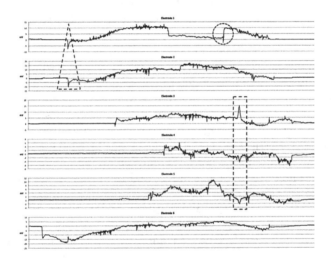

Fig. 4. Graphs of results

2.3 Step Sequencer

We programmed this device in Max with some data handling operations being dealt with in Java. First, we established a data recall system. Here, the user can define how fast they wish the electrical potential data to be recalled into the system in entries per second. Upon doing so, the system defines the frame rate for the time lapsed imagery, in order to play back the images in motion with perfect synchrony. As with any musical devices, the user interface is an integral part of its function. Within this device, the interface is built around the time lapsed imagery playback, inducing a connection between the user and the organism. Once in the system, each electrical potential entry is broken into its six individual readings and altered to become an absolute value. The system then steps through each measurement in a 360° order taking a reading at a user defined BPM. Steps only become active within the sequence once populated by the plasmodium. Until this time, no reading is taken. Once activated, the system looks for a level of change in electrical potential in order to retire steps from triggering sounds when the plasmodium is no longer active. This is achieved by storing readings over a short period of time and reviewing any oscillatory behaviour.

We decided to experiment with our sequencer in two different scenarios. The first looks at harnessing *P.polycephalum's* behaviour to extend the functionality of the conventional step sequencer by triggering different sounds as a function of each step's electrical potential reading. Here, the readings taken by the metronome are used to trigger one of four sound samples assigned to each step, which are associated with a voltage range. We tested this device using a set of piano samples all belonging to the key of C major. This sample set consisted of a variety of dynamic chords, notes and short phrases. These were assigned in a logical manner where samples we considered to have a higher value are triggered through elevated electrical potential readings.

The second scenario is novel and takes the form of a MIDI instrument. Here, the recorded behaviour is put through a sonification model where the user can change the parameters. Readings taken by the sequencer are used to trigger a set of nine MIDI notes that are programmed in by the user. All steps are allocated a set of four notes from the nine available, which are then each assigned to a voltage trigger range. When a note is triggered, its velocity is produced through scaling the step's current electrical potential value to the MIDI data range. In order to determine the duration of a note, the current average potential of all other steps (active and non-active) is calculated, and then compared to the triggered step's voltage to produce a potential difference value. The higher this value, the more significant the note duration will be within the sequence, with a maximum duration being four beats. The sequencer is limited to only allow six notes to sound at a time; if a note is triggered but is unavailable due to being made active by another step, the note with the closest value in the step's priority list will sound. To make this version of the sequencer versatile, we allow each step's note priority order to be changed in real-time. Furthermore, we implemented an interactive graph showing the combined electrical potential readings. This allows the user to change the current position of the data being recalled, creating means to restructure the output of the sequencer. Shown in Fig. 5 is the sequencer user interface.

3   Discussions

We explored two scenarios for the *P.polycephalum* step sequencer: sample and MIDI note triggering (for sound recordings see [21]). The output of our device in both scenarios produced a variety of interesting arrangements, which can be

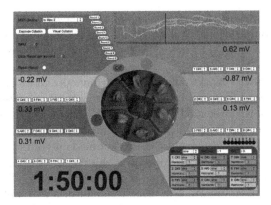

Fig. 5. The step sequencer user interface

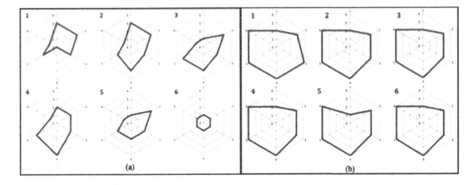

Fig. 6. Radar graphs depicting two sets of six consecutive sequencer loops. Set (a) shows the sequencer's most dynamic arrangement, while (b) shows a repetitive arrangement.

used by musicians in several different ways. In the sample-triggering scenario, we found that by allocating sounds to a relative voltage range - for example, higher velocity sounds to elevating voltages - a naturally progressive output is achieved (Fig. 6a). However, at certain points, the sample arrangement can become slightly repetitive (Fig. 6b). From a musical perspective, we believe the MIDI scenario gave more useful and interesting results. This version of the device outputs a progressive arrangement of notes, which correspond morphologically to the recorded foraging behaviour. As a sonification of behaviour, the produced output does convey auditory representation of voltage levels quite accurately. This is because each note's velocity is produced directly by the respective step's voltage - a parameter that directly relates to energy. Moreover, by producing each note's duration with a potential difference value, it is possible to compare activity on each step through listening. From a musical perspective, having note velocity controlled this way is slightly undynamic due to voltage levels also controlling which notes are triggered: each note is played with a similar velocity every time. As a compositional tool, we found this version of the sequencer useful for arranging sets of notes that we composed and applying interesting variations over time.

Currently, our device works offline, using behavioural data gathered from an experimental process beforehand. Such an experimental process creates a large obstacle that limits the extended usability of the sequencer. Using the same set of behavioural data will result in a similar output each time. This constraint could be avoided by gathering more behavioural data, but this process takes several days and would be tedious. Moreover, this constraint poses a detrimental obstacle to overcome if the device was ever to be used during a live performance. To address this problem, we are proposing to engineer a live, wetware version of the sequencer, harnessing the organism's vibrant intracellular activity.

3.1   Future Work

P.polycephalum oscillates protoplasm around its network of veins through the process of shuttle streaming. Shuttle streaming is the intracellular movement of protoplasm back-and-forth. Under a microscope, this streaming activity is visible and can be seen moving at rates in excess of $1\,mm/s$ [22]. Recently, researchers have been exploring how this behaviour may be used for various computational purposes, one example being logic gate schemes [12]. Cifarelli et al. have demonstrated that it is possible to load the organism with micro-particles, which are picked up and moved around with shuttle streaming [23]. We are interested in exploring how we could use the movement of such micro-particles to trigger sounds as they pass through certain areas of the organism. We intend to load the organism with micro-particles and place high magnification cameras over various parts of its network. Such cameras will feed into a system that is programmed to recognise when a micro-particle passes. In relation to a step sequencer, each camera will represent a step in the sequence where a sound event is triggered upon a particle's passing.

The ability to interact, control and repeat the behaviour of a composition tool is important to musicians. In our current device, these are all possible due to the device working off-line and using the same set of behavioural data. In the case of our proposed wetware sequencer, controlling the behaviour of *P.polycephalum* in real-time is still an active area of research in laboratories worldwide. In regards to controlling certain aspects of the shuttle streaming process, researchers have found that through gentle tactile stimulation of the protoplasmic vein, a person can change the direction and pause movement (see [24] for a video demonstration). It is possible that this stimulation method could be an approach for a composer to interact and play the wetware sequencer.

4   Conclusion

In this paper, we reported on our initial work into engineering a musical step sequencer with the biological organism *P.polycephalum*. *P.polycephalum* is currently gaining a lot of research interest in the field of unconventional computing. We have selected it as the biological computing substrate for our investigations into how new, non-classic, computational paradigms may provide new pathways for music and related technologies. It is a good candidate for such research due to its ease of application and open accessibility.

At this early stage in our research, we are spending a lot of time investigating and experimenting with what type of musical application *P.polycephalum* may be used in to go beyond our standard offering. The step sequencer presented here is an early example. The *P.polycephalum* step sequencer in the sample-triggering scenario adds a new dimension to our conventional sequencer devices by naturally progressing the arrangement of sound events. However, a similar result could be achieved through conventional automation and computer programming. The MIDI note scenario is slightly different; this harnesses a selection of sonification techniques and parameter mappings, creating an auditory representation of the recorded behaviour.

The limitations of working with *P.polycephalum* for music have become apparent from our experimentation. The time the organism takes to display behaviour is extensive, causing a large obstacle to overcome when designing musical systems. We have outlined our plans to develop a live wetware version of the sequencer, which will exploit the organism's unique intracellular movement. The implementation of such a device would be a large step forward for unconventional computing in music, being one of the first musical wetware devices.

To conclude, the intersection of music and unconventional computing is very much in its infancy. To begin understanding how this branch of computer science may be used in music, we need to immerse its application across the field. This process will widen our appreciation and lead to advances as the computing paradigm lends itself to certain applications.

References

1. Doornbusch, P.: Computer sound synthesis in 1951: the music of CSIRAC. Comput. Music J. **28**(1), 10–25 (2004)
2. Turing, A.M.: On computable numbers, with an application to the Entscheidungsproblem. Proc. Lond. Math. Soc. **42**(2), 230–265 (1936)
3. Von Neumann, J.: First draft of a report on the edvac. In: Randall, B. (ed.) The Origins of Digital Computers, pp. 383–392. Springer, New York (1982)
4. Toffoli, T.: Programmable matter methods. Future Gener. Comput. Syst. **16**, 187–201 (1998). Citeseer
5. Adamatzky, A., Teuscher, C.: From Utopian to Genuine Unconventional Computers. Luniver Press, Beckington (2006)
6. Stepney, S.: Programming unconventional computers: dynamics, development, self-reference. Entropy **14**(10), 1939–1952 (2012)
7. Braund, E., Miranda, E.: Unconventional computing in music. In: Proceedings of the 9th Conference on Interdisciplinary Musicology - CIM14, Berlin, Germany (2014)
8. Miranda, E.R.: Granular synthesis of sounds by means of a cellular automaton. Leonardo **28**(4), 297–300 (1995)

9. Miranda, E.R., Bull, L., Gueguen, F., Uroukov, I.S.: Computer music meets unconventional computing: towards sound synthesis with in vitro neuronal networks. Comput. Music J. **33**(1), 9–18 (2009)
10. Meyer, R., Stockem, W.: Studies on microplasmodia of physarum polycephalum V: Electrical activity of different types of microplasmodia and macroplasmodia. Cell Biol. Int. Rep. **3**(4), 321–330 (1979)
11. Adamatzky, A., Jones, J.: On electrical correlates of Physarum polycephalum spatial activity: Can we see Physarum Machine in the dark. Biophys. Rev. Lett. **6**(01n02), 29–57 (2011)
12. Adamatzky, A., Schubert, T.: Slime mold microfluidic logical gates. Mater. Today **17**(2), 86–91 (2014)
13. Adamatzky, A.: Towards slime mould colour sensor: Recognition of colours by Physarum polycephalum. Org. Electron. **14**(12), 3355–3361 (2013)
14. Tsuda, S., Zauner, K.P., Gunji, Y.P.: Robot control with biological cells. Biosystems **87**(2), 215–223 (2007)
15. Adamatzky, A.: Physarum Machines: Computers from Slime Mould, vol. 74. World Scientific, Singapore (2010)
16. Jones, J.: The emergence and dynamical evolution of complex transport networks from simple low-level behaviours. IJUC **6**(2), 125–144 (2010)
17. Miranda, E.R., Adamatzky, A., Jones, J.: Sounds synthesis with slime mould of physarum polycephalum. J. Bionic Eng. **8**(2), 107–113 (2011)
18. Miranda, E.R.: Harnessing the Intelligence of physarum polycephalum for unconventional computing-aided musical composition. IJUC **10**(3), 251–268 (2014)
19. Braund, E.: Unconventional Computer Music with Physarum Polycephalum. Master's thesis, Plymouth University (2013)
20. Braund, E., Miranda, E.: Music with unconventional computing: a system for physarum polycephalum sound synthesis. In: Aramaki, M., Derrien, O., Kronland-Martinet, R., Ystad, S.I. (eds.) CMMR 2013. LNCS, vol. 8905, pp. 175–189. Springer, Heidelberg (2014)
21. Braund, E.: Physarm polycephalum step sequencer examples (2015). https://soundcloud.com/ed-braund
22. Coggin, S., Pazun, J.: Dynamic complexity inPhysarum polycephalum shuttle streaming. Protoplasma **194**(3–4), 243–249 (1996)
23. Cifarelli, A., Dimonte, A., Berzina, T., Erokhin, V.: On the loading of slime mold physarum polycephalum with microparticles for unconventional computing application. BioNanoScience **4**(1), 92–96 (2014)
24. PhyChip: Tactile Stimulus x 2 of (Y-crossing), Physarum Polycephalum (2013). http://www.youtube.com/watch?v=nGRv4dzwGoU

Feature Discovery by Deep Learning
for Aesthetic Analysis
of Evolved Abstract Images

Allan Campbell$^{(\boxtimes)}$, Vic Ciesielksi, and A.K. Qin

School of Computer Science and Information Technology,
RMIT University, Melbourne, Australia
{allan.campbell,vic.cieskielski,kai.qin}@rmit.edu.au

Abstract. We investigated the ability of a Deep Belief Network with logistic nodes, trained unsupervised by Contrastive Divergence, to discover features of evolved abstract art images. Two Restricted Boltzmann Machine models were trained independently on low and high aesthetic class images. The receptive fields (filters) of both models were compared by visual inspection. Roughly 10 % of these filters in the high aesthetic model approximated the form of the high aesthetic training images. The remaining 90 % of filters in the high aesthetic model and all filters in the low aesthetic model appeared noise like. The form of discovered filters was not consistent with the Gabor filter like forms discovered for MNIST training data, possibly revealing an interesting property of the evolved abstract training images. We joined the datasets and trained a Restricted Boltzmann Machine finding that roughly 30 % of the filters approximate the form of the high aesthetic input images. We trained a 10 layer Deep Belief Network on the joint dataset and used the output activities at each layer as training data for traditional classifiers (decision tree and random forest). The highest classification accuracy from learned features (84 %) was achieved at the second hidden layer, indicating that the features discovered by our Deep Learning approach have discriminative power. Above the second hidden layer, classification accuracy decreases.

Keywords: Computational aesthetics · Deep learning · Evolved abstract images

1 Introduction

Having computers make aesthetic distinctions in digital media, that are comparable to the subtlety of human judgement is an open problem in computer science. Consider that even between humans there can be many levels of sophistication in aesthetic judgement, from that of a child drawn to bright colours to the refined sense of an art historian assessing art-works across a spectrum of visual, semantic and contextual levels. Computational aesthetics at present ranks lowly on this spectrum of capability. Given a class of simple abstract

© Springer International Publishing Switzerland 2015
C. Johnson et al. (Eds.): EvoMUSART 2015, LNCS 9027, pp. 27–38, 2015.
DOI: 10.1007/978-3-319-16498-4_3

images lacking semantic content for example, the accurate prediction of average human aesthetic judgement expressed as a simple high or low rating is considered a significant challenge. Most successful computational methods analyse not raw images themselves, but measurements of visual characteristics such as brightness, colourfulness and symmetry, which are computed from the images. These characteristics are termed "features". The particular features measured for some task are in most cases designed by human intuition. The optimality of designed features for their application of purpose is unknown and unlikely. A key idea behind Deep Learning is the automatic discovery of new representations for input data, which express salient features in a form that is more powerful than any feature set of human design. Deep Learning has shown recent success in a variety of tasks applied to images and these have inspired us to investigate a Deep Learning approach to discovering features that underpin the aesthetic value of evolved abstract images. We based our study on the Deep Belief Network, chiefly due to our greater experience with this architecture in comparison to alternatives such as deep convolution networks and deep auto-encoders. Deep Belief Networks are multi-layered probabilistic generative networks, so called because the output activations are regarded as probabilities of salient features of the input data from which plausible examples of the input can be reconstructed by the network. The top 2 layers of neurons in a Deep Belief Network are symmetrically connected and form an undirected associative memory while the lower layers have downward directed connections that enable the input to be reconstructed, given a set of probabilities of features in the associative memory. A Restricted Boltzmann Machine is a two layer probabilistic generative network that can be used as a module for composing Deep Belief Networks. Hinton in 2002 introduced the Contrastive Divergence algorithm [13] and in 2006 showed a greedy layer-wise approach to training Deep Belief Networks [12]. A diagrammatic representation of the composition of a Deep Belief Network from Restricted Boltzmann Machine modules is shown in Fig. 1.

A Restricted Boltzmann Machine trained by Contrastive Divergence learns a set of parameters for the model, that approximately maximizes the product of the probabilities output by the hidden nodes $p(h_i|\mathbf{v})$ for input vectors $\mathbf{v}$ drawn from the training set. If the learning has generalized well for the domain from which the training examples have been drawn, then $p(\mathbf{h}|\mathbf{v})$ represents the probability that the input $\mathbf{v}$ is a plausible example of the domain. The outputs of the nodes in the hidden layer $p(h_i|\mathbf{v})$ are considered to be probabilities of salient features of the input.

1.1 Research Questions

1. What is the nature of features discovered by a Deep Learning approach applied to high aesthetic value abstract evolved images.
2. What is the nature of features discovered by a Deep Learning approach applied to low aesthetic value abstract evolved images.
3. Can the aesthetic rating of an abstract evolved image be predicted from the features discovered by our Deep Learning approach.

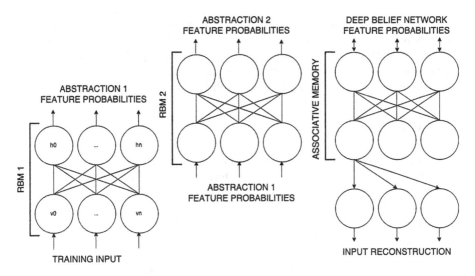

Fig. 1. Deep belief network composition

2   Related Work

The idea that aesthetic value is connected to features goes back at least to Birkhoff in the 1930s [1]. Hoenig [15] in 2005 comprehensively defined computational aesthetics as a field of study with emphasis on three important factors: computational methods, the human aesthetic point of view and the pragmatic need to focus on objective approaches. Datta in 2006 introduced machine learning as a computational approach to the investigation of features that underpin aesthetic value in artistic and photographic images [5]. Many subsequent studies have applied machine learning to photographic digital images and or art images with the goal of predicting the aesthetic rating of these images from features engineered to measure image properties such as colorfulness, brightness and texture. Examples are [2,3,8,20]. Most subsequent work focusses on photographic images and studies of art works have borrowed features engineered for photographs. For example Ciesielski et al. [3] base their study on the set of features designed and published by Datta et al. [5]. Three additional papers that invent image features that other researchers have used for further work are: Reaves [23], Ke et al. [16] and Datta et al. [4]. As machine learning extends learning from engineered feature sets toward a new paradigm of representational learning and feature discovery, computational aesthetics has begun to exploit these capabilities also. Lu et al. [19] present a method based on multi-column deep convolutional networks for predicting the aesthetic rating of photographic images in the AVA image dataset [21]. A number of recent publications related to computational aesthetics more generally, make reference to the developments in Deep Learning and how these intersect their topics. Ginosar et al. [9] argue for extending the evaluation of computer vision systems for object detection in images to corpora that include art works having characteristic abstractions such as part-reorganisation in Cubist paintings and blurring in Impressionist works. Spratt and Elgammal [25] re-examine the long held tension between the formal philosophical discourse on aesthetic theory and the steady encroachment of computer science, arguing for greater collaboration between science and humanities.

3 Methodology

We emphasize that classification performance has been secondary to our primary interest in feature discovery and analysis. Our methodology has therefore been focussed on unsupervised learning. However, to claim any significance of the features discovered in steps 1 to 5, they must be shown to be capable of discriminating the aesthetic category of the input. For this reason we conducted classification experiments in steps 6 and 7.

1. Formulate two datasets, one representing high aesthetic value images, the other low aesthetic value images;
2. Train independent Restricted Boltzmann Machine models for each dataset;
3. Compare the independent model receptive fields by visualization;
4. Join both datasets and train a Restricted Boltzmann Machine model on the joined dataset;
5. Analyse the joint model receptive fields by visualization;
6. Train a 10 layer Deep Belief Model on the joined dataset;[1]
7. Compute classification accuracy per layer for the 10 layer Deep Belief Model.

The set of weighted connections between a hidden node and all of its input nodes is referred to as a receptive field or a filter. A common way to visualize the receptive fields of a Restricted Boltzmann Machine is by rasterizing the connection weights and scaling the weight values to the range of pixel intensity values. Receptive fields operate as multiplicative constants on the input signal and the form or structure of visualized receptive fields provides a crude interpretation of the nature of features learned by the network.

Our motivation for training and analysing independent models on each aesthetic class was the starting assumption that if there are features associated with one aesthetic class but not the other, then we should be able to identify these by visualization of the receptive fields of each model. In the joint model we might recognize these same features and show that an input image of one class activates its associated features exclusively or predominantly. Steps 2 and 4 in the methodology indicate that Restricted Boltzmann Machine networks rather than Deep Belief Networks have been trained to model each class of input data. The first layer of a Deep Belief Network is equivalent to a Restricted Boltzmann Machine and can be considered to encode atomic level features, while layers above this encode "features of features". A focus on atomic level features was taken to be

---

[1] We arbitrarily decided 10 layers are sufficient to satisfactorily show any trend in classification accuracy with depth.

an obvious starting point for an exploratory study such as ours. Additionally, the higher level abstractions in Deep Belief Networks are not well understood. Various methods have been published for visualizing the receptive fields at these higher layers [6, 18] but no method for visualizing learned features in Deep Belief Networks is comprehensively illuminating. Our study has sought to investigate only the atomic layer features and for this purpose, only 1 layer of Restricted Boltzmann Machine modules was trained in steps 2 and 4.

4 Experiments

IMAGENE [27] is an evolutionary art generating program that creates abstract art images using a genetic programming approach. The program presents a population of images to the user who supplies IMAGENE with a fitness function by making aesthetic selections that guide the generation of further images. The result of an interactive run of the program is a set of images that have no semantic content but significantly varying degrees of aesthetic appeal. These provide what are believed to be suitable source data for experiments in computational aesthetics. A dataset of 2260 IMAGENE images studied in previous work [3] has been re-examined in this study. Three people independently rated the images on a scale of increasing aesthetic value from 1 to 7. The average rating for each image was then computed. In order to exaggerate the presence of distinguishing features at the high and low aesthetic extremes, the middle classes were excluded. This yielded 242 images at each end of the spectrum providing a training set of 484 images. The images were scaled from 600×600 to 32×32 pixels to make runtime practical. 100 Examples of each subset of the 32×32 pixel images are shown in Fig. 2.

A Restricted Boltzmann Machine trained by Contrastive Divergence is subject to incremental weight adjustments Δw_{ij} which are each calculated as a small proportion ϵ of the difference between two quantities.

$$\Delta w_{ij} = \epsilon(\langle v_i h_j \rangle_{data} - \langle v_i h_j \rangle_{model}) \tag{1}$$

The first quantity $\langle v_i h_j \rangle_{data}$ is the correlation between visible and hidden node outputs when the network is presented with data from the training set. The second quantity $\langle v_i h_j \rangle_{model}$ is the correlation between visible and hidden nodes when the network is presented with a reconstruction of the input, which the network itself generates, given a set of hidden node activations (from the previous input). The reconstructed input is the network's "opinion" of a plausible example of the input, given its current set of parameters and given a set of probabilities at the hidden nodes. Input reconstruction error can be computed as the sum of square differences between the training vectors and their reconstructions, averaged over the number of input nodes and the number of training vectors. Reconstruction error for the two independent models and the joint model are shown in Fig. 3.

Reconstruction error is expected to initially fall steeply and then trend generally in a negative direction and level out. This is broadly indicative that learning

Low Aesthetic Value   High Aesthetic Value

Fig. 2. Example training images

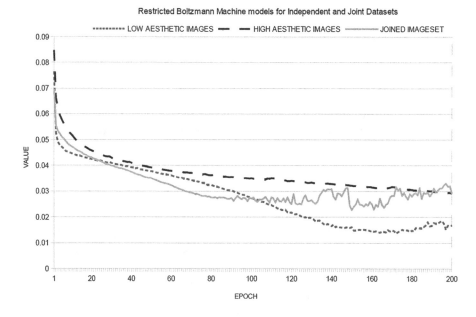

Fig. 3. Reconstruction error for joint and independent RBM models

is progressing. We note however that reconstruction error is not the function that
the Contrastive Divergence algorithm is optimizing [11]. A large or sustained
increase in the reconstruction error can indicate that learning is not progressing
but in Fig. 3 no such indication is evident. All models in all experiments were

trained with learning rate = 0.1, number of Gibbs sampling steps = 1, number of training epochs = 200. For the classification experiments an additional Deep Belief Network was trained for 50 training epochs. All layers in all models have $32 \times 32 \times 3 = 3072$ nodes. Each color component of each pixel in the 32 by 32 pixel images is input as a separate attribute. The left and right grids of 100 images each in Fig. 4 show the receptive fields for the models trained only with low and high aesthetic value images respectively.

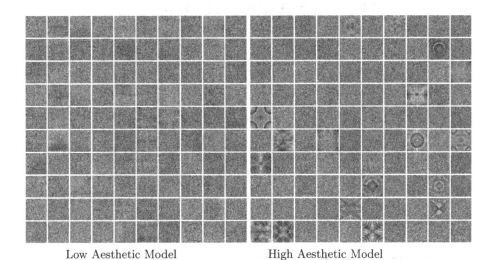

Low Aesthetic Model   High Aesthetic Model

Fig. 4. Receptive fields of independent restricted boltzmann machine models

Figure 4 shows a sample (100) of the total number (3072) of learned features of each model, but sampling any 100 adjacent nodes gives similar results. It is apparent that the high aesthetic model has discovered features having a form similar to the training images whereas the low aesthetic model has seemingly failed to discover features of any recognizable form. The apparent failure of the low aesthetic model might suggest that low complexity inputs are problematic for this class of architecture. Figure 5 shows the collection of 100 "well formed" receptive fields gathered from the first 1000 of the 3072 feature nodes of the high aesthetic value model. The yield in this independent high aesthetic model is roughly 10 % which we note only for comparison with other models. The similarity between training images and features is in contrast to the filters discovered using the same training algorithm applied to the MNIST benchmark dataset of hand-written digits [17] shown in Fig. 6. The MNIST filters shown on the right of Fig. 6 are interpreted as point and edge features and these are computed and visualized in the same way as the IMAGENE filters shown in Fig. 5 but using an architecture having only 500 neurons in the hidden layer.

It is possible that the similarity between features and training images reveals a property of the IMAGENE images, which are computed algorithmically and

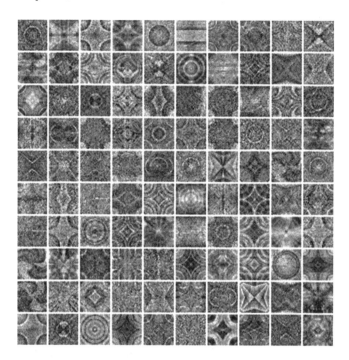

Fig. 5. High aesthetic image independent model receptive fields

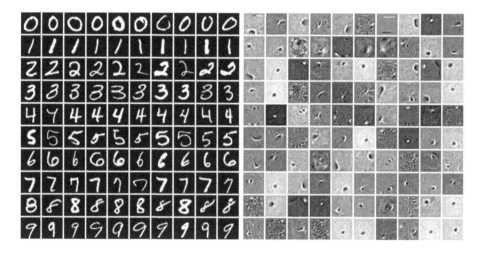

Fig. 6. MNIST data and features

may have a structural idiosyncrasy so that they are in a sense their own atoms and learned features are approximations to the images themselves. Another possibility is that feature learning has failed, exposing a poor configuration of the Restricted Boltzmann Machine to the empirical distribution of the training data.

The formal treatment of these networks with logistic nodes assumes binary input data, or that non binary values can be treated as probabilities [12]. This has not been verified for IMAGENE images. Over-fitting, due to the small number of training images in comparison to the large number of parameters also would contribute to the failure of feature learning. Training a joint model on both high and low aesthetic images improves the yield of "well formed" features to approximately 30 %, suggesting an insufficient number of training images, since the low aesthetic independent model absent these feature forms in Fig. 4(left) should not add to the set of features of the high aesthetic model. The difference then between the high aesthetic model and the joint model, and an explanation for the increased feature yield is the increased number of training images. An implication of the increased yield in the joint model is that we cannot associate these features exclusively with high aesthetic value images. We compared in the joint model, filters of output nodes activated with high probability by low aesthetic input images with filters activated by high aesthetic input images. Figure 7 shows example images input to the joint model and their respective filters for the 50 output nodes with highest activation probability. All filters shown have probability greater than 0.99. By visual inspection there is great similarity between strongly activated features of both aesthetic classes in the joint model, suggesting that such features may also be discovered in low aesthetic images given sufficient training data.

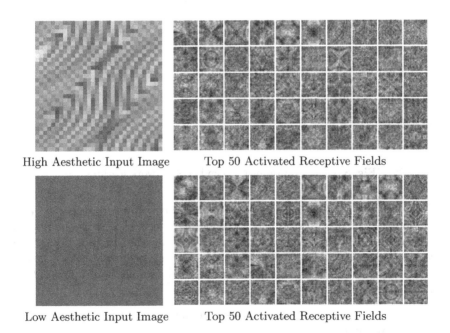

| High Aesthetic Input Image | Top 50 Activated Receptive Fields |

| Low Aesthetic Input Image | Top 50 Activated Receptive Fields |

Fig. 7. Input images and receptive fields of highest probability outputs

Classification performance has been secondary to our primary focus of feature discovery and analysis. It has not been our goal to better the previous best classification accuracy on this data set, but rather to validate the discovered features by demonstrating that they have discriminatory power. The previous best classification on this data is reported as 90 % by training a random forest on 55 engineered features computed over all 2260 IMAGENE images at 600×600 pixel resolution [3]. We trained a 10 layer Deep Belief Network on only 484 of these images, scaled down to 32×32 pixels and used the output activities at each layer as training data for traditional classifiers (decision tree and random forest) implemented in the Weka machine learning package [10][2].

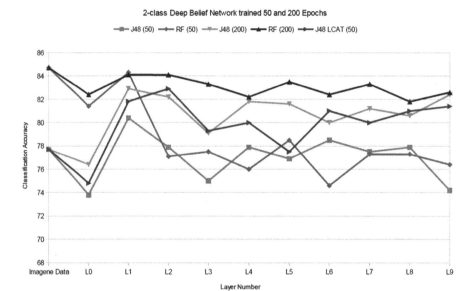

Fig. 8. Classification using deep belief network features

Figure 8 shows classification accuracy at each layer (L0 to L9) for two Deep Belief Networks, trained for 50 and 200 epochs respectively. The points on the vertical axis are classification accuracies achieved on the raw pixel data. The curve labelled "J48 LCAT (50)" shows classification accuracies at each layer where this layers outputs are laterally concatenated with all lower layers outputs to create the training records for the decision tree.

---

[2] WEKA J48 and RandomForest classifiers were run with all default settings and 10 fold cross validation.

5   Conclusions and Future Work

The conclusion to our first question is that features of high aesthetic IMAGENE images are an approximation to the form of high aesthetic images themselves. The similarity between training images and features may reveal a property of IMAGENE data. It is also possible that feature learning has failed, due to an unsuitability of some aspect of our approach or of over-fitting to the training data. For our second research question we conclude that there is insufficient complexity in the low aesthetic images to enable feature learning. We interpret the noise like receptive fields of the low aesthetic model to mean that the model views these images as featureless. However, the increased rate of feature discovery for the joint model (10 % to 30 %) suggests that similar features may be discovered in low aesthetic images given sufficient training data. One approach to expanding the training set is to sample image patches (say 500×500 pixels) from the 600×600 original images at random locations. The patches could further be distorted by a variety of suitable affine transforms. Such techniques for expanding available training data have been numerously reported in the literature, for example Simard et al. [24]. The conclusion to our third question is that the aesthetic rating of IMAGENE images can be predicted from the features discovered by our Deep Learning approach. Our best classification accuracy of 84 % supports this conclusion and warrants further investigation with more refined Deep Learning approaches. It is important to note that our Deep Learning approach is rudimentary. Future work could explore many Deep Learning advances that have been shown in the literature, such as Gaussian input units for real valued data [7], rectified linear units [22] or Maxout units [26] for hidden layers, Dropout regularisation [14] and indeed deep convolutional and autoencoder networks.

References

1. Birkhoff, G.D.: Aesthetic Measure. Mass, Cambridge (1933)
2. Campbell, A., Ciesielski, V., Trist, K.: A self organizing map based method for understanding features associated with high aesthetic value evolved abstract images. In: 2014 IEEE Congress on Evolutionary Computation (CEC), pp. 2274–2281. IEEE (2014)
3. Ciesielski, V., Barile, P., Trist, K.: Finding image features associated with high Aesthetic value by machine learning. In: Machado, P., McDermott, J., Carballal, A. (eds.) EvoMUSART 2013. LNCS, vol. 7834, pp. 47–58. Springer, Heidelberg (2013)
4. Datta, R.: Semantics and aesthetics inference for image search: statistical learning approaches. Pennsylvania State University (2009)
5. Datta, R., Joshi, D., Li, J., Wang, J.Z.: Studying Aesthetics in photographic images using a computational approach. In: Leonardis, A., Bischof, H., Pinz, A. (eds.) ECCV 2006. LNCS, vol. 3953, pp. 288–301. Springer, Heidelberg (2006)
6. Erhan, D., Bengio, Y., Courville, A., Vincent, P.: Visualizing higher-layer features of a deep network. Dept. IRO, Université de Montréal, Technical report (2009)
7. Fischer, A., Igel, C.: Training restricted boltzmann machines: An introduction. Pattern Recogn. **47**(1), 25–39 (2014)

8. Galanter, P.: Computational aesthetic evaluation: past and future. In: McCormack, J., d'Inverno, M. (eds.) Computers and Creativity, pp. 255–293. Springer, Heidelberg (2012)

9. Ginosar, S., Haas, D., Brown, T., Malik, J.: Detecting people in cubist art. arXiv preprint arXiv:1409.6235 (2014)

10. Hall, M., Frank, E., Holmes, G., Pfahringer, B., Reutemann, P., Witten, I.H.: The weka data mining software: an update. ACM SIGKDD Explor. Newslett. **11**(1), 10–18 (2009)

11. Hinton, G.: A practical guide to training restricted Boltzmann machines. Momentum **9**(1), 926 (2010)

12. Hinton, G., Osindero, S., Teh, Y.-W.: A fast learning algorithm for deep belief nets. Neural Comput. **18**(7), 1527–1554 (2006)

13. Geoffrey, E.: Training products of experts by minimizing contrastive divergence. Neural Comput. **14**(8), 1771–1800 (2002)

14. Hinton, G.E., Srivastava, N., Krizhevsky, A., Sutskever, I., Salakhutdinov, R.R.: Improving neural networks by preventing co-adaptation of feature detectors. arXiv preprint arXiv:1207.0580 (2012)

15. Hoenig, F.: Defining computational aesthetics. In: Neumann, L., Sbert, M., Gooch, B., Purgathofer, W. (eds.) Computational Aesthetics, pp. 13–18. Eurographics Association, London (2005)

16. Ke, Y., Tang, X., Jing, F.: The design of high-level features for photo quality assessment. In: 2006 IEEE Computer Society Conference on Computer Vision and Pattern Recognition, vol. 1, pp. 419–426. IEEE (2006)

17. LeCun, Y., Cortes, C.: The mnist database of handwritten digits (1998)

18. Lee, H., Ekanadham, C., Ng, A.Y.: Sparse deep belief net model for visual area v2. In: Platt, J.C., Koller, D., Singer, Y., Roweis, S. (eds.) Advances in Neural Information Processing Systems, pp. 873–880. MIT Press, Cambridge (2008)

19. Lu, X., Lin, Z., Jin, H., Yang, J., Wang, J.Z.: Rapid: Rating pictorial aesthetics using deep learning. In: Proceedings of the ACM International Conference on Multimedia, pp. 457–466. ACM (2014)

20. Machado, P., Cardoso, A.: Generation and evaluation of artworks. In: Proceedings of the 1st European Workshop on Cognitive Modeling, CM'96, pp. 96–39 (2010)

21. Murray, N., Marchesotti, L., Perronnin, F.: Ava: A large-scale database for aesthetic visual analysis. In: 2012 IEEE Conference on Computer Vision and Pattern Recognition (CVPR), pp. 2408–2415. IEEE (2012)

22. Nair, V., Hinton, G.E.: Rectified linear units improve restricted boltzmann machines. In: Proceedings of the 27th International Conference on Machine Learning (ICML 2010), pp. 807–814 (2010)

23. Reaves, D.: Aesthetic image rating (AIR) algorithm. Ph.D. thesis (2008)

24. Simard, P.Y., Steinkraus, D., Platt, J.C.: Best practices for convolutional neural networks applied to visual document analysis. In: 2013 12th International Conference on Document Analysis and Recognition, vol. 2, pp. 958–958. IEEE Computer Society (2003)

25. Spratt, E.L., Elgammal, A.: Computational beauty: Aesthetic judgment at the intersection of art and science. arXiv preprint arXiv:1410.2488 (2014)

26. Jost Tobias Springenberg and Martin Riedmiller. Improving deep neural networks with probabilistic maxout units. arXiv preprint arXiv:1312.6116 (2013)

27. Xu, Q., D'Souza, D., Ciesielski, V.: Evolving images for entertainment. In: Proceedings of the 4th Australasian Conference on Interactive Entertainment, p. 26. RMIT University (2007)

FuXi: A Fish-Driven Instrument
for Real-Time Music Performance

João Cordeiro[1,2](✉)

[1] Faculty of Creative Industries, University of Saint Joseph,
Rua de Londres, 16, Macau, China
joao.cordeiro@usj.edu.mo
[2] CITAR-Research Center in Science and Technology of the Arts,
Portuguese Catholic University of Portugal, Oporto, Portugal

Abstract. In this paper we present a system for real-time computer music performance (live electronics) and live visuals based on the behavior of a fish in an aquarium. The system is comprised of (1) an aquarium with a fish; (2) a computer vision module; (3) a visual display of the fish overlaid by graphical elements controlled by the user, (4) a sound synthesis module and (5) a standard MIDI controller. The musical expression and graphic generation is a combination of the fish movements and decisions made by the performer in real-time. By making use of a live animal, the system provides indeterminacy and natural gestures to the sound being generated. The match between sound and image shows some semantic redundancy, aiming at a more narrative compositional approach where the fish is the main character. The system is targeted to soundscape composition and electroacoustic music featuring a high degree of improvisation.

Keywords: Fish-driven instrument · Electroacoustic music · NIME · HCI · Improvisation · Indeterminism

1 Introduction

Music has evolved with mankind, shaping up to different eras and civilizations, serving as an expression of the ever-changing zeitgeists. Nonetheless, one may say that the *new music* of the XX century is based on such a disruptive approach when compared to the previous movements, that the sole definition of music had to be revised (an interesting contribution to the history of contemporary music can be found in [1] and [2]). It is within such unsettling but fruitful context that the first steps towards what is known today as Sound and Music Computing were given. The project that we present in this paper represents one of those examples of disruptiveness and experimentation that are frequently seen in academic and avant-garde artistic events. We introduce a fish-driven instrument where sound parameters and events are modified and triggered by the behavior of a fish and a human performer. Through this method we address two different issues of live electronics, first we introduce an organic gesture to

© Springer International Publishing Switzerland 2015
C. Johnson et al. (Eds.): EvoMUSART 2015, LNCS 9027, pp. 39–49, 2015.
DOI: 10.1007/978-3-319-16498-4_4

electronic music, contradicting the stiffness found in quantization and grid based methods, secondly we present a way to generate indeterminacy that will impact the course of the performance making each presentation unique. On the other hand, we also believe that our approach presents a good opportunity to close the gap between the audience and laptop artists, by matching visuals and sound in a direct and meaningful fashion. Throughout the next sections, we introduce the conceptual background and related areas behind the project, some examples of fish-based sound art, a detailed description of the system and a report of the first presentation of the system to an audience.

2   Related Areas

The system we propose links to several research and artistic fields, which combined give shape to an original interface for music creation. The artistic fields include (but are not limited to) improvisation, indeterminacy, soundscape composition, visuals and live electronics. The most relevant scientific fields addressed in this particular New Interface for Music Expression (NIME) include Computer Vision and System Control. A discussion on the way our system addresses each of the artistic and scientific fields mention above is presented next.

2.1   Indeterminacy

The concept of indeterminacy in music is broadly related with performance and compositional processes where the outcome is not totally controlled by the performer or composer. This concept shows some affinity with chance, aleatoric and stochastic music, depending on the production stage (performance vs. composition) and other intrinsic aspects of the production processes. No unified definition exists in literature that fully and unequivocally delimits these concepts or the way they relate with each other. Therefore, and because a deeper discussion is out of the scope of this paper, we assume the definition from John Cage, where a "composition is indeterminate with respect to its performance" [3]. It is during the performance that the musical work acquires "a unique form, which is to say a unique morphology of the continuity, a unique expressive content, for each performance" [3]. The system we present here shows greater empathy with indeterminacy, being suitable for music expressions characterized by a high level of freedom assigned to the performer, setting the stage for the improvisational aspect that drives the system's design and aesthetics. Our current use of the system has followed a macro-structural composition approach, using *action scores* "containing a description of how the sound should be produced rather than what it is to sound like. The production of sound was indicated by means of graphic signs; the optical image represented, as it were, the path or paths to be followed by the player in order to realise the musical intention" [4]. On the other side, the presence of a live organism such as a fish controlling different parameters of the sound production, will strongly determine the final result on the micro and mid levels of the piece, rendering it impossible to be represented by any notation.

The instrument constitutes a semi-autonomous performance system based on predefined rules, which can react to the fish's movements and performer actions. The performer's roll is to define the timbre properties of the instrument, tweak some of the pre-programed behaviours (of the system) in real-time and recall *scenes* (which correspond to snapshots of behaviours and timbre). There are several branches of electronic music instruments, ranging from those used in experimental musical approaches to the pop-culture synthesizer. The indeterminist essence of FuXi makes it suitable for experimental musical genres, with a certain affinity with soundscape compositions, due to the repetition of background sound events in different layers, timbres and cadencies. Moreover, the system is strongly anchored on the use of visuals, displaying a live animal overlaid by images that shape its environment. The music produced has a direct relation to the elements displayed and their interaction with the fish, emphasizing the idea of a soundtrack from a cinematography perspective.

2.2 Live Visuals

The use of live visuals during the performance of electronic music has been a common practice among different artists and a subject of debate among the scientific community. The visual element usually goes beyond the use of lighting, with an emphasis on computer generated graphics, video projection and video mapping for an increasing sense of depth. Conceptual discussions on this topic can be found in [5–8] and practical implementations of research in this area are detailed in [9–12]. In our opinion, the wide use of this resource is related with the dimmed activity usually associated with the performance of electronic music, where the performer usually stays on stage behind a laptop. The lack of expressive performing movements perceived by the audience tends to a visually dull show when comparing with other traditional music performances, where the cause-effect between gesture and sound is easily perceived. We are not judging the quality of this approach, only presenting a hypothesis for the generalized use of visuals in electroacoustic performances, where the ratio between the use of visuals seems to grow inversely to the gestural activity of the performers on stage. Our project addresses this issue by displaying synchronized figurative visuals, providing, a cause-effect relation between the image and the sound being produced.

2.3 System Control

The musical instrument presented here can be understood as an illusive hybrid ecosystem, where rule-based logical elements seemingly coexist with a live organism - the fish. However, the interaction between both is unidirectional - from the fish to the logical elements - since the images of the logic elements are invisible to the fish, thus having no impact on its behavior. Nonetheless, performer and audience perceive fish and logical elements as being part of an ecosystem confined to an aquarium, by watching both images seemingly projected onto a video canvas. While the fish behaves in a non-deterministic way, providing the system with random qualities, the logical elements are mostly comprised of linear function and piecewise linear function behaviors, producing a dynamic system with eventual tendency for chaos. The role of the performer is to act as an external control factor for the ecosystem, aiming at a meaningful auditory and visual display. That is possible by defining the occurrence and state of the logical elements which have pre-programed basic behaviors. This control can be characterized as an intuitive stochastic control, since random behaviors with limited probability distribution affect the evolution of the system (essentially the fish). This way, the user does not possess absolute control over the sound events (onset, volume, timbre, modulation, envelope) but can modify the overall system behavior in order to increase/decrease the chances for their occurrence, as well as the range of each parameter. For controlling the system, we propose Direct Manipulation Interfaces (DMI), such as knob-based/fade-based controllers and touch screen controllers (e.g. tablets).

3   Examples of Fish-Based Sound Art

It is not common to find musical instruments that make use of live animals as a constitutive part. While plans for a bizarre piano using cats (See Fig. 1) as the *sound engine* appear in literature [13], not many real examples are actually put in practice. Next we present three projects that use fish as the central element of a sound production artifact, which we consider an inspiration for the project described here.

Fig. 1. The cat organ. Bizarre instrument described by G. Schott in 1657.

3.1   Submersed Songs by Vivian Caccuri

In Submersed Songs, an interactive sound installation, sound input is processed by the movement of four fish in an aquarium (See Fig. 2). Users are asked to plug the output of their music players to a TRS plug, connecting their sound to a computer with a computer vision module. This way, "the fish carry the sound around the space and change the layers like a musical topography. The experience

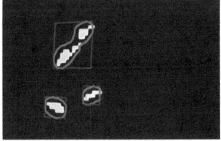

Fig. 2. View of the aquarium (left) and view of software for video tracking used in the sound installation Submersed Songs by Vivian Caccuri.

of this installation is to create an alternative physical / visual register for the songs that the participant is already used to, as well as to merge his personal music preferences to other people's" [14].

3.2 Quintetto by Quiet Ensemble

Quintetto is a sound installation/music performance project, where different layers (tracks) of a piece are manipulated based on the vertical movements of five fish in five different aquariums placed vertically side by side (See Fig. 3).

Fig. 3. View of the Quintetto Installation/Performance by Quiet Ensemble. In this case, five aquariums are used, each one with a single fish responsible for controlling one layer of the sound.

These movements are "captured by a videocamera, that translates (through a computer software) their movements in digital sound signals. (...) [we] have 5 different musical instruments creating a totally unexpected live concert" [15].

3.3 The Accessible Aquarium

This project was developed on the context of Informal Learning Environments (e.g., aquaria, zoos, science centers) to fulfill cognitive and aesthetic needs of visually impaired visitors to an aquarium. The Accessible Aquarium tracks the movement of the fish using a computer vision system in order to produce a meaningful soundscape through sonification techniques. It applies "methods of mapping fish movement to sounds, with the idea of providing some non-visual information about the attributes of the various fish being tracked, as well as their location and activities" [16]. Several experiments were accomplished by applying different mapping strategies, which conduct to distinct soundscapes. This project has progressed over time, with multiple approaches and implementations as reported in [17–21].

4 System Design and Implementation

Next we will present in detail the current implementation of the system, which can be augmented in future versions as described in the Future Work section. The system is comprised of (1) an aquarium with a fish; (2) a computer vision module, including a video camera for capturing the image of the fish; (3) a GUI displaying the fish image interleaved with graphical elements controlled by the user, (4) a computational sound module for the production of the auditory display and (5) a set of hardware devices for controlling the system. For the sake of stability, the graphic and sound tasks are accomplished using two different laptops (Fig. 4).

4.1 The Aquarium and the Fish

The fish chosen for this project is a Betta Splendens, commonly known by Siamese Fighting Fish (See Fig. 5). This species is quite popular in aquariums due to its vivid colors and beautiful fins. Around the age of six weeks, the fish develop a labyrinth organ, which allows them to breathe air at the surface of water. This way, it is not necessary to have oxygen pump or filter inside the aquarium, which contributes to keep the water calm and suitable for the computer vision task. The movements of the fish in the water are also interesting from the perspective of the musical expression, as it moves with light bumps followed by slowing movements, resulting in interesting musical gestures. The aquarium is custom made, in order to provide an optimal setup for the computer vision task. The priority was to restraint the fish to the field of view defined by the camera and avoid reflections caused by the water surface and the aquarium walls.

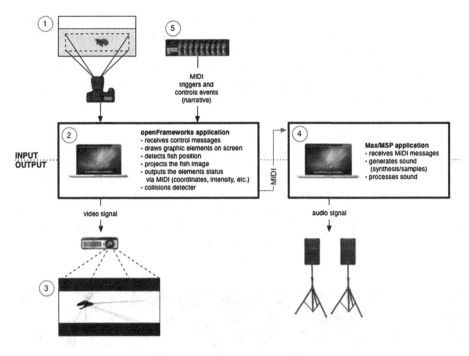

Fig. 4. FuXi system overview.

Fig. 5. Image of the Siamese fighting fish (scientific name: Betta splendens), used in our project.

4.2   Computer Vision

The computer vision module is comprised of a webcam (Logitech HD C510) connected via USB to a computer running a software program developed in openFrameworks. In order to keep the image processing faster, our approach was to accomplish the computer vision task over a smaller version of captured video and later scale the tracked position back to the original size (1080 × 720). Since in this version only one fish is utilized, the strategy proved to be quite effective, even under different light environments. The back of the aquarium is covered by white sticking paper and lighted from behind, using a costume made led wall. This way, the silhouette of the fish is very detailed, simplifying the computer vision process and producing a graphic image with a clean aesthetics.

4.3   Visuals / GUI

The GUI of the software (See Fig. 6) is the most visible part of the instrument, which is meant do be displayed on the up-stage wall where the performance takes place. The bottom line is that all triggered sounds have a corresponding visual event, either being the a fish touching walls of the aquarium, moving around, touching other visual elements, changing the size of the visual elements or changing the color. The goal of having the one-on-one matching is to provide audience with meaningful cause-effect sonic events.

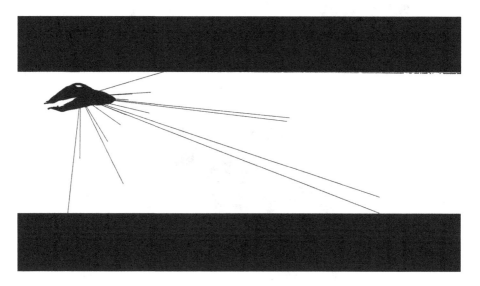

Fig. 6. GUI for FuXi. In this view the fish is overlaid with black lines that represent moorings.

4.4   Sound Synthesis

The sound synthesis module is programmed in Max/MSP and controlled through MIDI protocol directly from the MIDI controller. The sound module includes different elements, such as granular synthesis, additive synthesis, sample triggering and sound processing (reverb, delays, panning, etc.). The modular system architecture allows musicians with minimum programming skills in graphic programming languages, to adapt the sound identity of the system to different artistic concepts, by defining new sound sources and new mapping strategies between visual elements and sound output.

4.5 Mode of Interaction

The user, by means of hardware interfaces, controls several parameters of the logical elements within the system. Each type of element is programmed as an individual class using object-oriented programming (openFrameworks / C++) and is represented by a graphical element in the canvas, overlaying the image of the fish. The Graphic User Interface (GUI) is the same for the performer and audience. This way, by automating procedures, the instrument can easily be transformed into an interactive audiovisual installation making use of only one screen.

5 Discussion

This system was already tested and presented to an audience during the INTER-FACE International Conference on Live Interfaces, held in Lisbon on 21 November 2014. In this setup, two computers were used: one handling the computer vision task and the other the sound production, communicating with each other through the MIDI protocol (wireless) (See Fig. 7). From the performer's perspective the system is considered functional and stable. The audience also provided positive informal feedback, highlighting the surprise and hypnotic effect caused by the movements of the fish and its corresponding sounds.

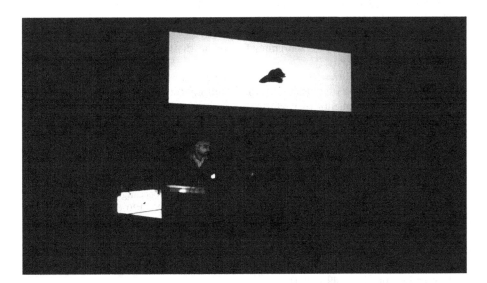

Fig. 7. View of the performance. On stage are the performer, an aquarium (on the left), two laptops (one for sound, one for live visuals), a webcam and a MIDI controller.

6   Future Work

Future developments in this project include experimenting with a higher number of fish, increasing the possibilities of narrative/compositional concepts. Additionally, combining more powerful video cameras with different lighting setups should provide further detail to the image of the fish, opening the door for more realistic aesthetic approaches. Future developments also include providing feedback to the fish, in order to close the feedback loop that characterizes interactive processes.

Acknowledgments. We would like to acknowledge the valuable artistic inputs coming from Prof. Álvaro Barbosa, Dr. José Alberto Gomes and Ana Cristina Dias; the expertise and encouragement from Professor David Flores Gonalves in the field of biology and fish behavior; and the financial support from GAES, which made possible the presentation of this work abroad.

References

1. Taruskin, R.: Music in the Late Twentieth Century: The Oxford History of Western Music. Oxford University Press, New York (2009)
2. Chadabe, J.: Electric Sound: The Past and Promise of Electronic Music. Pearson Education, Upper Saddle River (1996)
3. Cage, J.: Silence, 1st edn. Wesleyan University Press, Middletown (1961)
4. de Leeuw, T.: Music in Twenty Century: A Study of Its Elements and Structure. Amsterdam University Press, Amsterdam (2005)
5. Collopy, F.: Color, form, and motion: Dimensions of a musical art of light. Leonardo **33**(5), 355–360 (2000)
6. DeWitt, T.: Visual music: searching for an aesthetic. Leonardo **20**(2), 15–122 (1987)
7. Paradiso, J., O'modhrain, S.: Current trends in electronic music interfaces. J. New Music Res. **32**(4), 345–349 (2003). (Guest Editors' Introduction)
8. Peacock, K.: Instruments to perform color-music: two centuries of technological experimentation. Leonardo **21**(4), 397–406 (1988)
9. Franco, E., Griffith, N., Fernström, M.: Issues for Designing a flexible expressive audiovisual system for real-time performance & composition. In: Proceedings of the 2004 Conference on New Interfaces for Musical Expression (2004)
10. Levin, G., Lieberman, Z.: Sounds from shapes: audiovisual performance with hand silhouette contours in the manual input sessions. In: Proceedings of the 2005 Conference on New Interfaces for Musical Expression, pp. 115–120 (2005)
11. Levin, G.: Painterly interfaces for audiovisual performance. Ph.D. thesis, Massachusetts Institute of Technology (2000)
12. Lew, M.: Live Cinema: designing an instrument for cinema editing as a live performance. In: Proceedings of the 2004 Conference on New Interfaces for Musical Expression, pp. 144–149 (2004)
13. Schott, G.: Magia universalis natura et artis. Number, vol. 1 in Magia universalis natura et artis (1657)
14. Caccuri, V.: Canções Submersas (2008)
15. Quiet Enseble: Quintetto (2009)

16. Walker, B.N., Godfrey, M.T., Orlosky, J.E., Bruce, C., Sanford, J.: Aquarium sonification: Soundscapes for accessible dynamic informal learning environments. In: Proceedings of the 12th International Conference on Auditory Display, pp. 238–241. Citeseer (2006)
17. Walker, B.N., Kim, J., Pendse, A., Others: Musical soundscapes for an accessible aquarium: Bringing dynamic exhibits to the visually impaired. In: Proceedings of the International Computer Music Conference (ICMC 2007), Copenhagen, Denmark (2007)
18. Pendse, A., Pate, M., Walker, B.N.: The accessible aquarium: identifying and evaluating salient creature features for sonification. In: Proceedings of the 10th International ACM SIGACCESS Conference on Computers and Accessibility, Assets 2008, pp. 297–298. ACM, New York (2008)
19. Bruce, C., Walker, B.: Designing effective sound-based aquarium exhibit interpretation for visitors with vision impairments. In: Proceedings of the 12th International ACM SIGACCESS Conference on Computers and Accessibility, pp. 251–252. ACM (2010)
20. Jeon, M., Winton, R., Yim, J., Bruce, C., Walker, B.: Aquarium fugue: interactive sonification for children and visually impaired audience in informal learning environments. In: Proceedings of the 18th International Conference on Auditory Display, Atlanta (2012)
21. Jeon, M., Winton, R.J., Henry, A.G., Oh, S., Bruce, C.M., Walker, B.N.: Designing interactive sonification for live aquarium exhibits. In: Stephanidis, C. (ed.) HCII 2013, Part I. CCIS, vol. 373, pp. 332–336. Springer, Heidelberg (2013)

Chorale Music Splicing System: An Algorithmic Music Composer Inspired by Molecular Splicing

Clelia De Felice, Roberto De Prisco, Delfina Malandrino,
Gianluca Zaccagnino, Rocco Zaccagnino$^{(\boxtimes)}$, and Rosalba Zizza

Dipartimento di Informatica,
Università degli Studi di Salerno, Via Giovanni Paolo II, 132,
84084 Fisciano, SA, Italy
zaccagnino@di.unisa.it

Abstract. *Splicing systems* are a formal model of a generative mechanism of words (strings of characters), inspired by a recombinant behavior of DNA. They are defined by a finite alphabet $\mathcal{A}$, an initial set $\mathcal{I}$ of words and a set $\mathcal{R}$ of rules. Many of the studies about splicing systems focused on the properties of the generated languages and their theoretical computational power.

In this paper we propose the use of splicing systems for algorithmic music composition. Although the approach is general and can be applied to many types of music, in this paper, we focus the attention to the algorithmic composition of 4-voice chorale-like music. We have developed a Java implementation of this approach and we have provided an evaluation of the music output by the system.

1 Introduction

Modern computers are powerful means for creating, enjoying, and sharing art, music, film, and much more. Beside mere computations, computers are able to produce "creative" results, especially when the creation process is driven by clever algorithms. In the field of music, theory and application of new and existing technologies have been successfully employed in many aspects, such as sound synthesis, digital signal processing, sound design, and so on. A specific music problem which has been tackled with the use of computers is that of algorithmic (music) composition. In this paper we are interested in such a problem which can be defined as the problem of giving a formal process whose goal is that of producing music with no (or minimal) human intervention.

Algorithmic composition has always fascinated both computer scientists and musicians. The literature is full of examples, starting from the ILLIAC suite proposed by Hiller [1,2], to our knowledge the first piece of music written with the aid of a computer, to more recent efforts, such as, the works by Cope [3–5] and Miranda [6–10].

Various tools or techniques have been used to devise algorithms for music composition: random numbers, formal grammars, cellular automata, fractals,

© Springer International Publishing Switzerland 2015
C. Johnson et al. (Eds.): EvoMUSART 2015, LNCS 9027, pp. 50–61, 2015.
DOI: 10.1007/978-3-319-16498-4_5

neural networks, evolutionary algorithms, genetic algorithms (DNA and protein-based). The book by Miranda [11] provides a survey of several of these approaches.

In this paper we investigate the use of biological environment features, specifically those that characterize *splicing systems*, to develop a new system for algorithmic composition. To our knowledge, no other algorithmic composer has used splicing systems as the basis for the creation of music.

Splicing is a language-theoretic word operation, introduced by Head [12], which models a DNA recombination process, namely the action of two compatible restriction enzymes and a ligase enzyme on two DNA strands. Abstracting from the physical phenomenon, splicing is formalized as an operation on two words (strings) that generates new words. It concatenates a prefix of one string with a suffix of another string, under some conditions, represented as a (splicing) rule. A splicing system consists of a set $\mathcal{I}$ of words, the initial language, defined over an alphabet $\mathcal{A}$, and a set $\mathcal{R}$ of splicing rules. The language generated by a splicing system contains every word that can be obtained by repeated applications of rules to pair of words in the initial language and in the set of generated words. Splicing systems are a relatively old research topic in computer science and much early research effort has been devoted to the study of the computational power of such formal systems. The computational power mainly depends on the level of the Chomsky hierarchy that $\mathcal{I}$ and $\mathcal{R}$ belong to. For instance, the class of languages generated by splicing systems with a finite initial language and a finite set of rules, often referred to as finite splicing systems, contains all finite languages and it is strictly contained in the class of regular languages. This result has been proved in several papers by using different approaches (see [13,14]). Splicing systems theory is still an interesting field of research, with complex open problems, as shown by more recent literature on this topic, such as [15–18].

Contribution of this paper. In this paper we propose a new approach for algorithmic composition of 4-voice (chorale) music based on splicing systems, that we call *chorale music splicing systems*. Since splicing systems generate languages of words, the basic idea of our approach is to treat music compositions as words and to view the music compositional process as the results of operations on words. We focus our attention on a specific type of music composition, namely chorales and we build a music splicing system using as basis some Bach's chorales. The system exploits a ground set consisting of some chorales written by Bach. From this ground set we extract information about the chords in each beat of the music and we create the set of rules according to some well-established rules in classical music composition. The system has been implemented in Java.

In order to assess the quality of the produced music the output has been compared with another system that produces similar compositions, i.e., EvoBass-Composer, a multi-objective genetic algorithmic composer for 4-voice music [19].

Related Work. Writing automatic composers for 4-voice chorale-like music has been already considered in different works. For example Ebcioglu [20] and Schottstedt [21] described automatic composers based on rules and expert-systems.

Another system capable of composing 4-voice chorales (and not only) is the EMI system by Cope [3,5]; the EMI system uses a combination of techniques (formal grammars, analysis, pattern matching). Lehmann [22] uses an approach based on neural networks. Phon-Amnuaisuk [23] investigated the use of heterogeneous cellular automata. In [19] a multi-objective genetic algorithm has been used.

Among the works on automatic composers that use genetic algorithms we cite the work by Horner and Goldberg [24] for thematic bridging, the work by Biles [25] for Jazz solos, the work by Jacob [26] which use an interactive genetic algorithm (i.e., it needs human intervention). Horner and Ayers [27] use genetic algorithms to harmonize chords progressions. The paper by De Prisco and Zaccagnino [28] provides a genetic algorithm that solves the *figured* bass problem, that is, the input already contains the chords to be used for each bass note. Hence the algorithm has to find only the position of the voices for each chord in the input.

Other works that are closer to our paper are those by McIntyre [29] and by Wiggings [30]. In these two papers, automatic composers that use a genetic algorithm are presented.

To the best of our knowledge the system proposed in this paper is the first attempt to define an algorithmic composer based on splicing systems.

2   Background

In this section we briefly recall the needed background to understand the rest of the paper. We assume that the reader is already familiar both with music concepts (tonality, chords, harmony rules, etc.) and with splicing systems; this section is intended only to recall such notions, the former for the benefit of the computer scientist not versed in music and the latter for the benefit of the musician not acquainted with splicing systems.

2.1   Music Background

We consider the tempered music system used in western countries. Tempered music is based on the notion of tonality. Roughly speaking, a tonality is a group of notes which form a scale. Starting from each of the 12 notes in an octave one can have a tonality (there are various kinds for each note, like major, minor, etc.). A piece has a main tonality, and notes of the corresponding scale are considered more important than notes outside the scale. Western music, starting from the common practice period, is based upon harmonic and melodic rules for the tempered system, which are very well-established. A description of such rules is discussed in [31]. Here we recall only some important concepts relevant to our paper.

We focus our attention on music composed in 4 voices; unparalleled examples of such type of compositions are Bach's chorales. A chorale consists of 4 independent voices, corresponding to *bass*, *tenor*, *alto* and *soprano*. The range of notes that the 4 voices can play/sing covers approximately 4 octaves that we call octave 3, 4, 5 and 6 (with respect to the 7 octaves of the piano keyboard).

A piece of music consists of a sequence of *measures*, each consisting of a given number of *beats*. In each beat the 4 voices play or sing a note (this a simplification of what really happens since a composition may have also other notes which are not part of the harmony). The vertical set of notes in a beat is a *chord*. The notion of chord is fundamental. It is largely accepted that some sequences of chords are more pleasant and/or have a better function, than others. For example, the cadence II - V - I, is very common.

For further details see [31].

2.2 Splicing Systems

In [12] Head has formalized the biochemical operation of splicing as an operation on strings. Following Head's work there have been further development of such an abstraction, in particular Păun [32] and Pixton [33] have introduced alternative operations. Each of these operations take as input two words and can generate either one new word, 1-splicing, or 2 new words, 2-splicing.

In this paper we will use the 2-splicing operation introduced by Păun.

A Păun's 2-splicing rule r is explicited in the form $r = u_1 \# u_2 \$ u_3 \# u_4$, where u_1, u_2, u_3, u_4 are strings over a given alphabet $\mathcal{A}$ such that $\#, \$ \notin \mathcal{A}$. The words $u_1 u_2$ (concatenation of u_1 and u_2), and $u_3 u_4$ (concatenation of u_3 and u_4) are called *sites* of r. Roughly speaking, a site is a substring of the input words where we can "cut" the input words. Hence a rule identifies two points where we can cut the input strings.

Given such a rule r, and two words x and y belonging to the current language, if x contains the first site $u_1 u_2$, that is $x = x_1 u_1 u_2 x_2$, and y contains the second site $u_3 u_4$, that is $y = y_1 u_3 u_4 y_2$, rule r produces the strings $z = x_1 u_1 u_4 y_2$, $w = y_1 u_3 u_2 x_2$. We denote this operation by $(x, y) \vdash_r (z, w)$. Notice that if an input words contains a site multiple times, then the operation can be applied multiple times so that 2 new words are generated for each pair of 2 sites in the input words.

Example 1. Let $r = a \# b \$ c \# d$ and consider $x = eabf$ and $y = gcdh$. Then *eadh* and *gcbf* are generated by splicing. If we consider $x = eabfiabl$ and $y = gcdh$, then *eadh*, *gcbfiabl*, *aebfiadh* and *gcbl* are generated.

Splicing systems are models for generating languages based on the splicing operation. In order to generate a language using a splicing system we start from an initial set of words (often called the initial language) and we apply the rules of the splicing system to produce new words which are added to the initial set.

More formally a *splicing system* is a triple $\mathcal{S} = (\mathcal{A}, \mathcal{I}, \mathcal{R})$, where $\mathcal{A}$ is a finite alphabet such that $\#, \$ \notin \mathcal{A}$, $\mathcal{I} \subseteq \mathcal{A}^*$ is the initial language and $\mathcal{R} \subseteq \mathcal{A}^* \# \mathcal{A}^* \$ \mathcal{A}^* \# \mathcal{A}^*$ is the set of rules. A splicing system $\mathcal{S}$ is finite if $\mathcal{I}$ and $\mathcal{R}$ are both finite sets. Let $L \subseteq \mathcal{A}^*$. We set $\sigma'(L) = \{w', w'' \in \mathcal{A}^* \mid (x, y) \vdash_r (w', w''), x, y \in L, r \in \mathcal{R}\}$.

The splicing operation on languages is defined as follows:

$$\sigma^0(L) = L,$$
$$\sigma^{i+1}(L) = \sigma^i(L) \cup \sigma'(\sigma^i(L)), \ i \geq 0,$$
$$\sigma^*(L) = \bigcup_{i \geq 0} \sigma^i(L).$$

Definition 1 (Păun splicing language). *Given a splicing system* $\mathcal{S} = (\mathcal{A}, \mathcal{I}, \mathcal{R})$, *the language generated by* $\mathcal{S}$ *is* $L(\mathcal{S}) = \sigma^*(\mathcal{I})$. *A language* L *is* $\mathcal{S}$-*generated (or is a* Păun *splicing language) if there exists a splicing system* $\mathcal{S}$ *such that* $L = L(\mathcal{S})$.

3   Chorale Music Splicing System

In this section we describe the chorale music splicing system, i.e., an algorithmic composer based on splicing systems that generates chorale-like music. The basic idea is the following. We start from a ground data set of Bach's chorales, representing them as words; such words are the initial set of the splicing system. Then we apply the splicing system to produce a language from the initial set. Such a language will contain many words; the actual number depends on the initial set and the set of rules of the splicing system. We remark that the process is deterministic. In ordered to generate the final language the splicing process has to be applied many times. This process might take a very long time, so for practical applications, such as the one we are proposing, we may stop the generation at some point and proceed with the language generated so far. Once we stop the splicing process we need to choose one single word from the generated language as the output of the system.

In the following we provide details about the application of the above described idea to 4-voice chorale-like music. The first thing we need is a representation of music in terms of words, and a mechanism of combination of music compositions in terms of rules. As we have said in the previous section, a splicing system $\mathcal{S}$ consist of three components: an alphabet $\mathcal{A}$ of the symbols used, an initial set $\mathcal{I}$ of words and a set $\mathcal{R}$ of rules. In the following we will give these components for the chorale music splicing system $\mathcal{S}_{\text{CMSS}} = (\mathcal{A}_{\text{CMSS}}, \mathcal{I}_{\text{CMSS}}, \mathcal{R}_{\text{CMSS}})$.

3.1   The Alphabet $\mathcal{A}_{\text{CMSS}}$

The alphabet we need has to allow us to specify the notes for each voice. Let $\mathcal{A}_V = \{\beta, \tau, \alpha, \sigma\}$ be the voice alphabet, where β stands for bass, τ for tenor, α for alto and σ for soprano. Let $\mathcal{A}_N = \{C, C\#, Db, D, D\#, Eb, E, F, F\#, Gb, G, G\#, Ab, A, A\#, Bb, B\}$ be the notes alphabet and $\mathcal{A}_O = \{3, 4, 5, 6\}$ be the octaves alphabet. Then let $\mathcal{A}_{\text{CMSS}} = \mathcal{A}_V \cup \mathcal{A}_N \cup \mathcal{A}_O$.

Using $\mathcal{A}_{\text{CMSS}}$ we can represent 4-voice chorale-like music as words. Notice that the "composition" that we will represent are sequences of chords. They might represent an entire chorale but also a fragment of it consisting of a few measures or even a single chord. A chord contains the notes sung (or played) in a specific beat by the bass, the tenor, the alto and the soprano voice (or instrument). Hence a 4-voice composition is a sequence $C = (c_1, \ldots, c_n)$ where each c_i is a chord, for each $1 \leq i \leq n$.

We can represent chord c_i as a word over $\mathcal{A}_{\mathrm{CMSS}}$, more precisely, c_i, for each $1 \leq i \leq n$, can be represented as $w_i = \beta x_i \tau y_i \alpha v_i \sigma z_i$, where $x_i, y_i, v_i, z_i \in \mathcal{A}_N \mathcal{A}_O$.

An entire composition $C = (c_1, \ldots, c_n)$ is represented as $w(C) = w_1 w_2 \cdots w_n$.

Let $\mathcal{C} = \{C_1, \ldots, C_k\}$ be a set of 4-voice compositions (entire compositions, fragments or even single chords). The set of words associated to $\mathcal{C}$ is $\mathcal{W}(\mathcal{C}) = \{w(C_1), \ldots, w(C_k)\}$. We also say that $\mathcal{C}$ is the set of 4-voice compositions associated to $\mathcal{W}$.

Example 2. Let us consider the 4-voice music fragment C in Fig. 1 (a fragment of Chorale BWV 32.6), $C = (c_1, c_2, c_3, c_4)$. We have $w_1 = \beta G4\tau B4\alpha D5\sigma G5$, $w_2 = \beta F\#4\tau A4\alpha D5\sigma A5$, $w_3 = \beta G4\tau G4\alpha D5\sigma B5$, $w_4 = \beta D4\tau G4\alpha D5\sigma A5$, so $w = \beta G4\tau B4\alpha D5\sigma G5 \beta F\#4\tau A4\alpha D5\sigma A5 \beta G4\tau G4\alpha D5\sigma B5 \beta D4\tau G4\alpha D5\sigma A5$.

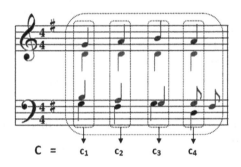

Fig. 1. A fragment of BWV 32.6

3.2   The Initial Set of Words $\mathcal{I}_{\mathrm{CMSS}}$

In order to define the initial set of words we have selected some Bach's chorales. Namely, we chose the following 10 chorales: BWV 3.6, BWV 10.7, BWV 11.6, BWV 12.7, BWV 13.6, BWV 14.5, BWV 20.7, BWV 20.11, BWV 31.9 and BWV 32.6. Each one of these chorales was transposed in every tonality so our ground data set, which we will denote with $\mathcal{G}$, contained 10*12=120 words, each one representing a chorale, with each group of 12 words being the same chorale in 12 tonalities. The set $\mathcal{I}_{\mathrm{CMSS}}$ contains the 120 words that represent the chorales in $\mathcal{G}$.

Moreover we will also insert into $\mathcal{I}_{\mathrm{CMSS}}$ some single chords as we will specify later in the next section. (These chords will come up in the definition of the rules.)

3.3   Rules Definition

The definition of the rules is very important because the rules determine the language being generated. We would like to provide rules that produce good patterns of music. In order to do so we analyze and extract single chords from the chorales in the ground data set $\mathcal{G}$ so that we can (sort of) reproduce music that is similar to that in the ground data set. During the chord extraction we attach to the extracted chord also information about its original function, that is, the degree of the scale on which the chord is built. This information will be crucial in re-arranging the chords, by means of splicing rules, so that specific sequences of chords (e.g., cadences) will be produced. As done for the initial set, we have transposed each extracted chord in all 12 tonalities.

In more details, we have extracted $13 * 12 = 156$ chords from the BWV 3.6, $18 * 12 = 216$ chords from the BWV 10.7, $9 * 12 = 108$ chords from the BWV 11.6, $17 * 12 = 204$ chords from the BWV 12.7, $19 * 12 = 588$ chords from the BWV 13.6, $7 * 12 = 228$ chords from the BWV 14.5, $5 * 12 = 60$ chords from the BWV 20.7, $16 * 12 = 192$ chords from the BWV 20.11, $16 * 12 = 192$ chords from the BWV 31.9, $18 * 12 = 216$ chords from the BWV 32.6, for a total of 2160 chords. We call $Chords(\mathcal{G})$ the set of these chords. The reason why we selected only some chords in each chorale and not every one was to keep the cardinality of $Chords(\mathcal{G})$ to a reasonable size.

For each extracted chord $c \in Chords(\mathcal{G})$, we store the information, provided by the harmonic analysis, about the degree on which the chord is built. We denote with $Degree(c)$ the degree of c. The set of words associated to $Chords(\mathcal{G})$ is $\mathcal{W}(Chords(\mathcal{G}))$.

We model the set of splicing rules on the basis of the classical harmonic rules (see Sect. 2.1). In particular we have decided to model as splicing rules the following musical cadences:

1. V → I
2. II → V
3. VI → II
4. V → VI
5. IV → V
6. IV → I
7. III → VI.

Moreover we also want that a composition starts and ends with a chord built on the first (I) degree of the scale, since this is what happens normally. We remark that for each of these situations (each cadence, and the starting and ending of the composition) we will define several rules of the splicing system.

Thus we can group all the rules in three sets of rules:

Rules for starting with I: For each pair of chords $c_1, c_4 \in Chords(\mathcal{G})$, such that $Degree(c_1) = I$, we define a rule $r = w_1 \# \epsilon \$ \epsilon \# w_4$ where ϵ is the empty word, w_1 is the word associated to c_1 and w_4 is the word associated to c_4. Moreover we also insert w_1 in $\mathcal{I}_{\text{CMSS}}$.

Rules for cadences: For each quadruple of chords $c_1, c_2, c_3, c_4 \in Chords(\mathcal{G})$, such that both $Degree(c_1) \to Degree(c_4)$ and $Degree(c_3) \to Degree(c_2)$ are cadences, we define the rule $r = w_1 \# w_2 \$ w_3 \# w_4$ where w_i is the word associated to c_i, for $i = 1, 2, 3, 4$.

Rules for ending with I: For each pair of chords $c_1, c_4 \in Chords(\mathcal{G})$, such that $Degree(c_4) = I$ we define a rule $r = w_1 \# \epsilon \$ \epsilon \# w_4$ where w_1 is the word associated to c_1 and w_4 is the word associated to c_4. Word w_4 is also inserted into $\mathcal{I}_{\mathrm{CMSS}}$.

The above set of rules, applied to the ground set $\mathcal{G}$ yields a total of $1,658,880$ in $\mathcal{R}_{\mathrm{CMSS}}$.

4 Choosing the Output

In the previous sections we have described the 3 components of the system $\mathcal{S}_{\mathrm{CMSS}} = (\mathcal{A}_{\mathrm{CMSS}}, \mathcal{I}_{\mathrm{CMSS}}, \mathcal{R}_{\mathrm{CMSS}})$. What remains to describe is how we produce the output composition. In order to do so, we use the system $\mathcal{S}_{\mathrm{CMSS}}$ to generate the language $L = L(\mathcal{S}_{\mathrm{CMSS}})$. As an implementation detail we remark that the generation of the complete language L (by complete we mean including all the possible words that can be generated) might require too many applications of the splicing rules. Hence our system will stop after a fixed number of iterations. Each iteration corresponds to one application of all the rules in $\mathcal{I}_{\mathrm{CMSS}}$ to all possible pairs of words in the current language. We will denote with $L_k(\mathcal{S}_{\mathrm{CMSS}})$ the language obtained after k iterations. In the tests we have used the following values for k: $10, 50, 100, 500, 1000$.

Once the language $L_k(\mathcal{S}_{\mathrm{CMSS}})$ has been generated we need to choose one single word $w \in L_k(\mathcal{S}_{\mathrm{CMSS}})$ as the output of the algorithmic composer. Obviously, the output of the composer is the composition represented by such a word.

In order to choose the output word (composition) we use a function that measures the harmonic quality of the composition whose definition (given in the following) is based on "weights" assigned to pairs of consecutive chords. Such weights have been chosen so that good harmonic pattern have heavier weights. We remark that this measure is the same that we have used in [19].

	I	ii	iii	IV	V	vi	vii°
I	250	200	50	200	250	50	10
ii	100	100	100	150	2000	150	10
iii	100	100	100	200	100	250	10
IV	250	150	100	200	1500	100	10
V	2000	100	100	100	250	150	10
vi	100	200	150	150	200	200	10
vii°	1000	50	150	50	50	100	200

Major

	i	2°	3°	4°	5°	6°	7°
i	250	250	50	200	250	50	10
2°	100	100	100	150	250	150	10
3°	100	100	100	200	100	250	10
4°	250	150	100	200	200	100	10
5°	250	100	100	100	250	150	10
6°	100	200	100	100	200	200	10
7°	250	50	150	50	10	10	200

Minor

Fig. 2. Weights for stepping between chords in the same tonality. In the right side we used $2°, 3°$ etc. because in a minor tonality on these degrees we can have several types of chords (e.g. on the second degree we can have ii or $ii°$).

Given a composition $C = (c_1, \ldots, c_n)$, the harmonic value $h(C)$ of C is obtained by giving a weight for (c_i, c_{i+1}), with $i = 1, 2, \ldots, n - 1$, as follows:

- if c_i and c_{i+1} are chords in the same major tonality, the weights are given in Fig. 2 (left side).
- if c_i and c_{i+1} are chords in the same minor tonality, the weights are given in Fig. 2 (right side).

In a similar way we assign weights to the pair (c_i, c_{i+1}) when c_i and c_{i+1} modulate, that is c_i belongs to a tonality and c_{i+1} belongs to another tonality. Due to lack of space we omit the tables that show the weights for these cases. The value of $f_h(C)$ is given by the sum of the weights for each pair (c_i, c_{i+1}) for $i = 1, 2, \ldots, n - 1$.

Let's consider as an example the sequence of chords I-IV-VI-V-IV-I-V-I; the harmonic value of such sequence is $200+100+200+100+250+250+2000 = 3100$.

Since the generated language contains words of different lengths, we use an average value of the harmonic function to select the best word as follows. For each $w \in L_k(\mathcal{S}_{\text{CMSS}})$ we consider the composition $C(w)$ corresponding to w, we compute the harmonic value $f_h(C(w))$ and we consider the average value computed over the length of composition, $f_h^{ave}(C(w)) = f_h(C(w))/(n-1)$, where n is the length of the composition. In other words $f_h^{ave}(C(w))$ is the average weight per pair of consecutive chords.

The output of the algorithmic composer is simply the composition of $L_k(\mathcal{S}_{\text{CMSS}})$ that maximizes $f_h^{ave}(C(w))$.

We remark that the output of the system is deterministic and it depends on the initial language $\mathcal{I}_{\text{CMSS}}$ (which depends on the ground set $\mathcal{G}$) and on the set of rules $\mathcal{R}_{\text{CMSS}}$ (which depends on $\mathcal{G}$ and on the set of cadences).

5   Comparison with EvoBassComposer

In order to evaluate the music produced by the Chorale Music Splicing System $\mathcal{S}_{\text{CMSS}}$, we have compared its output with that of another algorithmic composer that we have developed in the past, namely the EvoBassComposer [19]. EvoBassComposer is an algorithmic composer that takes as input a bass line and produces a 4-voice composition with that bass line.

To compare the two systems we have generated 5 outputs of $\mathcal{S}_{\text{CMSS}}$ using the following number of iterations: $10, 50, 100, 500, 1000$.

Then for each output, we have run EvoBassComposer giving it as input the bass line of each of the 5 outputs of $\mathcal{S}_{\text{CMSS}}$. Since EvoBassComposer is a genetic algorithm, and thus it runs for a given number of generations, we have used a number of generations that is equal to the number of iterations used in $\mathcal{S}_{\text{CMSS}}$.

The output of the EvoBassComposer depends also on the size of the initial population (see [19] for more details). Because of this, we have used it 5 times with population sizes $10, 20, 30, 40$ and 50 and to compare the harmonic value of the output with that of $\mathcal{S}_{\text{CMSS}}$ we have computed the average value over the 5 executions.

The comparison is shown in Fig. 3.

The x axis represents the number of generations for EvoBassComposer and the number of iterations for $\mathcal{S}_{\text{CMSS}}$, while the y axis shows the average harmonic value of the output of the two systems.

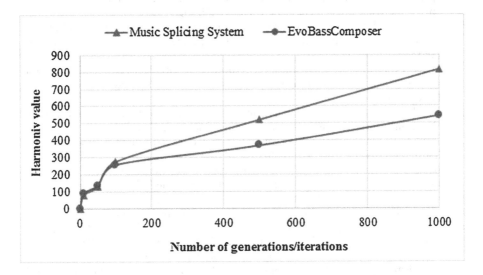

Fig. 3. Comparison between the Music Splicing System $\mathcal{S}_{\text{CMSS}}$ and EvoBassComposer

As can be seen from the figure, from about generation/iteration 100 the output of $\mathcal{S}_{\text{CMSS}}$ is, on average, better than that of EvoBassComposer, according to the harmonic evaluation function.

6 Conclusion

Various biological and natural processes have inspired systems for automatic music composition: cellular automata, fractals, neural networks, evolutionary algorithms, genetic music (DNA and protein-based music). In this work we described the splicing model, a generative mechanism of linear words, inspired by a recombinant behavior of linear DNA. To the best of our knowledge, this is the first attempt to use such formal systems to produce music.

Future work involve a deeper investigation of the potential of the approach presented in this paper. In particular it would be interesting to study the behavior of the system by changing the ground data set that determines the output. It would be interesting also to introduce rules that target the structure of the composition so that the output might have a better overall structure modeled over that of the chorale (the current rules concern only the initial and ending chords, and pair of consecutive chords).

References

1. Hiller, L.: Computer music. Sci. Am. **201**(6), 737–759 (1959)
2. Hiller, L., Isaacson, L.: Experimental Music. McGraw-Hill, New York (1959)
3. Cope, D.: Experiments in Musical Intelligence. A-R Editions, Madison (1996)
4. Cope, D.: The Algorithmic Composer. A-R Editions, Madison (2000)
5. Cope, D.: Virtual Music. The MIT Press, Cambridge (2004)
6. Gimenes, C., Miranda, E., Johnson, C.: On the learning stages of an intelligent rhythmic generator. In: Sound and Music Computing, Salerno, Italy, pp. 244–253 (2005)
7. Gimenes, C., Miranda, E., Johnson, C.: Towards an intelligent rhythmic generator based on given examples: a memetic approach. In: Sound and Music Computing, Glasgow, UK (2005)
8. Miranda, E.: On the music of emergent behaviour: what can evolutionary computation bring to the musician? Leonardo **36**(1), 55–58 (2003)
9. Miranda, E.: On the evolution of music in a society of self-taught digital creatures. Digit. Creativity **1**(1), 29–42 (2003)
10. Miranda, E., Kirby, S., Todd, P.: On computational models of the evolution of music: from the origins of musical taste to the emergence of grammars. Contemp. Music Rev. **22**(3), 91–111 (2003)
11. Miranda, E.: Composing Music with Computers. Focal Press, Oxford (2001)
12. Head, T.: Formal language theory and dna: an analysis of the generative capacity of specific recombinant behaviours. Bull. Math. Biol. **49**, 737–759 (1987)
13. Head, T., Păun, G., Pixton, D.: Language theory and molecular genetics: generative mechanisms suggested by dna recombination. In: Rozenberg, G., Salomaa, A. (eds.) Handbook of Formal Languages, vol. 2, pp. 295–360. Springer, Heidelberg (1996)
14. Zizza, R.: Splicing systems. Scholarpedia **5**(7), 9397 (2010)
15. Bonizzoni, P., de Felice, C., Zizza, R.: The structure of reflexive regular splicing languages via schützenberger constants. Theor. Comput. Sci. **334**(1–3), 71–98 (2005)
16. Bonizzoni, P., Jonoska, N.: Regular splicing languages must have a constant. In: Mauri, G., Leporati, A. (eds.) DLT 2011. LNCS, vol. 6795, pp. 82–92. Springer, Heidelberg (2011)
17. Head, T., Pixton, D.: Splicing and regularity. In: Esik, Z., Martín-Vide, C., Mitrana, V. (eds.) Recent Advances in Formal Languages and Applications. SCI, pp. 119–147. Springer, Heidelberg (2006)
18. Kari, L., Kopecki, S.: Deciding whether a regular language is generated by a splicing system. In: Stefanovic, D., Turberfield, A. (eds.) DNA 2012. LNCS, vol. 7433, pp. 98–109. Springer, Heidelberg (2012)
19. De Prisco, R., Zaccagnino, G., Zaccagnino, R.: Evobasscomposer: a multi-objective genetic algorithm for 4-voice compositions. In: GECCO, pp. 817–818, ACM (2010)
20. Ebcioglu, K.: An expert system for harmonizing four-part chorales. Machine Models of Music, pp. 385–401. MIT Press, Cambridge (1992)
21. Schottstaedt, B.: Automatic species counterpoint. Technical Report, Stanford, STAN-M-19, May 1984
22. Lehmann, D.: Harmonizing melodies in real-time: the connectionist approach. In: Proceedings of the International Computer Music Association, pp. 27–31 (1997)
23. Phon-Amnuaisuk, S.: Composing using heterogeneous cellular automata. In: Giacobini, M., Brabazon, A., Cagnoni, S., Di Caro, G.A., Ekárt, A., Esparcia-Alcázar, A.I., Farooq, M., Fink, A., Machado, P. (eds.) EvoWorkshops 2009. LNCS, vol. 5484, pp. 547–556. Springer, Heidelberg (2009)

24. Horner, A., Goldberg, D.: Genetic algorithms and computer assisted music composition. Technical report, University of Illinois (1991)
25. Biles, J.A.: Genjam: a genetic algorithm for generating jazz solos. In: International Computer Music Conference, pp. 131–137 (1994)
26. Jacob, B.L.: Composing with genetic algorithms. Technical report, University of Michigan (1995)
27. Horner, A., Ayers, L.: Harmonization of musical progression with genetic algorithms. In: International Computer Music Conference, pp. 483–484 (1995)
28. De Prisco, R., Zaccagnino, R.: An evolutionary music composer algorithm for bass harmonization. In: Giacobini, M., Brabazon, A., Cagnoni, S., Di Caro, G.A., Ekárt, A., Esparcia-Alcázar, A.I., Farooq, M., Fink, A., Machado, P. (eds.) EvoWorkshops 2009. LNCS, vol. 5484, pp. 567–572. Springer, Heidelberg (2009)
29. McIntyre, R.: Bach in a box: the evolution of four part baroque harmony using the genetic algorithm. In: International Conference on Evolutionary Computation, pp. 852–857 (1994)
30. Wiggins, G., Papadopoulos, G., Amnuaisuk, S., Tuson, A.: Evolutionary methods for musical composition. In: CASYS98 Workshop on Anticipation, Music and Cognition (1998)
31. Piston, W., DeVoto, M.: Harmony. W. W. Norton, New York (1987)
32. Păun, G.: On the splicing operation. Discrete Appl. Math. **70**, 57–79 (1996)
33. Pixton, D.: Regularity of splicing languages. Discrete Appl. Math. **69**(1–2), 101–124 (1996)

Towards an Evolutionary Computational Approach to Articulatory Vocal Synthesis with PRAAT

Jared Drayton[✉] and Eduardo Miranda

Interdisciplinary Centre for Computer Music Research,
Plymouth University, Plymouth, UK
jared.drayton@students.plymouth.ac.uk,
eduardo.miranda@plymouth.ac.uk

Abstract. This paper presents our current work into developing an evolutionary computing approach to articulatory speech synthesis. Specifically, we implement genetic algorithms to find optimised parameter combinations for the re-synthesis of a vowel using the articulatory synthesiser PRAAT. Our framework analyses the target sound using Fast Fourier Transform (FFT) to obtain formant information, which is then harnessed in a fitness function applied to a real valued genetic algorithm using a generation size of 75 sounds over 50 generations. In this paper, we present three differently configured genetic algorithms (GAs) and offer a comparison of their suitability for elevating the average fitness of the re-synthesised sounds.

Keywords: Articulatory vocal synthesis · Vocal synthesis · Evolutionary computing · Speech · PRAAT · Genetic algorithms

1 Introduction

Computing technology has advanced at a rapid frequency over the last eighty years. As computers are becoming more ubiquitous in our everyday lives, the need to communicate with our technology is increasing. Speech synthesis is the artificial production of human speech and features in an increasing amount of our digital devices. We can see the use of speech synthesis in a wide span of technologies, ranging from car GPS navigation to video games. Currently, there are three main approaches to artificially producing speech: concatenative synthesis, formant synthesis and articulatory synthesis. Out of these three, concatenative synthesis is the approach that dominates.

Concatenative speech synthesis is a sound synthesis approach where small sound units of pre-recorded speech are selected from a database, and sequenced together to produce a target sound or sound sequence. This approach currently offers the highest amount of intelligibility and naturalness when compared to the other techniques available. Because the technique relies on the arranging

© Springer International Publishing Switzerland 2015
C. Johnson et al. (Eds.): EvoMUSART 2015, LNCS 9027, pp. 62–70, 2015.
DOI: 10.1007/978-3-319-16498-4_6

of sound recordings from human speakers, it bypasses some of the drawbacks inherent in other methods; for example, the unnatural timbre of formant synthesis, or an imperfect physical model used in articulatory synthesis. However, there are a number of limitations on concatenative synthesis systems that result from its reliance on pre-recorded speech. The corpus of sounds that concatenative synthesis relies on is finite, and the segments themselves cannot be modified extensively without negatively impacting the quality and naturalness of the sound. This severely limits the capacity to modify prosody in relation to the text given. Therefore, to account for different types of prosody, it must be accounted for in the creation of the original corpus.

Articulatory synthesis is widely considered to have the biggest potential out of all current speech synthesis techniques [1]. However, as it stands, articulatory speech synthesis is largely unexploited and undeveloped. This is largely attributed to the difficulty of producing a robust articulatory Text To Speech (TTS) system that can perform on a par with existing concatenative solutions. This is due to the highly complex and non-linear relationship between parameters and the resultant sound. There have been a number of different approaches attempted for extracting vocal tract area functions, or articulatory movements. These range from using methods of imaging the vocal apparatus during speech (using machines such as an X-Ray [2] or MRI [3]) to attaching sensors to the articulators themselves. Inversion of parameters from the original audio has also been attempted [4].

In this paper we present a framework for developing an evolutionary computing approach to articulatory speech synthesis together with some initial results. The primary motivation for this research is to explore approaches to an automatic system of obtaining vocal tract area functions from recorded speech data. This is highly desirable in furthering the field of articulatory synthesis and the field of speech synthesis in general.

2 Background

2.1 Articulatory Synthesis

Articulatory synthesis is a physical modelling approach to sound synthesis. These physical models emulate the physiology of the human vocal apparatus. They simulate how air exhaled from the lungs is modified by the glottis and larynx, then propagated through the vocal tract and further modified by the articulators such as the tongue and lips. Control of this synthesis method is achieved by passing numerical values to parameters that correspond to individual muscles or muscles groupings. Therefore, any set of parameter values can be thought of as describing an articulatory configuration or articulatory movement i.e. describing a vocal area tract function (Fig. 1).

There are a number of different approaches when it comes to the design of articulatory synthesisers. Some synthesisers favour the use of a simplified periodic signal in place of physically modelling the larynx. This allows the fundamental frequency or pitch to be defined manually, and decrease the complexity of the model. By not attempting to simulate the lungs and larynx, the realism

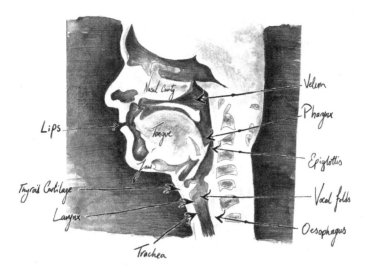

Fig. 1. Mid-Sagittal View of the Human Vocal Apparatus

in terms of phonetic quality is reduced. Breathing patterns also have a great impact on prosody, and are also essential for accurately modelling of fricatives and plosive speech sounds.

2.2 Evolutionary Computation

Within the field of evolutionary computing, there is a group of heuristic search techniques known as evolutionary algorithms that draw inspiration from the neo-Darwinian paradigm of evolution and survival of the fittest. These evolutionary algorithms work on an iterative process of generating solutions and testing their fitness and suitability using a fitness function, then combining genetic material from the fittest candidates. This is done by using genetic operators such as selection, crossover and mutation.

Genetic Algorithms were developed by John Holland and put forward in the seminal text "Adaptation in Natural and Artificial Systems" [5]. They have been employed in a variety of different optimisation tasks [6], especially in tasks where the search space is large and not well understood. The approach of using evolutionary computing for non-linear sound synthesis applications is not a new concept, and has been explored by a number of researchers. Several different EC techniques are given in "Evolutionary Computer Music" [7] for musical applications, with Chaps. 5–7 specifically implementing GA's. Parameter matching with Frequency Modulation (FM) synthesis has also been explored [8,9].

3 Methods

The articulatory synthesiser used in this project is the PRAAT articulatory synthesiser [10]. PRAAT is a multi-functional software package with tools for a large range of speech analysis and synthesis tasks developed by Paul Boersma and David Weenink [11]. Whilst having a fully-fledged graphical user interface, PRAAT also provides the ability to use its own scripting language, allowing the majority of operations to be executed autonomously. This functionality allows a genetic algorithm to be implemented in conjunction with PRAAT without a great deal of retrofitting that would be required with other available synthesisers such as VTDemo or Vocal Tract Lab 2. Additionally the provided analysis tools for speech make the integration of an appropriate fitness function highly convenient, and minimises the need for using external tools.

The physical model constraints are configured to use an adult male speaker. Control of the synthesiser is done by passing a configuration file that contains a list of all parameters for the model. The model used in PRAAT has 29 parameters that can be specified. Therefore the encoding approach taken in this GA is a real value representation, with each individual stored as a vector of 28 numbers. Each number of the vector represents a parameter and can take any value in the range $-1 \leq x \leq 1$. Where p_1 = Interarytenoid, p_2 = Cricothyroid, p_3 = Vocalis, p_4 = Thyroarytenoid etc.

$$[p_1\ p_2\ p_3\ p_4 \cdots p_n]$$

Therefore a randomly generated individual may be initialised with parameter values such as Interarytenoid = 0.82, Cricothyroid = -0.2, Vocalis = -0.48, Thyroarytenoid = 0.1 etc.

$$[0.82, -0.2, -0.48, 0.1 \ldots p_n]$$

Only one parameter uses prior knowledge. The lungs are set to a predefined value of 0.15 at the beginning of the articulation, then 0.0 at 0.1 seconds. PRAAT automatically interpolates values between these two discrete settings. The reasoning behind this choice is that unlike the other parameters, the lungs parameter needs to be changed over time to provide energy or excitation of the vocal folds necessary for phonation. This parameter is kept the same for every individual generated and is not altered by any GA operations, hence the reason individuals are represented as vectors with a length of 28, and not 29.

The fitness function is implemented by using a FFT for analysis of features of the target sound. Four frequencies are extracted from each sound. The first is the fundamental frequency or "pitch" of the sound. The next three frequencies are the first three formants produced. This analysis is performed on the target vowel sound, and then subsequently performed on each individual sound in every generation. Fitness is based on the differences between the four frequencies in the target sound, and the respective frequencies in each individual. A penalty is introduced for each formant that is not present in the candidate's solution, which replaces the difference in frequency with a large arbitrary value (10,000).

The natural state of the fitness function in this application is a minimisation function, as the goal is to minimise the differences between features of two sounds rather than maximise some sort of profit. It is therefore necessary to scale the fitness for each individual in order to implement a fitness proportional selection scheme. This is achieved through dividing one by each candidate's fitness.

Because of the inherent use of stochastic processes in Genetic Algorithms, any analysis of results must take this into account. Each experiment is run multiple times to ensure that there is no bias due to the stochastic process. Pseudorandom numbers are used for any stochastic processes and are provided by the built-in random function in Python, which uses a Mersenne twist algorithm. Mutation of allele values is done using a Gaussian distribution where $\mu = 0$ and $\sigma = 0.25$. Any mutation that results in allele values outside of the constraints $-1 \leq x \leq 1$ are rounded to 1.0 or -1.0.

4 Results

Three differently configured genetic algorithms are presented, with the results displayed using a performance graph, as shown in Figs. 2, 3 and 4. These graphs show the average fitness of the population at every generation, and the fitness of the best candidate from each population at every generation. All experiments are carried out with the same size populations and number of generations, with number of generations set to 50 and a population size of 75. The generation at 0 on each performance graph is the initial randomly generated population without having any genetic operations performed. This would be a random voice configuration.

4.1 Experiment 1 - Elitism Operator

The first run is not strictly a genetic algorithm, as there is no exchange of genetic material between individuals generated in each population. It is more akin to a hybrid parallel evolutionary strategy. This first experiment was a proof of concept to demonstrate the ability that the fitness function worked as it should, and that it could differentiate. As displayed in Fig. 2, the results of this show the average fitness of each population steadily increasing. This exploratory measure confirms the basic viability and behaviour in this domain.

4.2 Experiment 2 - Fitness Proportional Selection with One Point Crossover

This experiment sees the introduction of fitness proportional selection (FPS), combined with one point crossover for exchange of genetic material between candidate solutions.

An example of one point crossover is shown below. Two parent candidates are selected by making two calls to the FPS function which returns a candidate for each call. A random crossover point is generated and used to combine values from both parents before and after this point. For this example a shortened range of 10 parameters is used.

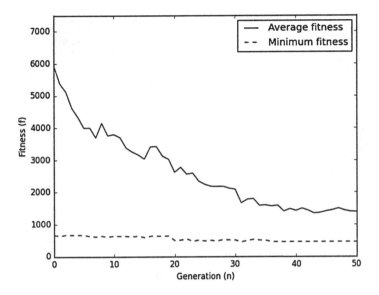

Fig. 2. Performance Graph of Using Only an Elitism Operator

$$Parent1 \begin{bmatrix} 0.25, -0.32, -0.97, 0.6, -0.23, -0.5, -0.31, 0.89, 0.4, 0.93 \end{bmatrix}$$

$$Parent2 \begin{bmatrix} -0.4, -0.24, 0.64, -0.35, 0.51, 0.7, 0.93, 0.19, -0.83, 0.18 \end{bmatrix}$$

After one point crossover with a value of three, an offspring or child candidate is created by combining the first three allele values from parent 1 and then the last seven values from parent 2. This then creates a new solution containing genetic material from both parent candidates.

$$Offspring \begin{bmatrix} 0.25, -0.32, -0.97, -0.35, 0.51, 0.7, 0.93, 0.19, -0.83, 0.18 \end{bmatrix}$$

This process if then repeated until a new population has been generated. In Fig. 3, it shows the average fitness converges much quicker than when using just elitism. However there is stagnation of genetic diversity from around the 23rd generation where both the average fitness and best candidate of each generation shows very little change.

4.3 Experiment 3 - Fitness Proportional Selection with One Point Crossover and Mutation

Here, the FPS operator is kept for selection. A mutation operator is also implemented with each allele value having a probability of 0.1 to mutate.

As it can be observed in Fig. 4 there is a rapid improvement in average fitness, after which it settles down into smaller fluctuations. The fitness of the best candidate at each point improves more slowly early on, but more consistently. The voice model is clearly converging towards the target sound.

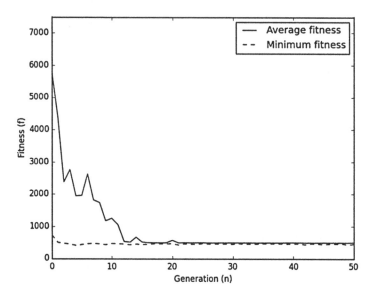

Fig. 3. Performance Graph Using Fitness Proportional Selection and One Point Crossover

5   Discussions

5.1   Observations

It is clear that the elitism operator - because there is no combination of candidates - causes the average of each population to move steadily towards the target, but will not generate new candidates outside of a random search. Removing the elitism operator and replacing it with a fitness proportional selection operator, as done in Experiment 2, causes the rapid increase in the optimisation of the average population but leads to a stagnation of genetic diversity. With the incorporation of the mutation operator in experiment 3, the average fitness fluctuated more than in the previous experiments, but this also produced the best results with respect to the fittest candidate in each population. In general GAs seem to be able to optimise the PRAAT parameters.

5.2   Future Work

As this is an early work in progress there are several areas identified for extensive improvement and future research, these will be focused on the following.

– **Fitness Function:** The fitness function is a crucial aspect of any genetic algorithm. This is especially true when using a multimodal one. As it is the only metric that can guide the search process, it is therefore imperative that it accurately represents the suitability of a candidate solution. If the fitness of an individual is miss-represented, then regions of the search space may

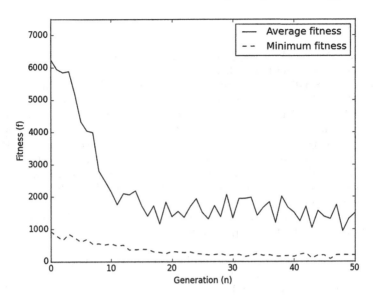

Fig. 4. Performance graph using Fitness Proportional Selection, One Point Crossover and Mutation operators.

be exploited that are not conducive to finding good solutions. A number of shortcomings are clear with the current fitness function. For example the current analysis takes a FFT using a window size equal to the entire length of the sound. This does not account for things such as vocal breaks, intensity of phonation, modulation of pitch etc.

- **Genetic Operator Additions:** The fitness proportional selection scheme, when applied to other optimisation tasks, has been found to be in certain cases an inferior operator. Therefore, a Rank-Based Selection to bring a change in selection pressure will be implemented. Trials with different crossover operators will also be explored, such as uniform crossover and two point crossover.
- **Genetic Algorithm Parameters:** The relationship between number of generations, population size, and mutation rate will all have a large impact on convergence and population diversity. As the synthesis of each individual is computationally expensive, minimising the total number of individuals in a run is desirable. Further experiments with different mutation rates, population sizes and number of generations need to be taken to ascertain optimal values.

To conclude, our results indicate that GAs are a viable method of optimisation for the parameters of PRAAT, and therefore articulatory synthesis. A substantial number of improvements have been identified, which when implemented may improve the robustness and effectiveness of the genetic algorithm for use in mapping sounds to articulatory configurations.

References

1. Shadle, C., Damper, R.: Prospects for articulatory synthesis: a position paper. In: 4th ISCA Tutorial and Research Workshop (2002)
2. Schroeter, J., Sondhi, M.: Techniques for estimating vocal-tract shapes from the speech signal. IEEE Trans. Speech Audio Process. $2(1)$, 133–150 (1994)
3. Kim, Y.C., Kim, J., Proctor, M., Toutios, A., Nayak, K., Lee, S., Narayanan, S.: Toward automatic vocal tract area function estimation from accelerated three-dimensional magnetic resonance imaging. In: ISCA Workshop on Speech Production in Automatic Speech Recognition, Lyon, France, pp. 2–5 (2013)
4. Busset, J., Laprie, Y., Cnrs, L., Botanique, J.: Acoustic-to-articulatory inversion by analysis-by-synthesis using cepstral coefficients. In: ICA - 21st International Congress on Acoustics, vol. 2013 (2013)
5. Holland, J.H.: Adaptation in natural and artificial systems: an introductory analysis with applications to biology, control, and artificial intelligence. U Michigan Press, Ann Arbor (1975)
6. Goldberg, D.E.: Others: genetic algorithms in search, optimization, and machine learning, vol. 412. Addison-wesley, Reading (1989)
7. Miranda, E.R., Al Biles, J.: Evolutionary Computer Music. Springer, London (2007)
8. Horner, A., Beauchamp, J., Haken, L.: Machine tongues XVI: genetic algorithms and their application to FM matching synthesis. Comput. Music J. $17(4)$, 17–29 (1993)
9. Mitchell, T.J.: An exploration of evolutionary computation applied to frequency modulation audio synthesis parameter optimisation. Ph.D. thesis, University of the West of England (2010)
10. Boersma, P.: Praat, a system for doing phonetics by computer. Glot Int. $5(9/10)$, 341–345 (2001)
11. Boersma, P.: Functional phonology: Formalizing the interactions between articulatory and perceptual drives. Holland Academic Graphics/IFOTT (1998)

The Sound Digestive System: A Strategy for Music and Sound Composition

Juan Manuel Escalante$^{(\boxtimes)}$

Media Arts and Technology, University of California Santa Barbara,
Santa Barbara, USA
jmd@umail.ucsb.edu

Abstract. Sound Digestive System is an audio visual project that uses the digestive system processes into algorithmic sound composition. This project proposes different strategies to bring bio-data, translations and interpretations of living processes into the sound domain, thus generating an artistic result based on scientific data.

Keywords: Sound synthesis · Music · Generative · Algorithm

1 Introduction and Context

Since the second half of the 20th century, the music field opened dramatically to new sound possibilities. Specifically, the development of new technologies (from tape recorders, analog synthesizers and computers) created what we understand as electronic and digital acoustic reality [1]. During that period, the relationship of sound creation and image was also taken into account, with notable works from György Ligeti, Cornelius Cardew, Anestis Logothetis and Iannis Xenakis UPIC System [2].

In the age of bioinformatics, bio art and computer generated simulations in science, new ways of arranging and composing sound from these fields, could open new musical and sound genres. The Sound Digestive System (SDS), proposes a new arrangement, not exclusively based on biodata, but also with a strong focus on the process and its translation into the acoustic and visual field.

2 The System

2.1 Definition

The SDS is an audiovisual piece that uses the human digestive system logics into algorithmic sound composition. If we conceive this system as conduits (esophagus, gastrointestinal tract) and spaces, then we can throw sound particles into these objects. A computer simulation would generate the journey of these particles as the system builds itself over time.

© Springer International Publishing Switzerland 2015
C. Johnson et al. (Eds.): EvoMUSART 2015, LNCS 9027, pp. 71–77, 2015.
DOI: 10.1007/978-3-319-16498-4_7

2.2   Composition

Sound agents are divided into the following categories:

A. Sound particles (food)
B. Spaces (major organs)
C. Conduits (connections between spaces)
D. Actions

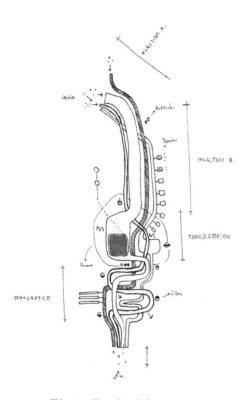

Fig. 1. Sketch of the system

A. Sound particles (food) - A sound particle is understood as food. Each sound particle has a different composition, as each type of food presents different nutritional properties. For this study, food is divided into seven major categories: *I. Carbohydrates,* [3] *II. Fibers, III. Vitamins,* [4] *IV. Proteins, V. Lipids (not including III), VI. Water, VII. Waste.* Each component is assigned a different sound. At the beginning of the process, all of this sounds are mixed (uninteresting). However, as the digestion process starts, these components will be separated and treated as a separate entities. The nutritional ones will be absorbed and the waste will be disposed (Fig. 1).

B. Spaces (major organs) - Each organ is treated as an architectural space with reverberation properties [5]. Therefore, the scale of the stomach (experienced from the inside) would be radically different than, for example, a liver or a spleen.

C. Conduits (connections between spaces) - Transitional spaces between major organs, have the same importance as transitional passages in music composition. From the biological point of view, important stages of the process occur at these steps. For example, pancreatic enzymes along with substances from the gallbladder join the digestive mix in the duodenum. For this piece, the esophagus is also treated as a conduit.

D. Processes / Actions - Food breaks, and changes its own composition, excessive water is handled by the spleen, an overdose of sugar causes chemical reactions in the liver and pancreas and so forth. All of these operations are transformed into sound operations: substraction, multiplication, addition, pitch and phase shifting (Fig. 2).

2.3   Duration and Proportions

The average timescale of the digestion process is also taken into account. Away from traditional music composition dogmas, each sound passage is controlled by the behavior of the digestive system (Fig. 3).

Table 1. Proportional durations for the piece according to action, space and time.

Action	Space	Duration
Chewing/swallowing	Mouth and esophagus	0.1 %
Food breaking	Stomach	14.5 %
Absorption (95 %)	Upper gastro intestinal tract	17 %
Absorption and fermentation (mostly water)	Lower gastro intestinal tract	67 %
Release	Interior(rectum) and exterior	0.1 %

3   Sound Synthesis

This project is conceived as a live-performance piece where sound and image are being processed in real time. This means, according to the type of food thrown into the system during an specific performance, it generates a different experience every time (Table 1).

For sound synthesis Super Collider (an environment and programming language by James McCartney [6]) is used. Each synthesizer (or *synth*) could produce one or three sounds. Depending on the code of each *synth*, different sound generators (also known as unit generators: UGens), envelopes, and other types of parameters could be assigned. The total number of *synths* for this piece is 21.

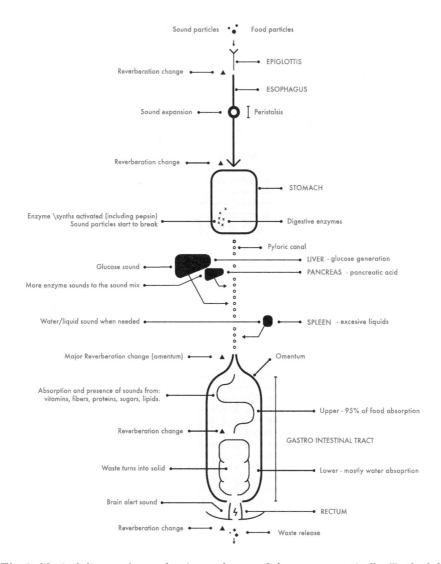

Fig. 2. Musical diagram/score showing each part of the process vertically. To the left: the organ names and behaviors. To the right: sound translation of such processes.

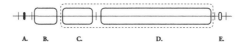

Fig. 3. Total time proportions. A: mouth, B: stomach, C: Upper intestinal tract, D: Lower intestinal tract, E: rectum.

```
// This \synth receives  x, y, mul, vol. values, each numbers 13 for each UG
SynthDef(\gingerPerc, { |
x1 = 6000, y1 = 3.2, mul1 = 2.002, vol1 = 0.1,
x2 = 6000, y2 = 4.2, mul2 = 2.002, vol2 = 0.1,
x3 = 6000, y3 = 4.2, mul3 = 2.002, vol3 = 0.0001,
att = 0.1, rel = 0.83, vol = 0.5, canal = 0, gate = 1|
// Local Variables
var sen, env;
// Signals compound
sen = GbmanL.ar(x1, y1, mul1) * vol1;
sen = sen + (GbmanL.ar(x2, y2, mul2) * vol2);
sen = sen + (GbmanL.ar(x3, y3, mul3) * vol3);
// Envelope
env = EnvGen.kr( Env.perc(att, rel), 1, doneAction:2 );
// Our signal
Out.ar( canal, (sen*vol)*env );
}).send(s);
);
x = Synth( \ginger, [\canal, 9]); // Ch.9 output, high non-linear texture
y = Synth( \ginger, [
\x1, 10000, \y1, 29.12, \mul1, 1.002, \vol1, 0.0033011,
\x2, 10000, \y2, 19.12, \mul2, 1.002, \vol2, 0.0033011,
\vol3, 0.000001, \rel, 10, \att, 18,
\canal, 10]); // Channel 10 output, very high frequencies
x = Synth( \ginger, [
\x1, 500, \y1, 29.12, \mul1, 1.002, \vol1, 0.033011,
\x2, 500, \y2, 19.12, \mul2, 1.002, \vol2, 0.03011,
\x3, 500, \y3, 39.12, \mul3, 1.002, \vol3, 0.01533011,
\rel, 5, \canal, 11]); // Channel 11 oscillator from left to right side
```

[SuperCollider code shows an example of one \synth (ginger). In this case, used for a protein sound. Notice how different function calls (shown after the \synth is declared) represent different types of proteins.]

```
// Two simple oscillators
sen = SinOsc.ar( freq, 0, vol/3 ) + Dust.ar( 10 );
sen = sen + Saw.ar( freq-2,  vol/6, 0 );
// Fixed frequency sine oscillators
sen = Klank.ar('[ (1..13)*freq, 1/(1,2..13), nil ], PinkNoise.ar(0.005));
// Seven Ring filter with decay time
sen =  Mix.arFill(7 , {
Ringz.ar(exciter,XLine.kr(exprand(freqMin,freqMax), exprand(freqMin,freqMax),
tiempo),  vol)
});
// Three linear interpolating sound generators
sen = GbmanL.ar(x1, y1, mul1) * vol1;
sen = sen + (GbmanL.ar(x2, y2, mul2) * vol2);
sen = sen + (GbmanL.ar(x3, y3, mul3) * vol3);
// Gaussian function oscillator
sen = LFGauss.ar(XLine.kr(inicio, 0.001, 20), 0.02) * 0.4;
```

[UGens extract of the most important oscillators and functions used in this project]

Each \synth -or variations of a given one- was assigned to the following objects: *esophagus walls, breaking food, stomach enzymes, stomach contractions, blue glucose, breaking white/red cells, pancreatic juice, B.E.R. (Basal Electrical Rhythm), rectum to brain signal, release, upper gastro intestinal tract, lower gastro intestinal tract and each component of a food particle(carbohydrates, fibers, vitamins, proteins, fats, water and waste).*

4   Graphic Score and Diagram

The arrangement of sounds throughout time is controlled with the open source software Processing. Three main libraries are used for the project: supercollider, oscP5 [7] and netP5 Visual cues distributed in space (represented in two dimensions) would trigger an specific reverberation, or sound particle transformation, according to its own position (which is also a visual approximation of the whole

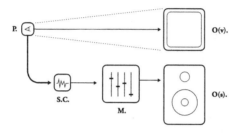

Fig. 4. All sounds are sent through 64 channels into a mixing software -in this case, Apple Logic X-, for live space sculpting and sound control on each channel. P: Processing, S.C.: SuperCollider, M: Mixing and space sculpting software, O(s): Sound output, O(v): Visual output.

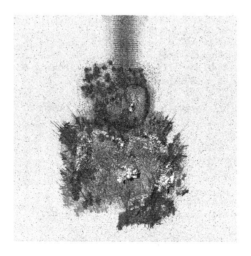

Fig. 5. Result after throwing two particles.

system). Visual cues positioned vertically higher would represent an early stage of the sound digestive process, while sounds positioned vertically lower are closer to full absorption and waste release (Fig. 4).

In this artificially controlled system, there could be hundreds of sound particles digested at different times and speeds. This ultimate concept is also a new difference between algorithmic composition and a traditional approach: multiple timelines instead of a linear one. A greater quantity would require also a proportional computational power (Fig. 5).

5   Conclusion

The final result of this project is an algorithmic -visual and sound- composed piece, based on the human digestive system. This project allows to explore - in the future- new major systems abstractions, based on the human body. Or, going ever further, new paths of sound arrangement in time (and space) based on biological processes using computer simulations. An open field where scientific data in music could help artistic intuition to generate new types of work. Future revisions should explore other sonification techniques that allow a greater mixture between sound and image (tools as the Sonification Sandbox [8] or software explorations by Clarence Barlow).

To hear the result and browse additional material visit the following address: http://goo.gl/DT1Wy0.

Acknowledgment. This project was built, designed and composed under the guidance of electronic music composer Curtis Roads, at the Xenakis Studio, UCSB, US.

References

1. Chadab, J.: Electronic Sound: The Past and Promise of Electronic Music, pp. 21–23, 36, 40, 43. Prentice Hall, New Jersey (1996)
2. Xenakis, I.: Formalized Music: Thought and Mathematics in Composition, p. 329. Prendagon Press, New York (2014)
3. Harvard School of Public Health, Carbohydrates and Blood Sugar. http://www.hsph.harvard.edu/nutritionsource/carbohydrates
4. Harvard Health Publications: Listing of Vitamins. http://www.health.harvard.edu/newsweek/Listing_of_vitamins.htm
5. Roads, C.: The Complete Music Tutorial, pp. 30–62, 160–187. MIT Press, Cambridge (1996)
6. Jones, D.: SuperCollider library for Processing. http://www.erase.net/projects/processing-sc/
7. OscP5 library for Processing written by Schlegel, A. based on Open Sound Control protocol by Wright, M., Freed, A. http://www.sojamo.de/libraries/oscP5/
8. Walker, B.: Sonification Sandbox, Georgia Institute of Technology. http://sonify.psych.gatech.edu/research/sonification_sandbox/
9. Roads, C.: Composing Electronic Music: The Nature of Sound. Oxford University Press, Oxford (2014)

Avoidance Drawings Evolved Using Virtual Drawing Robots

Gary Greenfield[✉]

University of Richmond, Richmond, VA 23173, USA
ggreenfi@richmond.edu

Abstract. We introduce a generative system for "avoidance drawings", drawings made by virtual drawing robots executing a random walk while simultaneously avoiding the paths of other robots. The random walk method is unique and is based on a curvature controlling scheme initially introduced by Chappell. We design a fitness function for evaluating avoidance drawings and an evolutionary framework for evolving them. This requires us to follow principles we elucidate for simulated evolution where the generative system is highly stochastic in nature. Examples document the evolutionary system's efficacy and success.

1   Introduction

To execute his self-avoiding random walk drawings, Chappell [1] introduces a model for random walks based on curvature. Chappell's point that moves in the plane and executes a self-avoiding random walk can be viewed as virtual drawing robot. Using a variation of Chapelle's random walk model we introduce a generative system that uses a small number of virtual drawing robots that each executes a random walk while simultaneously avoiding all other robot paths. Thus, in effect, n such robots create paths that partition the canvas into n simply-connected regions. Examining examples of these "avoidance drawings" that are generated using several different initial configurations leads to an aesthetic evaluation criterion that can be implemented as a fitness function. However, due to the chaotic nature of the generative system, we are forced to evolve avoidance drawings using only a limited number of the available parameters and adopting a very conservative evolutionary framework. The evolutionary system is successful in evolving novel and interesting avoidance drawings.

This paper is organized as follows. In section two we review self-avoiding random walks. In section three we consider Chappell's model for random walks based on curvature. In section four we provide some background on drawing robots. In section five we give the details of the design of our virtual drawing robot. Section six shows examples of avoidance drawings. In section seven we develop our fitness function and in section eight we describe our evolutionary framework. Section nine discusses the evolved avoidance drawings we obtained while section ten gives our summary and conclusion.

© Springer International Publishing Switzerland 2015
C. Johnson et al. (Eds.): EvoMUSART 2015, LNCS 9027, pp. 78–88, 2015.
DOI: 10.1007/978-3-319-16498-4_8

2 Self-Avoiding Random Walks

Self-avoiding walks arise in the physics and chemistry literature because of their application to protein folding and other polymer-related problems [2]. Usually self-avoiding walks are implemented using lattices [3], and in this case it is known that there are algorithms for infinite self-avoiding walks [4]. In order to generate smooth self-avoiding random walks Chappell introduced a model for random walks in the plane based on curvature [1]. Then, by formulating rules based on readings from sensory apparatus — two sets of "feelers" attached to the point executing the walk — and incorporating a stylized line, Chappell generated drawings of points executing prolonged self-avoiding walks such as the one shown in Fig. 1. More recently, Greenfield used a similar random walk curvature model, but a different sensory system and line stylization method to generate self-avoiding walks resulting in labyrinths such as the one also shown in Fig. 1.

3 Random Walks Based on Curvature

The random walk algorithm based on curvature introduced by Chappell [1] is parametrized by arc length. To cut to the chase, if after the point has traveled a distance s, the point has tangential angle (i.e., direction) $\theta(s)$, curvature $\kappa(s)$ and position $(x(s), y(s))$ then at distance $s + \Delta s$ the behavioral update equations are given by:

$$\kappa(s + \Delta s) = \kappa(s) + \kappa_0 X(s),$$
$$\theta(s + \Delta s) = \theta(s) + \kappa(s + \Delta s)\Delta s$$

where $X(s)$ is a stochastic random variable assuming values $+1$ and -1 and κ_0 is a "small" constant, while the positional update equations are given by:

$$x(s + \Delta s) = x(s) + \cos(\theta(s + \Delta s))\Delta s,$$
$$y(s + \Delta s) = y(s) + \sin(\theta(s + \Delta s))\Delta s.$$

In fact, it is through the use of more elaborate update formulas for θ that Chappell implements his self-avoidance rules, but the details will not concern us here since we will consider a simpler model below.

4 Drawing Robot History

Because they have sensory apparatus, obey rules that act as controllers, and incorporate stylized line drawing methods, it is clear that points executing self-avoiding walks such as the ones described by Chappell and Greenfield can be viewed as virtual drawing robots. If the walks were in 3D rather than 2D, they might also fall within the category of agents in swarms potentially following rules such as the flocking rules of Reynolds [5] or Jacob et al. [6].

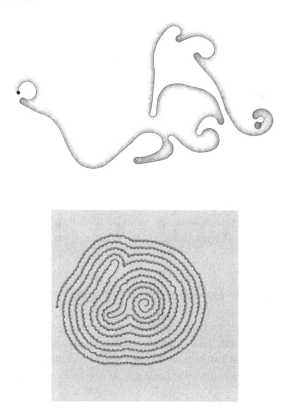

Fig. 1. Top: An example of a point in the plane performing a self-avoiding random walk using Chappell's model. (Copyright 2014 David Chappell. Reprinted from [1] with permission.) Bottom: SA Labyrinth #8352, a self-avoiding random walk using Greenfield's model. (Copyright 2014 Gary Greenfield. Reprinted from http://gallery. bridgesmathart.org/exhibitions/2015-joint-mathematics-meetings/gary-greenfield.)

There is a brief history of drawing robots in evolutionary art. The most famous *physical* drawing robots are undoubtedly those of Moura, Ramos, and Pereira [7,8] who referred to their collective robotic swarm drawings as "non-human art". Bird et al. [9] engaged in a more scientific experiment by attempting to evolve controllers for line drawing primitives for a single robot. Recently, a team led by Monmarché has posted video of experiments conducted with small groups of drawing robots [10]. We assume details of their work will be forthcoming. On the virtual drawing robot front, numerous agent based generative art systems might be viewed as qualifying for virtual robot status. Due to their focus on agents marking and establishing territory two deserve particular attention: Annuziato's system [11] which drew attention in the graphics and artificial life communities at the start of computer generated generative art, and more recently an homage to that work done by McCormack [12]. A series of papers by Greenfield was devoted to virtual robot drawings. His virtual robots were modeled

after Khepera robots. He evolved robot paintings using as genomes initial placement configurations [13], evolved encoding tables such that DNA data could be
used to drive controllers [14], explored a variation of the robot wherein the pen
moved transversely to the robot's straight line motion in order to provide the
ability to draw curvilinear lines [15], and evolved programs for his virtual robots
in a higher level language modeled after video game controller languages [16].

5   Our Virtual Drawing Robot

With one exception, the behavior for our point mass virtual robot is exclusively
controlled by updating κ as its position changes. The exception is an avoidance
turn. If the robot is not executing an avoidance turn, then the update equation
for κ uses 0.4 for the distance increment Δs, lets $\kappa_0 = 0.04$, and takes $X(s)$
to be zero for seven consecutive updates before letting it be a random number
between -1 and $+1$. Over time this smoothness condition on the robot's turning
yields a random walk that causes the robot to transition back and forth between
a flowing line and a tight spiral. If the robot is executing an avoidance turn,
then it does not modify κ at all, so $\kappa(s + \Delta s) = \kappa(s)$, but when it completes the
avoidance turn it resets κ using the formula

$$\kappa(s + \Delta s) = -\kappa(s)/4 + \kappa_r/2 + \kappa_0 Y(s)$$

where κ_r is the value saved prior to initiating the turn, Δs and κ_0 are as above,
and $Y(s)$ is a random number between -1 and $+1$. The idea is to try to transition
from the avoidance turn back to the previously interrupted course.

Avoidance turns are induced from sensing. Sensing occurs after each position
update. The robot has two "feelers" extending 17 units from its point mass and
located 15° to each side of its forward heading. The feelers can sense canvas
boundaries and the paths of other robots. The feelers also transmit the distance
to such obstacles. If an obstacle is detected that is distant, then the robot initiates
a turning sequence away from it by saving the current value of κ and assigning κ
the magnitude 0.15 with sign opposite to that of the saved value. This effectively
causes the robot to veer off and initiate a "tight" turn that lasts 25 update steps.
If an obstacle is detected that is deemed close, then it takes more drastic action
by completely reversing course; that is, it increments θ by 180° ± 30°. Note
that it does not otherwise cancel any avoidance turn which is in progress. The
demarcation between distant and close is 10 units.

The mark making ability of our drawing robot is anti-climactic. It has an
assigned color, and after each change in position it deposits a 3×3 pixel splat of
that color as well as an identifier so that its path can be sensed by other robots.
Note that since it takes multiple updates to traverse a pixel, the use of a splat
helps anti-alias the curve the robot draws.

6   Examples of Avoidance Drawings

To explore the type of drawings the virtual robots described above can create,
we conducted three experiments using a 600×600 canvas and allowing 400,000

position updates per robot. For all three experiments there were four drawing robots, each assigned a distinct color. By using different seeds for the pseudo random number generator, we generated 40 drawings where (a) the robots were uniformly spaced around a circle all pointing outward (b) the robots were uniformly spaced around a circle all pointing inward and (c) and the robots were uniformly spaced along a horizontal bisector all pointing upward. Figure 2 shows the drawings from the outward pointing and upward pointing experiments that we felt were most aesthetically pleasing. It also reveals how the drawings might be interpreted as the outcome of a competition among the four robots to stake out a simply-connected region of the canvas where they are free to meander in.

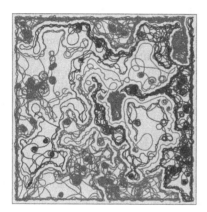 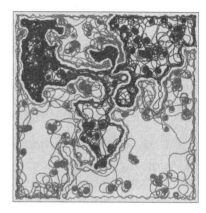

Fig. 2. Left: Avoidance drawing where the four robots were initially uniformly spaced around a circle all pointing outward. Right: Avoidance drawing where the four robots were initially uniformly spaced along a horizontal bisector all pointing upward.

7   The Fitness Function

In considering the 120 drawings we had pseudo randomly generated we came to the realization that the ones we found most interesting were the ones where the robot paths were most clearly delineated and no robot had gotten hemmed in resulting in its path looking like a region that had been flood filled. One crude way to measure the extent to which flood fill has been *avoided* is to consider $N(i)$, the number of adjacent background pixels summed over all pixels of the canvas that have been marked by robot i. The robot with the *smallest* value of N should be one that was most hemmed in. Therefore, if we maximize over the minimum of the N values, we should be able to identify drawings where all four paths are most clearly delineated. This argument suggests assigning drawing D fitness

$$f(D) = \min_i \{N(i)\}.$$

As we shall see, this fitness function does not address aesthetic issues such as region balance or canvas coverage. Be that as it may, even though the problem of designing fitness functions is known to be hard [17], past experience suggests simplistic fitness criteria can often yield positive results.

8   The Evolutionary Framework

The 120 avoidance drawings we generated from our preliminary experiments were ample testimony to the chaotic nature of our generative process and its sensitivity to perturbations and initial conditions. To apply evolutionary techniques we formulated principles to help must constrain the system in order to have some hope of obtaining meaningful results. The rationale for the principles is to yield drawings that arise from an evolutionary process, not random search.

Our first principle is that the fitness landscape be well-defined. To that end, our implementation first sets aside a fixed sequence of pseudo random numbers to present to the robots as the need arises by reserving the first 400,000 pseudo randomly generated numbers from the `lrand48()` generator using seed 121314. Note that using month/day/year format, 12/13/14 is the last sequential date of the 21st century. We then re-seed the pseudo random number generator so that it can oversee the genetics of our evolutionary algorithm.

Our second principle is that the initial configuration is the same for every drawing, save for parameters under evolutionary control. We initialize robots so that their initial headings all point upward i.e., we set $\theta(0) = \pi/2$ and $\kappa(0) = 0$ for each robot. This means that our avoidance drawing is now completely determined by the initial positions of the four robots, whence if robot i has *integral* initial position $(x_i(0), y_i(0))$ where each coordinate lies in the interval $[20, 580]$, there are essentially $560^8 \approx 9.6 \times 10^{21}$ genomes of the form

$$(x_1(0), y_1(0), x_2(0), y_2(0), x_3(0), y_3(0), x_4(0), y_4(0))$$

to consider.

Designing a genetic framework to use for our genomes also presents difficulties. We adopt a very conservative approach which arises as a consequence of our third principle: at least at the genomic level, change must be gradual. In our implementation, a new genome is produced from an old one by cloning it and mutating one randomly selected robot position as follows: 75 % of the time a new position that lies in the 15×15 neighborhood of the old position is randomly selected, and 25 % of the time a completely new position is randomly selected. As this portends, our re-population scheme selects and retains the most fit genome from the population of size P and then clones and applies our mutation operator to provide $P-1$ genomes for the next generation. Thus an evolutionary run lasting G generations considers $P + (G - 1)(P - 1)$ genomes. Clearly this scheme does make evolution slow and gradual and make its dynamics easy to trace and understand. Note that as a bonus the evolutionary process can easily be interrupted and resumed simply by writing out the most fit genome and subsequently reading it back in.

9   Evolved Avoidance Drawings

For the evolutionary runs described here we set the population size $P = 12$ and the number of generations $G = 90$, so that each run considered $12 + (89)(11) = 991$ genomes. A run takes approximately 12 hours. A run usually yields no more than 3 genomes beyond a transient phase lasting, say, 10 generations indicating fitness improvements for the best individual after that stage of evolution typically occur infrequently. This reflects the slow, gradual and careful hill-climbing nature of our evolutionary design. It also reinforces our belief that the constrained fitness landscape is very rugged with local maximums abundant and easily found. Further evidence is obtained by noting that within each generation the population of mutated clones exhibits fitness values that fall off dramatically. Thus, it is not unusual to observe a fairly uniform spread in the 12 individual fitnesses ranging from, for example, 4000 to 24000. We discuss the results from two sample runs.

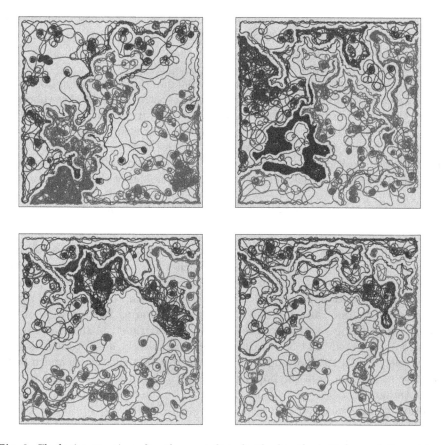

Fig. 3. Clockwise, starting after the most fit individual in the initial population at top left, are the three sequentially mutated improved individuals found at generations 3, 23, and 79 respectively.

Fig. 4. Clockwise, starting after the most fit individual in the initial population at top left, are the three sequentially mutated improved individuals found at generations 49, 87, and 88 respectively.

Table 1. The most fit genomes from an evolutionary run. Leftmost column shows generation number g, rightmost column shows fitness value f, and column r_i shows the initial position of the i-th robot.

g	r_1	r_2	r_3	r_4	f
0	(268, 321)	(24, 356)	(524, 533)	(528, 38)	24372
3	(268, 321)	(24, 356)	(517, 537)	(528, 38)	28956
23	(394, 122)	(24, 356)	(517, 537)	(528, 38)	29008
79	(390, 129)	(24, 356)	(517, 537)	(528, 38)	29444

For the first run, Table 1 shows that the most fit individual in the initial population had fitness 24372 and there were three subsequent improvements occurring at generations 3, 23, and 79 leading to a top fitness score of 29444. Further, these improvements resulted from finding a nearby new starting position

Fig. 5. Enlargement of the bottom left avoidance drawing from the previous figure — the most fit individual we have successfully evolved.

for robot #3 at generation 3, and a completely new position for robot #1 at generations 23 and 79. This means the mutated individual from generation 23 could have been skipped if the one from generation 79 had been encountered earlier. But, in looking at the avoidance drawings (phenomes) for these four individuals shown in Fig. 3, in our opinion that would have been a loss because we feel it was the best of the four. On the other hand, even though the two later drawings greatly reduce the flood fill phenomena found in the two earlier ones, they are both too top heavy with too much open space in the center of the composition.

The second run, again yielding only four genomes, seemed to avoid such problems, and in the next to last generation found the best avoidance drawing we have evolved to date. The four genomes are shown in Table 2 and the phenomes in Fig. 4. This time we observe that first a nearby position for robot #4 was found, then a new position for robot #3 was located, and finally a nearby position for robot #1 was obtained. To better appreciate the evolved result, and to give a sense of the detail found in avoidance drawings, we show an enlargement of the most fit individual from this run in Fig. 5.

Table 2. The most fit genomes from an evolutionary run. Leftmost column shows generation number g, rightmost column shows fitness value f, and column r_i shows the initial position of the i-th robot.

g	r_1	r_2	r_3	r_4	f
0	(183, 77)	(445, 60)	(456.245)	(287, 55)	29144
49	(183, 77)	(445, 60)	(456, 245)	(292, 49)	30022
87	(183, 77)	(445, 60)	(194, 319)	(292, 49)	30570
88	(188, 82)	(445, 60)	(194, 319)	(292, 49)	31544

10   Summary and Conclusion

We introduced a generative system for avoidance drawings, drawings made by virtual drawing robots executing a random walk based on a curvature while simultaneously avoiding the paths of other robots. We designed a fitness function for evaluating such drawings and an evolutionary framework for evolving them. We provided examples to document the system's efficacy. The main contribution of this work is the set of principles we developed to design an evolutionary framework for a generative system that is highly stochastic in nature.

References

1. Chappell, D.: Taking a point for a walk: pattern formation with self-interacting curves. In: Greenfield, G., et al. (eds.) Bridges 2014 Conference Proceedings, pp. 337–340. Tessellations Publishing, Phoenix (2014)
2. Madras, N., Slade, G.: The Self-Avoiding Walk. BirkHauser, Boston (1993)
3. Vanderzande, C.: Lattice Models of Polymers. Cambridge University Press, New York (1998)
4. Kremer, K., Lyklema, J.: Infinitely growing self-avoiding walk. Phys. Rev. Lett. **54**, 267–269 (1985)
5. Reynolds, C.: Flocks, herds, and schools: a distributed behavioral model. Comput. Graph. **21**(4), 25–34 (1987)
6. Jacob, C., Hushlak, G., Boyd, J., Sayles, M., Nuytten, P., Pilat, M.: Swarmart: interactive art from swarm intelligence. Leonardo **40**(3), 248–254 (2007)
7. Moura, L., Pereira, H.: Man + Robots: Symbiotic Art. Institut d'Art Contemporain, Lyon/Villeurbanne (2004)
8. Moura, L., Ramos, V.: Swarm paintings – nonhuman art. In: Maubant, J., et al. (eds.) Architopia: Book, Art, Architecture, and Science, pp. 5–24. Institut d'Art Contemporain, Lyon/Villeurbanne (2002)
9. Bird, J., Husbands, P., Perris, M., Bigge, B., Brown, P.: Implicit fitness functions for evolving a drawing robot. In: Giacobini, M., et al. (eds.) EvoWorkshops 2008. LNCS, vol. 4974, pp. 473–478. Springer, Heidelberg (2008)
10. Monmarché, M. et al., 2014. http://youtu.be/GrxthHngARU
11. Annunziato, M.: The Nagual experiment. In: Soddu, C., (ed.) Proceedings 1998 International Conference on Generative Art, pp. 241–251 (1998)

12. McCormack, J.: Creative ecosystems. In: McCormack, J., d'Inverno, M. (eds.) Computers and Creativity, pp. 39–60. Springer, Heidelberg (2012)

13. Greenfield, G.: Robot paintings evolved using simulated robots. In: Rothlauf, F., et al. (eds.) EvoWorkshops 2006. LNCS, vol. 3907, pp. 611–621. Springer, Heidelberg (2006)

14. Greenfield, G.: Evolved look-up tables for simulated DNA controlled robots. In: Li, X., et al. (eds.) SEAL 2008. LNCS, vol. 5361, pp. 51–60. Springer, Heidelberg (2008)

15. Greenfield, G.: On simulating drawing robots with straight line motion but curvilinear pen paths. In: Roeschel, O., Santos, E., Yamaguchi, Y., (eds.) 14th International Conference on Geometry and Graphics, International Society for Computer Graphics, Conference DVD (2010)

16. Greenfield, G.: A platform for evolving controllers for simulated drawing robots. In: Machado, P., Romero, J., Carballal, A. (eds.) EvoMUSART 2012. LNCS, vol. 7247, pp. 108–116. Springer, Heidelberg (2012)

17. McCormack, J.: Open problems in evolutionary music and art. In: Rothlauf, F., et al. (eds.) EvoWorkshops 2005. LNCS, vol. 3449, pp. 428–436. Springer, Heidelberg (2005)

A Genetic Programming Approach to Generating Musical Compositions

David M. Hofmann$^{(\boxtimes)}$

Institute for Musicology and Music Informatics,
University of Music Karlsruhe, Karlsruhe, Germany
hofmann@hfm.eu

Abstract. Evolutionary algorithms have frequently been applied in the field of computer-generated art. In this paper, a novel approach in the domain of automated music composition is proposed. It is inspired by genetic programming and uses a tree-based domain model of compositions. The model represents musical pieces as a set of constraints changing over time, forming musical contexts allowing to compose, reuse and reshape musical fragments. The system implements a multi-objective optimization aiming for statistical measures and structural features of evolved models. Furthermore a correspondent domain-specific computer language is introduced used to transform domain models to a comprehensive, human-readable text representation and vice versa. The language is also suitable to limit the search space of the evolution and as a composition language for human composers.

Keywords: Automated music generation · Multi-objective genetic programming · Domain-specific languages

1 Introduction

Since the beginning of the computer era it has been a question if computers could ever be considered creative. The idea of computer-generated music goes back to 1843, when Ada Lovelace mentioned the "Analytical Engine's potential for automated composition" [1]. Since then, numerous attempts have been made to create music with computer programs. Applied programming techniques include pseudo-randomly generated musical sequences, generative grammars, recursive transition networks, Markov models, artificial neural networks and cellular automata [2]. Another approach is the application of evolutionary algorithms (EAs). A widely held belief is that the highest observable extent of creativity exhibited by computer programs is limited by the creativity of the programmer. However, the application of evolutionary algorithms is especially promising because at times results of considerable innovative and subjectively perceived "creative" quality are produced. These results often surprise experts, including the programmer [3]. In this paper, a system inspired by genetic programming (GP, which is a subset of evolutionary algorithms) is presented.

© Springer International Publishing Switzerland 2015
C. Johnson et al. (Eds.): EvoMUSART 2015, LNCS 9027, pp. 89–100, 2015.
DOI: 10.1007/978-3-319-16498-4_9

2   Related Work

A number of relevant systems have been proposed, most of which are based on genetic algorithms (GAs) [3]. Horner and Goldberg proposed an approach to thematic bridging, evolving transitions from an initial musical pattern to another pattern [4]. Biles created an interactive system named *GenJam* which evolves jazz solos using musically meaningful mutation and crossover operators [5,6]. Horowitz focused on evolving rhythmic patterns [7]. GAs have also been applied to the problem of harmonization, adhering to a number of constraints according to traditional music theory [8,9]. Jacob developed a composition system named *variations* [10,11]. It uses three GA-based components which are responsible for generating, evaluating and arranging music respectively. A system generating short melodies using GP was introduced by Johanson and Poli [12]. Specialized crossover and mutation operators were used by Marques et al. [13] and a grammar-based approach was proposed by de la Puente et al. [14]. *SARAH* is a composition language introduced by Fox [15], enabling to define musical phrases and arrange them hierarchically. A GA-based program named *GenDash* was developed by Waschka II [16], in which the whole evolutionary process, transforming musical user input, represents the composition.

3   Motivation

The intended purpose of the proposed model is to overcome some limitations inherent in genetic representations of previous works. In most of the models, the evolution is focused on only one or few musical aspects such as pitches or rhythms. Misleadingly, "music" is often regarded as simply a sequence of notes and rests. In fact, these elements have to be seen within their context, taking metre, rhythm, tonal system, tonal center, harmony, scale and loudness into account. In many of the mentioned systems these contexts are hard-coded and are not part of the actual evolution. The proposed model is designed to (a) represent a large number of musical aspects and parameters, (b) encode compositions of arbitrary complexity and length with minimal redundancy, (c) allow not only the evolution of one-dimensional sequences, but also their hierarchical context, (d) enable to reuse and vary existing material rather than introducing new material all the time and (e) incorporate some mechanisms of human creativity, as explained in the next section. None of the systems mentioned above combine all of these characteristics in their representation.

4   Creativity and Constraints

It is highly implausible that all aspects of human creativity can ever be modeled by a computer. However, the proposed software system tries to incorporate some aspects of human creativity. Boden outlines an interesting relation between constraints and creativity as follows: "Constraints – far from being opposed to creativity – make creativity possible. To throw away all constraints would be to destroy the capacity for creative thinking" [17]. As soon as constraints are present in creative processes, three common principles of creativity can be applied: **Exploration**, where the space of possibilities is searched, **Combination**, where aspects in the possibility space are combined in order to form new ideas and **Transformation**, in which the constraint space itself is modified, leading to a different, mostly larger space of possibilities [18].

5   Domain Model

The proposed model represents compositions in terms of musical constraint sets changing over time. Possibilities in this space can be explored, aspects can be combined and the space can be transformed by a computer program. This is accomplished by arranging the following elements in a tree-based structure: Musical *constraints*, constraint *modifiers*, constraint *generators* and *control structures*. Constraints include basic compositional elements such as tonal systems, instruments, beats, rhythms, harmonies, chords, scales and pitches. Compositions are often structured in such a way that established constraints are not completely changed, but only slightly modified in order to reshape already introduced material. Constraint modifiers represent modifications such as rhythmic and tonal variations, inversions, displacements and transpositions. Generators have the functionality of generating new constraints based on already existing ones in a specific pattern. For example, an *arpeggio generator* is responsible for generating pitch constraints based on the current harmony using the current rhythm and a specified pattern of sequentially sounding chord notes.

5.1   Example

The function of the individual components is explained using a constraint model of the first four measures of Bach's *Prelude in C major* from *The Well-Tempered Clavier (BWV 846)* which is shown in Fig. 1. The nodes are arranged in an acyclic graph structure. Every model has a root node which is displayed labeled *composition*. Models are evaluated from top to bottom, aggregating all constraints at the leaf nodes. This implies that every leaf node has a musical context, which is defined as a set of all constraints in the path from the root node to the leaf node. Multiple child nodes are interpreted as a consecutive sequence of constraints. If a path contains a constraint of the same type more than once, the constraint which is nearest to the leaves overwrites all upper constraints of that type. This model architecture allows temporary transformations of previously established constraint spaces, enabling to model surprising musical twists in a composition. The model supports modularization in the form of fragments. These are reusable subtrees which can be referenced from anywhere else in the model as long as no cycle is produced. In this way musical ideas can be reused and even reshaped by creating child nodes under the reference node, supporting context-dependent variations. The model also features control structures (e.g. repetitions and iterations). Polyphonic compositions are represented using a control structure named *parallelization* indicating that its child nodes are arranged concurrently in time.

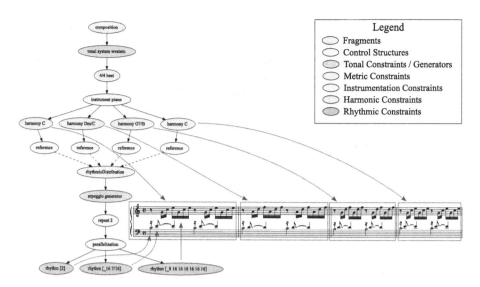

Fig. 1. Constraint model of the first four measures of Bach's *Prelude in C major* from *The Well-Tempered Clavier (BWV 846)*

6   The Domain-Specific Language

A domain-specific language (DSL) correspondent to the introduced model was developed. Its name is MC³L, abbreviating **M**usical **C**onstraint, **C**ontext and **C**omposition **L**anguage. Its main purpose is to provide a comprehensive textual representation of models. Thus the evolutionary process can be monitored in a very convenient way as the progress can be persisted in simple text files at any time. The process also works vice versa which enables users to express musical compositions in terms of constraint spaces. By this means, a "side-product" of the system is a comprehensive computer language that can be used by human composers to capture compositions and ideas. This makes the language a multi-purpose tool for both traditional and algorithmic composition.

6.1   Language Syntax

The language syntax is demonstrated with a code example which is equivalent to Fig. 1. As demonstrated in the first lines, model fragments can be distributed over several files in order to minimize redundancy. The language allows users to specify custom tonal systems and instruments. The grammar features a basic expression language which enables to formulate parameters using arithmetical and logical expressions, whereupon functions can be invoked. The explanation of the complete language syntax, however, would go beyond the scope of this paper.

```
1   import"../../tonalSystems/western.mcl"
2   import "../../instruments/piano.mcl"
3   title "Prelude in C major"
4   composer "J.S. Bach"
5   root {
6       tonalSystem western {
7           beat 4/4 {
8               instrument piano {
9                   harmony C {
10                      fragmentRef rhythmicDistribution
11                  }
12                  harmony Dm/C {
13                      fragmentRef rhythmicDistribution
14                  }
15                  harmony G7/B {
16                      fragmentRef rhythmicDistribution
17                  }
18                  harmony C {
19                      fragmentRef rhythmicDistribution
20                  }
21              }
22          }
23      }
24  }
25  fragment rhythmicDistribution {
26      arpeggioGenerator [startOctave 3, numberOfNotes 5, noteIndexSequence 0 1 2
        3 4 2 3 4, includeBassNote true]
27      {
28          repeat 2 {
29              parallel {
30                  rhythm 2
31                  rhythm _16 7/16
32                  rhythm _8 16 16  16 16 16 16
33              }
34          }
35      }
36  }
```

Listing 1.1. Syntactical Representation of the Prelude Constraint Model in Fig. 1

7   Transformation Infrastructure

The system supports a number of transformations in order to produce graphical and audible material from models. Graphical representations of models, as already seen in Fig. 1, are generated using a graph language called *DOT*. Models can be transformed to a sequential *stream model*. This is accomplished by a compiler which traverses the tree structure until it reaches a leaf node. It then evaluates the constraint space and writes sequences of constraints, one for each constraint type, into a corresponding timeline depending on the parallelization context. Stream models can in turn be converted into a *score model* containing score-specific events such as notes, rests and loudness instructions. Currently an export module to the music notation language *LilyPond* is implemented which enables to export the score as PDF and MIDI files.

8   Evolutionary Composition System

The core of the automated composition system is inspired by the genetic programming paradigm. An initial constraint space and the fitness function configuration are given as input. The initial constraint space can either be unbounded (which means virtually any composition can be the result) or contain constraints limiting the possibility space of the evolution. For example, a set of applicable instruments, musical fragments to be incorporated or musical forms and structures can be purported. The initial constraint space can conveniently be specified using MC^{3}L. Note that it is possible to define which parts of the initial constraint space may be modified during the evolution. This is possible using two keywords: The *fixed* keyword indicates that the correspondent node must not be moved or removed. The *final* keyword indicates the same policy applied recursively for a whole subtree. Additionally, no more child nodes may be added to a final subtree. For example, if the user would like the output to be a canon with three voices, the initial constraint space shown in Listing 1.2 could be specified. It defines a parallelization with three voices, each of which references the same fragment named *melody*. The references of the second and third voice are delayed by two respectively four whole measures of rests. This effectively limits the evolution to happen under the last repetition node.

```
1   root final {
2       parallel {
3           fragment voice1 {
4               fragmentRef melody
5           }
6
7           fragment voice2 {
8               rhythm _2!
9               fragmentRef melody
10          }
11
12          fragment voice3 {
13              rhythm _4!
14              fragmentRef melody
15          }
16      }
17  }
18  fragment melody fixed {
19      repeat 3 fixed
20  }
```

Listing 1.2. Syntactical Representation of a Constraint Space Yielding a Canon with Three Voices

9   Fitness Function

A particularly challenging part when generating music using evolutionary algorithms is the design of a suitable fitness function to evaluate and compare the evolved compositions on a scalar basis. Considering that every human has a different taste in music which in turn is dependent on cultural influences, personal experiences, social periphery and probably also the mood of the person, there apparently can not be a universal fitness function for music. The approach in the proposed system is a configurable, modular fitness function which is optimized in respect of statistical measures and structural features. The system implements a multi-objective optimization process that aims to minimize the total absolute distance from optimum values for all modules, which can be weighted individually. The author is currently investigating which module configurations yield musically appealing results.

9.1 Statistical Fitness Function Modules

Implemented fitness function modules regarding statistical musical measures are listed in Table 1. All measures starting from the third row can be applied to either the global composition or to a single voice (respectively instrument) in the piece. Some modules are explained in greater detail below.

Table 1. List of statistical fitness function modules

Name	Description
Duration	Optimizes the piece to span a specified duration in beats or measures
Number of voices	Biases the system to favor compositions with a given number of instruments or voices
Note duration	Optimizes note length average and standard deviation
Rest duration	Optimizes rest length average and standard deviation
Note duration ratio	Considers the ratio between the total duration of notes and rests
Global dissonance	Analyzes simultaneously sounding notes in order to compute an average dissonance value and its standard deviation
Dissonance distribution	Considers simultaneously sounding notes and aims for a given distribution of interval occurrences
Dissonance in rhythmic context	Optimizes dissonance values depending on the point of time they appear in a measure
Interval leap distribution	Analyzes consecutively sounding note intervals and aspires a given distribution of interval leaps
Chord compliance	Checks the relative occurrence of notes matching their context harmony
Scale compliance	Aims for a relative occurrence of notes matching a scale corresponding to the context harmony or tonal center

9.2 Dissonance Analysis

A measure to compare the perceived dissonance of two simultaneously sounding notes is the Tenney Harmonic Distance or Tenney Height, defined as $log_2 ab$, where $\frac{a}{b}$ is the ratio between the two note frequencies [19, p. 407]. Tenney Heights

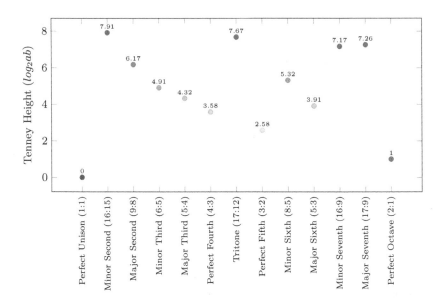

Fig. 2. Dissonance values of simultaneously sounding note intervals within an octave

for common intervals are visualized in Fig. 2. To compute a dissonance value of more than two simultaneously sounding notes, all combinations of intervals are analyzed. For example for an A minor chord the intervals A-C, A-E and C-E are analyzed. The dissonance value is then determined by calculating the average dissonance value of all note combinations in the chord. The system is capable of optimizing compositions regarding their global average dissonance value and its standard deviation. Furthermore the system can be instructed to aim for a given frequency distribution of simultaneously sounding intervals. In order to be independent from the total number of notes in the piece, the relative frequencies (i.e. the number of times an interval appears divided by the total number of intervals detected) can be specified as part of the fitness function.

Another approach is to optimize simultaneously sounding note intervals depending on the rhythmic context (i.e. the point of time they appear in a measure). In order to address points of time in a measure (i.e. pulses in a metric context) independently from the beat signature, the pulses are given numbers according to their importance in the metric context. The formula, yielding the pulse strengths of any multiplicative metre, was developed by Barlow [20, pp. 44–47]. For the quarter notes of a $\frac{4}{4}$ beat, for example, the formula yields the pulse strengths (or "indispensabilities", as referred to by Barlow) 3 0 2 1. The higher the number, the higher is the importance of the pulse. For a metre with 5 pulses the formula produces the series 4 0 3 1 2 and for the six eighth notes in a $\frac{3}{4}$ bar 5 0 3 1 4 2. A distribution of dissonance values depending on the pulse indispensability can be specified as fitness function objective.

9.3   Interval Leap Analysis

Not only is it functional to analyze simultaneously sounding intervals, but also to take consecutively played intervals into account. Therefore, the system compares all pitches of notes played in direct succession. Analyzing the distribution of successively played intervals for human compositions, it is remarkable that interval leaps of two semitones appear far more often (with a frequency of occurrence up to nearly 40 % dependent on the musical style) than intervals of 1 or 0 semitones [21, p. 218ff.]. In general the probability of intervals greater than two semitones decreases with ascending interval size with local minima at tritones and major sevenths as well as a local maximum for octaves. It is possible to define a target distribution of interval leaps as part of the fitness function for ascending as well as descending intervals (i.e. the distribution does not necessarily have to be symmetric).

9.4   Structural Fitness Function Modules

Since compositions are represented using tree-structured model instances, it is possible to define additional fitness function modules considering structural features of the model as shown in Table 2.

Table 2. List of structural fitness function modules

Module	Description
Tree depth	Controls the maximum tree depth of the model
Superfluous elements	Aims to eliminate nodes in the model which are syntactically allowed but semantically obsolete
Modifier ratio	Prefers compositions with a specified ratio of modifiers and constraints. The higher the ratio, the more compositions in which existing material is reshaped are preferred
Reference count	Favors compositions which reuse existing material by referencing fragments from different places in the model
Canonic pattern detector	Detects structures in which a fragment is successively referenced from different voice contexts (as applied in canons or fugues, for example)
Variation pattern detector	Promotes compositions repeating existing musical material in a varied form

10   Mutation and Crossover Operators

The following basic mutation operators are applied: node additions, replacements and removals are carried out for all types of nodes. The elements are either added as child nodes to existing ones or inserted between two already existing nodes. Replacements and removals can either happen for a single node (node replacement mutation) or whole subtrees (subtree mutation) [22]. For rhythmic constraints the following specialized mutations are applied: adding, removing or replacing single rhythmic notes or rests and turning rhythmic notes into rests and vice versa. For pitch constraints individual pitches are added, removed or replaced.

The system applies three different crossover operators. The first one swaps random subtrees of two compositions determined by roulette wheel selection. Another operator selects on average 50 % of the nodes of a specific type in a model. Nodes of the same type are randomly selected from the other model and exchanged with the previously selected ones. The third operator works similarly to the second one, though it additionally mixes sequences (e.g. pitches or rhythmic notes) contained in the nodes. During the evolution the system assures that neither the root node nor any of the locked model nodes (as described in Sect. 8) are replaced or removed, that no referential cycles are produced and that referenced fragments are copied to the target models recursively.

Note that the system does not differentiate between terminal and non-terminal nodes like in conventional genetic programming. In fact, all constructable models that have a root node are syntactically correct. Models that produce little or no output are semantically obsolete and will become extinct quickly as they are considered inferior in terms of fitness.

11   Results

The system successfully evolves compositions largely complying with the requested features. An example fitness function configuration is shown in Table 3. Although the compositions meet the statistical requirements, the pieces are only partially aesthetically pleasing. Evolved pieces clearly become more appealing when optimizing for high ratios of chord compliance and scale compliance in combination with a normally distributed, symmetric frequency distribution of consecutive intervals. This aligns with previous research with systems producing musically pleasant results by considering notes in a harmonic context and thereof derived scale context (e.g. [5,6,13,15]). When increasing the allowed standard deviation for note durations, the rhythms sound unstructured and random. This can be improved by implementing fitness functions analyzing pulse strengths in the metric context or considering approaches proposed by Horowitz [7]. Another weakness of the system is probably that there are no restrictions regarding the arrangement of the model nodes. A layer-based approach, where nodes of the same hierarchy level have the same type (with less strict conditions at the leaf node levels) similar to Fig. 1 could help to organize the evolved compositions. Then it is possible to develop enhanced crossover and mutation operators. The ones used in the current implementation seem to be too generic for the task of musical composition, so "musically intelligent" operators are required (as proposed by [6,13,15]). The system can be further improved by introducing more specialized modules, such as algorithms considering voice leading rules, harmonic progressions and redundancy measures of several musical aspects.

Table 3. Example fitness function configuration

Module	Target value(s)
Duration	16 measures
Average note duration	0.25 (quarter note)
Note duration σ	0.15
Note duration ratio	80 %
Global average dissonance	3.5
Superfluous elements	0
Interval leap distribution	Symmetric distribution centered at perfect unisons: 5 % with ± minor seconds: 10 %, ± major seconds: 17.5 %, ± minor thirds: 5 %, ± major thirds: 5 %, ± perfect fourths: 2.5 %, ± perfect fifths: 2.5 %, ± perfect octaves: 5 %
Chord compliance	60 %
Scale compliance	90 % relative to default scale matching the harmony

12   Conclusions and Future Work

The application of genetic programming in the field of automated music generation is promising considering that the system is capable of generating short musical pieces which are at least tonally pleasing. Improvements are still to be implemented for other aspects such as rhythms and harmonic progressions. Another goal to be pursued is to extend the system in such a way that it generates longer pieces with multiple sections which have different statistical and structural properties. The next ambition is to establish mechanisms which connect different sections in a musically satisfying way. Furthermore additional node types for relative harmonic constraints and modifiers are planned as well as a real-time capable compiler for direct playback of the compositions.

References

1. Collins, N.: Introduction to Computer Music. Wiley, Chichester (2010)
2. Nierhaus, G.: Algorithmic Composition: Paradigms of Automated Music Generation. Springer, New York (2009)
3. Fogel, D.B.: Evolutionary Computation: Toward a New Philosophy of Machine Intelligence. Wiley, Hoboken (2006)
4. Horner, A., Goldberg, D.E.: Genetic algorithms and computer-assisted music composition. In: Belew, R., Booker, L. (eds.) Proceedings of the Fourth International Conference on Genetic Algorithms, pp. 437–441. Morgan Kaufmann, San Mateo (1991)

5. Biles, J.A.: GenJam: a genetic algorithm for generating jazz solos. In: Proceedings of the 1994 International Computer Music Conference, ICMA, San Francisco, pp. 131–137 (1994)
6. Biles, J.A.: Improvizing with genetic algorithms: GenJam. In: Miranda, E.R., Biles, J.A. (eds.) Evolutionary Computer Music, pp. 137–169. Springer, London (2007)
7. Horowitz, D.: Generating rhythms with genetic algorithms. In: Proceedings of the 1994 International Computer Music Conference, ICMA, San Francisco, pp. 142–143 (1994)
8. McIntyre, R.A.: Bach in a box: the evolution of four part baroque harmony using the genetic algorithm. In: Proceedings of the IEEE Conference on Evolutionary Computation, vol. 14, No 3. IEEE Press, New York, pp. 852–857 (1994)
9. Horner, A. and Ayers, L.: Harmonization of musical progressions with genetic algorithms. In: Proceedings of the 1995 International Computer Music Conference, ICMA, San Francisco, pp. 483–484 (1995)
10. Jacob, B.: Composing with genetic algorithms. In: Proceedings of the 1995 International Computer Music Conference, ICMA, San Francisco, pp. 452–455 (1995)
11. Jacob, B.: Algorithmic composition as a model of creativity. Organised Sound 1(3), 157–165 (1996)
12. Johanson, B., Poli, R.: GP-Music: an interactive genetic programming system for music generation with automated fitness raters. In: Koza, J.R., et al. (eds.) Genetic Programming 1998: Proceedings of the Third Annual Conference (GP 1998), pp. 181–186. Morgan Kaufmann, San Francisco (1998)
13. Marques, M., Oliveira, V., Vieira, S., Rosa, A.C.: Music composition using genetic evolutionary algorithms. In: Proceedings of the IEEE Conference on Evolutionary Computation 2000. IEEE Press, New York (2000)
14. de la Puente, A.O., Alfonso, R.S., Moreno, M.A.: Automatic composition of music by means of grammatical evolution. In: Proceedings of the 2002 Conference on APL, pp. 148–155. ACM Press, New York (2002)
15. Fox, C.: Genetic hierarchical music structures. In: Proceedings of the 19th International FLAIRS Conference. AAAI Press, Menlo Park (2006)
16. Waschka II, R.: Composing with genetic algorithms: GenDash. In: Miranda, E.R., Biles, J.A. (eds.) Evolutionary Computer Music, pp. 117–136. Springer, London (2007)
17. Boden, M.A.: Creativity and computers. In: Dartnall, T. (ed.) Artificial Intelligence and Creativity: An Interdisciplinary Approach, pp. 3–26. Kluwer Academic Publishers, Dordrecht (1994)
18. Boden, M.A.: Creativity and Art: Three Roads to Surprise. Oxford University Press, Oxford (2010)
19. Deza, M.M., Deza, E.: Encyclopedia of Distances. Springer, Heidelberg (2013)
20. Barlow, C.: On musiquantics. Technical report, Johannes Gutenberg-Universität Mainz (2012)
21. Patel, A.D.: Music, Language, and the Brain. Oxford University Press, New York (2008)
22. Poli, R., Langdon, W.B., McPhee, N.F., Koza, J.R.: A Field Guide to Genetic Programming (2008). Published via http://lulu.com and freely available at http://www.gp-field-guide.org.uk

AudioInSpace: Exploring the Creative Fusion of Generative Audio, Visuals and Gameplay

Amy K. Hoover[✉], William Cachia,
Antonios Liapis, and Georgios N. Yannakakis

Institute of Digital Games, University of Malta,
Msida MSD 2080, Malta
amy.hoover@gmail.com,
{william.cachia.07,antonios.liapis,
georgios.yannakakis}@um.edu.mt

Abstract. Computer games are unique creativity domains in that they elegantly fuse several facets of creative work including visuals, narrative, music, architecture and design. While the exploration of possibilities across facets of creativity offers a more realistic approach to the game design process, most existing autonomous (or semi-autonomous) game content generators focus on the mere generation of single domains (creativity facets) in games. Motivated by the sparse literature on multifaceted game content generation, this paper introduces a multifaceted procedural content generation (PCG) approach that is based on the interactive evolution of multiple artificial neural networks that orchestrate the generation of visuals, audio and gameplay. The approach is evaluated on a spaceship shooter game. The generated artifacts — a fusion of audiovisual and gameplay elements — showcase the capacity of multifaceted PCG and its evident potential for computational game creativity.

1 Introduction

Computer games are a creative outlet for players tasked with solving problems and designers and artists who create a game's multiple facets (e.g. audio, visuals, gameplay, narrative, level architecture and game design) [1]. Often both the creative expression of video game designers and the players' immersion in the game are significantly impacted by the interplay between audio facets (e.g. character themes, sound effects, foreshadowing) and visuals facets (e.g. object and level design) [1]. Historically in popular video games like Super Mario Bros. [2] and Sonic the Hedgehog [3], game composers and developers interweave these facets by assuming that a player will *linearly* progress through known game states. However as players are increasingly drawn toward dynamically constructing their own personalized and replayable game experiences (i.e. *nonlinear* games), game composers and designers are challenged to maintain meaningful interaction between these audio and visual game facets [4].

Procedural content generation (PCG) methods can alleviate some of the demands on game designers, developers, and artists by fully automating the

© Springer International Publishing Switzerland 2015
C. Johnson et al. (Eds.): EvoMUSART 2015, LNCS 9027, pp. 101–112, 2015.
DOI: 10.1007/978-3-319-16498-4_10

process of creating game facets or within computer-aided tools designed to assist the human creator [5]. With a few notable exceptions [6,7], until recently these PCG methods have focused on generating single game facets (e.g. visuals, levels) that are then incorporated into the standard game development pipeline [8].

Instead, this paper introduces a *multifaceted* PCG approach that simultaneously generates audio, visuals, and gameplay facets. Represented by a special type of artificial neural network called a compositional pattern producing network (CPPN) [9], the audio and visual facets are generated with respect to each other (i.e. audio generation considers the currently displayed visuals and vice versa). This paper explores the idea through an extension to a space shooting game introduced by Cachia et al. [10] called AudioInSpace. Players control a spaceship in this test bed game and progress through levels while shooting at enemies and avoiding obstacles. Through *implicit* interactive evolutionary computation (IEC) [11] of the audio and visual CPPNs, over the course of the game players shape their experience by shooting weapons with the most desirable trajectories and colors, and evolving the audio to suit their sound preferences and bullet trajectory needs. The results are personalized weapons and soundtracks created through *mixed-initiative co-creativity*, where the machine mediates the bidirectional relationships between the audio and the visuals while the human player controls the aesthetic outcome via the firing of weapons.

2   Background

While there are many approaches to procedurally generating video game facets (e.g. visuals, audio, narrative, game design, level design and gameplay), the focus is often on a single facet rather than how generated facets combine for a complete game experience. For instance, world maps in *Civilization V* [12], dungeons in *Diablo* [13], racing tracks [14], petal colors and shapes in Petalz [15], and weapons in *Borderlands* [16] are all procedurally generated to provide the player with increased personalization and replayability. Similarly, *Audiosurf* [17] generates game levels from sound files provided by the player. While these generated elements may increase replayability and alleviate authorial burden on developers, these approaches serve as means to an end rather than celebrating the creativity of procedural content generation itself.

Other approaches aim to interweave procedurally generated elements to enhance the game experience. For instance, *Galactic Arms Race* [18] encourages players to interactively evolve weapon visuals and bullet trajectories to their aesthetic and gameplay preferences, while *Game-o-matic* [19] helps players visually construct the topic of their game and then procedurally generates the rules and visuals, challenging players to interpret the designer's intent on topics like religion or politics. *A Rogue Dream* [7] is 2D maze game that gathers and parses internet data to discover relationships between natural language concepts to create visual and gameplay facets. Proteus [20] is a completely procedurally generated pixel-art world with open-ended gameplay encouraging players to spatially and sonically explore a generated island. However, the sonic output does not affect the previously generated landscapes. Even in these integrated environments, the output of one procedurally generated facet has little affect on the output of the other.

A notable exception is that of *AudioOverdrive*, a side-scrolling space shooter where players compose music by progressing through the game. It has bidirectional communication between enemies, gameplay, and level visuals [21], but the approach requires heavy human initiative by the developers. The approach in this paper extends ideas from AudioOverdrive by creating a game environment called AudioInSpace with closely coupled audio and visuals that requires minimal hard coding (initiative) from the developers. In this test bed space shooter, the audio, visuals, and gameplay are integrated to generate the appearance of the spaceship's weapons (e.g. color), gameplay effects (e.g. whether it hit an enemy), and the game soundtrack. The soundtrack then influences the firing rate, color and movement patterns of the weapon's particles, thus ensuring a bidirectional communication across three creative facets. While both AudioInSpace and AudioOverdrive explore similar goals, themes, and creative game facets, AudioInSpace specifically uses information on the spaceship's gameplay behavior and on-screen visuals rather than treating gameplay events such as firing a weapon solely on account of its sound effect.

3   Approach

While many PCG approaches focus on creating single game facets to augment the developers' creativity, the approach in this paper is to explore multiple generated game facets that are combined through mixed initiative co-creativity [1], where the machine and the player create and collectively augment the player's gameplay and creative experience. In particular, the machine's creativity is enhanced through a conceptual blending of the audio and visual modules in Fig. 1 where audio outputs inform the visual module, which in turn is input to the audio module. This model is implemented in a proof-of-concept space shooter game called AudioInSpace (see Sect. 3.1 for details) where players control space ships and fire at enemies. The ways in which the weapons fire (i.e. the bullet trajectories), their shapes, speeds, and colors are affected by the audio, while the audio in turn effects the trajectories. Both audio and visuals are affected by gameplay as players exercise their own creativity through selecting preferred weapons and audio for the soundtrack in AudioInSpace. To co-evolve the individual audio and visual facets, each PCG module bases decisions on information gathered from both domains.

The relationships between the domains and generated outputs are represented by a special type of artificial neural network (ANN) called a compositional pattern producing network (CPPN; shown in Fig. 2) [9]. Like traditional ANNs, each CPPN is an interconnected network of nodes and connection weights that when provided input, calculate an output value that can theoretically approximate any function [22]. However, unlike traditional ANNs that only compute sigmoid functions at their hidden nodes, CPPNs can compute any function

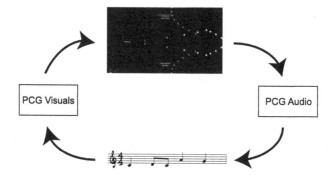

Fig. 1. Mixed-Initiative Co-Creativity with Multiple Facets. In AudioInSpace, weapon visuals and audio are represented by two separate modules that each provide relevant domain information to the other (i.e. the visual module is not only informed by current visual elements in the level, but also by the concurrently generated audio and vice versa). The human initiative in AudioInSpace comes from gameplay and the selection of weapons.

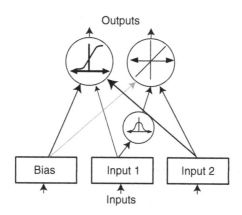

Fig. 2. Compositional Pattern Producing Network (CPPN). This feedforward CPPN is an interconnected network of nodes that take input values (at bottom) from a domain to calculate the output values (at top). Starting from the inputs, at each hidden node (middle) and output node, a value is computed depending on the node's activation function and activation sum, the latter determined by a weighted sum of the values of nodes connected below. Unlike traditional ANNs, a node's activation function can be any function many of which can bias the CPPN toward certain regularities including bilateral symmetry, repetition, and repetition with variation.

(e.g. Gaussian, sigmoid, sine, ramp, etc.), effectually making them pattern generators biased toward the particular regularities indicated by the hidden node activation functions. Through this representation, the aim is that both weapon visuals and audio are represented as patterns of each other.

Each PCG module is represented by a separate CPPN that inputs domain information and outputs instructions for generating either audio or visual patterns that not only affect player immersion but also gameplay. To personalize the relationship between audio, visuals, and gameplay, these CPPNs can be evolved through a process similar to animal breeding called interactive evolutionary computation (IEC), wherein the human rather than an explicit fitness function determines the fitness of candidate individuals. CPPNs are evolved through the NeuroEvolution of Augmenting Topologies (NEAT; [23]) algorithm that was originally developed to solve control and decision tasks but generates audio and visuals in this paper. Through (NEAT), each CPPN can start minimally and complexify as necessary over evolutionary time. By adding hidden nodes and connections, and changing activation functions and weight values, each new individual can expand the relationship between inputs and hidden nodes. Thus, player selection is an important aspect of this approach and toward facilitating mixed-initiative co-creativity.

3.1   AudioInSpace: The Game

The multifaceted PCG approach is evaluated in a space shooter, called AudioIn-Space, which extends approaches by Hastings et al. [18] for weapon particle generation through the integration of an audio component. As the game progresses, the player moves through different space-based game levels encountering obstacles and hostile enemies (as shown in Fig. 3).

The player encounters large rocks to avoid, and small rocks to avoid and shoot, while implicitly evolving weapon trajectories and aesthetics, and audio based on the amount of time the user has the weapon and audio track equipped. With each bullet fired, a weapon is assigned a preference point while the audio is rated for each new note. The longer each weapon and audio CPPN are in play, the higher that CPPN is rated. It is assumed that the longer weapons and visuals are in play, the more preferable they are to a particular player. Therefore through IEC players evolve the visual and audio networks toward their aesthetic preferences. By directing the two CPPNs to create patterns from information gathered from both domains, this approach incorporates mixed-initiative co-creativity while combining two different PCG modules.

Upon launch, the colors and trajectory of the first bullet are calculated when a random note from the C Major pentatonic scale is played and input to the visual CPPN in Fig. 4a. Together with the pitch information from the initially random MIDI note, this CPPN also inputs the $(\delta x, \delta y)$ position between where the bullet was fired and where it is currently located with respect to where it was fired, and the time t since firing. Note that before the bullet is fired, the initial $(\delta x, \delta y) = (0, 0)$ and $t = 0$. Outputs of the visual CPPN determine the red, green, and blue (RGB) color values for each bullet, and the (x', y') outputs dictate the bullet's new position (i.e. its trajectory). The color and trajectory of each bullet is calculated every time a new note sounds.

New notes are fired when the bullet hits an enemy or otherwise at the end of the current note's duration. As seen in Fig. 4b, the music CPPN determines the pitch and the note's duration through the respective Pitch and DeltaTime

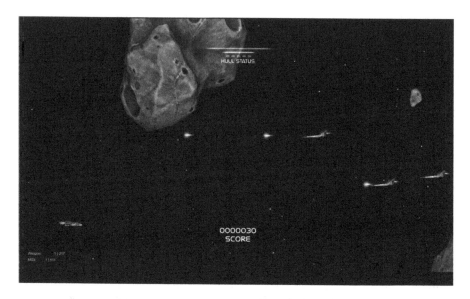

Fig. 3. AudioInSpace. In AudioInSpace, the user controls the spaceship on the left side of the screen while moving through each space level. The health of the ship is shown at the top of the screen as "hull strength" while the weapon score is displayed at the bottom. Two mirrored visual beams project from the player's spaceship shooting patterns directed by the current visual CPPN. The rate of fire and the pitches heard result from the audio CPPN's outputs.

outputs. These values are based on the (x, y) position of where the last bullet was fired, time since firing t, whether the bullet struck an enemy h, and its RGB values.

4   Experiments

Experiments in this section illustrate the potential of this multifaceted PCG proof-of-concept by exploring the impact of the audio and visual CPPNs on the game and on each other. In AudioInSpace, each CPPN module is evolved separately by the player. That is, the audio network is held constant while the weapon network is evolved and vice versa. The first set of experiments explores each network, one at a time. To start, three weapon CPPNs are evolved with a constant, simple audio input (i.e. a repeating eighth note at a pitch of MIDI value 72). After exploring the weapon effects with this repeated input, the audio CPPN is evolved for each of the weapon CPPNs. The results of the new and varied MIDI inputs are then explored through the weapon visuals. To further explore these effects, ascending and descending MIDI notes between MIDI values 20 and 90 are also input to the visual CPPN.

The second set of experiments explores the complete interaction between the two networks when evolved by players. In these experiments, a note in the

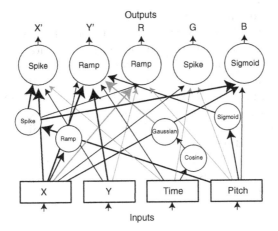

(a) Visuals and Gameplay (Weapon) CPPN

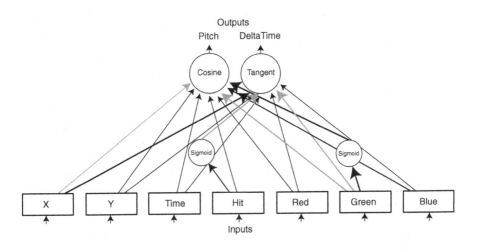

(b) Audio CPPN

Fig. 4. CPPNs for AudioInSpace. Each PCG module is enabled by its own CPPN. Darker connections represent a positive weight while lighter connections are a negative weight. The magnitude of each weight is represented by the line width where thicker lines indicate a higher absolute value. In (a), the inputs to the visual CPPN are the (x, y) coordinates from where the bullet is initially fired, the time since firing, and the current pitch being input from the CPPN in (b); it outputs a new (x', y') coordinate for the next frame and RGB values. On the other hand, (b) inputs the outputs from (a) as well as whether a bullet has just struck an enemy.

pentatonic C major scale is sent to the visual network. The visuals are then generated in loop with the MIDI notes.

In each of the experiments, tournament selection occurs amongst a population of fifty individuals, ten of which are rated by the player through IEC. Players can switch the current weapon or audio representation by pressing a button to activate a different CPPN chromosome whose effects are immediately heard and seen in AudioInSpace. The evolutionary parameters are set through preliminary testing, and the probability of adding a new node or connection is 30 % and 15 %, respectively. Similarly, the activation functions at any node can be replaced by one of the following with an even chance: Sigmoid, Hyperbolic Tangent, Sine, Cosine, Bipolar Sigmoid, Gaussian, Ramp, Step, Spike [18]. However, the activation function of any particular node is only changed with a 20 % chance. Weights are real values between $[-3, 3]$ that are mutated with a uniform 90 % chance. Occasionally (1 % chance), connections are disabled.

5   Results

Due to space constraints we will only present a number of indicative audio-visual patterns generated through the experiments conducted. For the interested reader several videos of the results presented in this section (and beyond) are available at http://music-ai.org/audioinspace/.

The first set of results explores the combination of visual and audio CPPNs by first examining the weapons with a predetermined MIDI pattern. MIDI note 67, or G, is input to the visual network in eighth note quantization. As shown in Fig. 5 and accompanying video, visuals generated from this single repeated note create a constant visual stream with a predictable trajectory dictated by the repeated eighth note inputs. Each visual CPPN has four inputs, five outputs, and in this result, which was evolved in fifty generations, also has six hidden nodes as shown previously in Fig. 4a. As these weapons are patterns created by human evolved CPPNs, many different colors and trajectory shapes are possible. As already noted, several additional examples are available at the website for the reader of this paper.

Once the audio CPPN is evolved by the player for the previously evolved weapon CPPN, the bullets still maintain much of the blue color present in Fig. 5a, but as shown in Fig. 5b also start shooting red colored bullets over time. The trajectory from the CPPN in Fig. 5(a) results in a predictable repetitive pattern. However, once the MIDI network is evolved in Fig. 5(b) the varied audio inputs impact the original path in Fig. 5(a). In fact, with this MIDI network, the bullets are fired with a slightly backwards trajectory that at times allows users to build posterior bullet defenses against potential upcoming enemies. In this way, players can simultaneously evolve networks suited for their individual game experiences.

Figure 6(a) shows a weapon CPPN that is evolved with a repeated MIDI input like Fig. 5a. However, Fig. 6(b) shows the same weapon from Fig. 6(a) but with MIDI notes that are input in ascending and descending order between 20 and 90. Over time, the overall trajectory shape of Fig. 6(a) is maintained, but

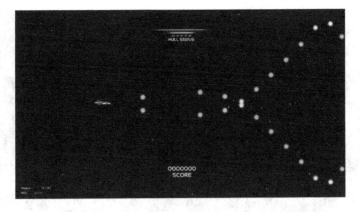

(a) Weapon with Repeated Single Eighth Note

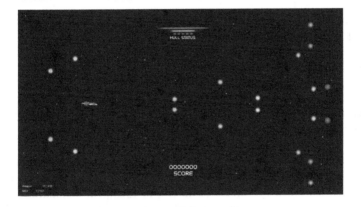

(b) Weapon with Repeated Variable Eighth Note

Fig. 5. Evolved weapon with repeated and variable notes. While the weapon in (a) maintains a steady trajectory due to the repeated eighth note input, the same weapon in (b) deviates in bullet timing, color, and trajectory once the MIDI network is evolved, thereby illustrating the influence of the MIDI CPPN.

the length of time between bullets increases and decreases according to the MIDI input. Videos of the complete system interaction are available at http://music-ai. org/audioinspace/ where the player cycles through several different weapons and MIDI CPPNs.

6   Discussion and Future Work

While this paper is a proof-of-concept of multifaceted game creativity as influenced by the player (mixed-initiative), it is important to investigate whether

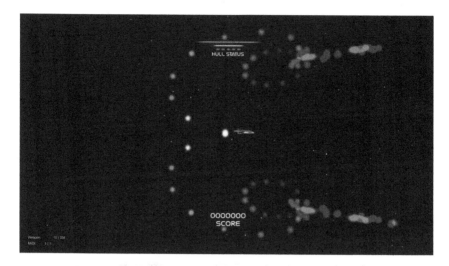

Fig. 6. Ascending and descending pitches. When ascending and descending notes between MIDI values 20–90 are sent to this weapon network, the smooth transitions between colors and trajectories are evident. The corresponding video is available at http://music-ai.org/audioinspace/.

players actually enjoy this new mixed-initiative experience. Future work aims to explore and evaluate players' appreciation of the visuals, audio, and gameplay, and whether the mixed-initiative interaction enhances the overall experience. The question is whether players prefer the sound of the additional audio and the control that it provides over the weapon visuals. AudioInSpace can be play tested — with the work by Cachia et al. [10] as a control — examining average game time, perceived enjoyment, generations per audio and visual CPPNs, and complexity of the relationships between inputs and outputs of each CPPN.

While it is currently assumed that the number of times a gun is fired and the length of time an audio network is heard reflect player preference, another interesting question is why players choose certain weapons and audio. For example, do players focus more on the look of the weapon or the rate of fire determined by the audio? Answers to these questions could help identify player styles and potential areas for more development.

There are also many different avenues for increasing the quality of the visuals and audio, and the cooperation between the two. Like Galactic Arms Race, for instance, the initial generation of weapon and audio CPPNs could be preselected for quality and gameplay. Furthermore, more constraints on the audio output (e.g. restriction to key) could enhance the sound of the output. Another interesting area of research is in adding "listeners" to generated audio and spawning monsters depending on the pitches and durations of note patterns. For instance, when low-pitched long notes play, a larger more important and difficult boss could appear, whereas higher pitched notes could signal intermittently approaching comets.

Future work includes incorporating more interwoven facets into this existing multifaceted PCG approach to explore the boundaries of the idea across different game types. While an obvious future direction is investigating level architecture facets, the complexity of extending the approach across a variety of games becomes greater with the generation of additional game facets. However, combining additional facets into a meaningful game that provides a positive player experience and potentially enhancing his or her creativity depends on more factors requiring more extensive experimentation.

7 Conclusion

This paper introduced an approach for procedurally generating multiple game facets simultaneously that depends on initiatives of both computational and human creators (mixed initiative co-creativity). Through a space shooter game called AudioInSpace, players evolve their own weapons and audio to suit their aesthetic tastes and tactical demands of the current level. Results from this proof-of-concept game illustrate that a significant impact is made on the visuals when combined with simultaneously generated audio patterns. While obtained results are already encouraging, there is room to improve the overall interaction between the player and the game and the generated audio in future version of the game. However, these initial results already suggest the potential of a multifaceted PCG approach toward realizing computational game creativity.

Acknowledgments. Special thanks to Luke Aquilina for his contributions to development. This research is supported, in part, by the FP7 ICT project C2Learn (project no: 318480) and by the FP7 Marie Curie CIG project AutoGameDesign (project no: 630665).

References

1. Liapis, A., Yannakakis, G.N., Togelius, J.: Computational game creativity. In: Proceedings of the Fifth International Conference on Computational Creativity (2014)
2. Nintendo: Super Mario Bros. (1985)
3. Sega: Sonic the Hedgehog (1991)
4. Collins, K.: An introduction to procedural music in video games. Contemp. Music Rev. **28**(1), 5–15 (2009)
5. Yannakakis, G.N.: Game AI revisited. In: Proceedings of the 9th Conference on Computing Frontiers, pp. 285–292 (2012)
6. Scirea, M.: Mood dependent music generator. In: Reidsma, D., Katayose, H., Nijholt, A. (eds.) ACE 2013. LNCS, vol. 8253, pp. 626–629. Springer, Heidelberg (2013)
7. Cook, M., Colton, S.: A rogue dream: automatically generating meaningful content for games. In: Proceedings of the AIIDE Workshop on Experimental AI and Games (2014)
8. Togelius, J., Shaker, N., Nelson, M.J.: Introduction. In: Shaker, N., Togelius, J., Nelson, M.J. (eds.) Procedural Content Generation in Games: A Textbook and an Overview of Current Research. Springer, Heidelberg (2014)

9. Stanley, K.O.: Compositional pattern producing networks: a novel abstraction of development. Genet. Program. Evolvable Mach. Spec. Issue Dev. Syst. **8**(2), 131–162 (2007)
10. Cachia, W., Aquilina, L., Martinez, H.P., Yannakakis, G.N.: Procedural generation of music-guided weapons. In: Proceedings of the IEEE Conference on Computational Intelligence and Games (CIG) (2014)
11. Togelius, J., Yannakakis, G.N., Stanley, K.O., Browne, C.: Search-based procedural content generation: a taxonomy and survey. IEEE Trans. Comput. Intell. AI Game. **3**(3), 172–186 (2011)
12. Firaxis Games: Civilization v (2010)
13. Blizzard: Diablo (1996)
14. Togelius, J., Nardi, R.D., Lucas, S.M.: Towards automatic personalised content creation for racing games. In: Proceedings of IEEE Symposium on Computational Intelligence and Games, IEEE, pp. 252–259 (2007)
15. Risi, S., Lehman, J., D'Ambrosio, D., Hall, R., Stanley, K.O.: Combining search-based procedural content generation and social gaming in the petalz video game. In: Proceedings of Artificial Intelligence and Interactive Digital Entertainment Conference (2012)
16. Gearbox Software: Borderlands (2009)
17. Audio Surf LLC: Audiosurf (2011)
18. Hastings, E.J., Guha, R.K., Stanley, K.O.: Automatic content generation in the galactic arms race video game. IEEE Trans. Comput. Intell. AI Game. **1**(4), 245–263 (2009)
19. Treanor, M., Blackford, B., Mateas, M., Bogost, I.: Game-o-matic: generating videogames that represent ideas. In: Proceedings of the FDG Workshop on Procedural Content Generation (2012)
20. Key, E., Kanaga, D.: Proteus (2011). http://www.visitproteus.com/
21. Holtar, N.I., Nelson, M.J., Togelius, J.: Audioverdrive: exploring bidirectional communication between music and gameplay. In: Proceedings of the 2013 International Computer Music Conference (2013)
22. Cybenko, G.: Approximation by superpositions of a sigmoidal function. Mathe. Control Signals Syst. **2**(4), 303–314 (1989)
23. Stanley, K.O., Miikkulainen, R.: Evolving neural networks through augmenting topologies. Evol. Comput. **10**, 99–127 (2002)

Toward Certain Sonic Properties of an Audio Feedback System by Evolutionary Control of Second-Order Structures

Seunghun Kim[1], Juhan Nam[1], and Graham Wakefield[2(✉)]

[1] Graduate School of Culture Technology,
Korea Advanced Institute of Science and Technology (KAIST),
Dahakro 291, Yuseong-gu, Daejeon, Republic of Korea
{seunghun.kim,juhannam}@kaist.ac.kr
[2] Digital Media, Visual Art and Art History, York University,
4700 Keele St., Toronto, Canada
grrrwaaa@yorku.ca

Abstract. Aiming for high-level intentional control of audio feedback, though microphones, loudspeakers and digital signal processing, we present a system adapting toward chosen sonic features. Users control the system by selecting and changing feature objectives in real-time. The system has a second-order structure in which the internal signal processing algorithms are developed according to an evolutionary process. Genotypes develop into signal-processing algorithms, and fitness is measured by analysis of the incoming audio feedback. A prototype is evaluated experimentally to measure changes of audio feedback depending on the chosen target conditions. By enhancing interactivity of an audio feedback through the intentional control, we expect that feedback systems could be utilized more effectively in the fields of musical interaction, finding balance between nonlinearity and interactivity.

Keywords: Audio feedback · Evolutionary algorithm

1 Introduction

We use the term audio feedback to refer to systems of positive acoustic/digital feedback in which signals received by one or more microphones are amplified and played through one or more loudspeakers with sufficient energy gain to create a persistent loop. Such systems support unique features, such as nonlinearity, emergence, self-organization and openness to the environment, and efforts to leverage these properties in music composition and sound art are numerous [1–5].

Many prior work with audio feedback systems have been characterized by an emphasis upon the emergent interactions the medium supports, while intentional control of sonic behaviours is given less emphasis. Where performer interventions are supported these are generally limited to deliberate sounds and parameter

© Springer International Publishing Switzerland 2015
C. Johnson et al. (Eds.): EvoMUSART 2015, LNCS 9027, pp. 113–124, 2015.
DOI: 10.1007/978-3-319-16498-4_11

changes, however due to the nonlinear dynamics of the medium the overall directions of tendencies remain unknown and thus unintentional. Our research aims to support intentional control through tendencies while preserving the attractive nonlinear characteristics of audio feedback, such as unpredictable yet rich transients, in order to open up new possibilities of musical application.

In this paper, we present a system adapting toward a certain chosen sonic properties such as average pitch, vibrato, tremolo, brightness, and spectral tonality: recognizable features of the feedback sound. The system allows users to select in real-time sonic characteristics as the target conditions of the system. Adaptation toward such conditions is achieved using a second-order structure which can organize and replace internal signal processing algorithms. This second-order structure uses an evolutionary process by selecting and changing the types and parameters of signal processing components. We evaluate a prototype through measurement of average and highest fitness curves over generations in several contexts.

2   Motivation

Although audio feedback is typically viewed as a problem to avoid in music and telecommunication industries, some performers have deliberately utilized feedback creatively. For example, *LIES(topology)* [5] is an improvisation performance based on the interaction between a feedback system and performers. The system is centred on a feedback delay network (FDN), in which several delay lines connected by a feedback matrix mediate the input and the output. Some feedback loops apply signal processing components, such as a ring modulator, frequency shifter, granulator, wave-shaper and reverberator. These form a complex network in which objects can be connected by a mixer or a ring modulator. Performers alter the topology by controlling amplitude changes of the recirculating signals and change the relations between the components by modifying parameters of the components.

Audible Eco-systemic Interface (AESI) [1] is a compositional work that interacts with its acoustic environment through sonic feedback, depending on ambient noise as its information source. The central idea is a self-feeding feedback loop, almost identical to the basic feedback structure. Features extracted from the received sound are compared with the original signal, and the difference is used to control parameters for sound synthesis, thereby adapting the system toward the room resonance.

Di Scipio notes how non-linear feedback systems may lead to new, emergent high-level behaviors, generated and maintained by a network of low-level components [6]. An implication is that specific performances cannot be formally defined or accurately predicted in advance. Instead, he directs attention to the technical conditions and sonic interactions of the system. As identities of feedback-based music systems are determined by the relations between low-level components, this results in fixed mappings from analysis parameters of the received signal to signal-processing parameters: the composer's role is to establish the mappings.

However, Kollias [4] criticizes that by doing so composer loses control over the overall sonic shape, as the system only determines microstructural sonic design.

Although high-level behaviors emerge through a bottom-up organization, control of them is a distinct issue. By referring to Mitchel's work [7], he instead suggests that adaptive systems must preserve a balance between bottom-up and top-down processes. He proposed *Ephemeron* [4,8], a feedback-based improvisation system, which is presented as a metaphorically living organism and consists of cells which are sonic units. This system is acoustically adaptive as the cells recognize environmental characteristics in an evolutionary process, yet also features both high- and low-level controls for producing music. Specifically, a composer proposes the emergence of certain sonic properties by design at a micro-structural level, while a performer controls the overall sonic result by modulating global parameters. This prevents the system's tendency toward a stable state. Nevertheless, direction of the tendency is unknown because the unpredictability of nonlinear dynamics hinders prediction.

Our motivation is to more deeply explore intentional control toward specified sonic properties without sacrificing attractive nonlinearities of the audio feedback itself. Intentional control means that people can observe desired tendencies in the feedback sound by setting and changing goal directions in real-time, enhancing interactivity through regulative processes. This would support idiosyncratic interactive applications that combine context-specificity, nonlinearity and interactivity; such as a sound installation sensitive to the acoustic environments according to audience's intentions, a generative improvisation system responding to its environment, or a sound generator that repeatedly generates new sound materials according to user-specified conditions.

3   System Design

Our system is built around three design ideas, outlined in the following subsections:

- Goal-directedness: sonic features are specified as target conditions, which can be controlled by users in real-time
- Second-order feedback structure: signal processing uses a modular approach to support diversity and dynamism
- Evolutionary process: the controller uses an evolutionary process for design of the second-order feedback structure.

Figure 1 shows an overview of the system. The controller, which designs the second-order feedback structure, uses an evolutionary process. This removes the necessity of manually searching for the optimal structure for a target condition. We do not need to care about the specific design, only the final characteristics: we provide the goal, and the system evaluates several structures to achieve it.

3.1   Goal-Directedness Toward a Specific Sonic Condition

A control method in cybernetic systems is presenting a goal and designing the system to follow it: it is referred to as goal-directed behavior [9]. An autonomous

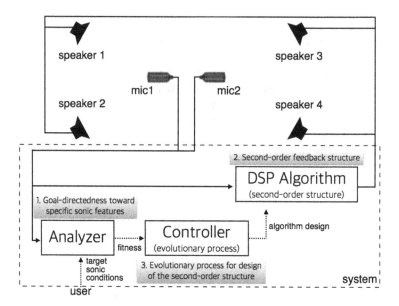

Fig. 1. Conceptual diagram of our system, which proposes (1) specific sonic features as target conditions, (2) second-order feedback structure and (3) evolutionary process for design of the second-order structure. Solid lines represent audio-rate signal flows while dotted lines sub-audio rate (data) signal flows.

system pursues its own purpose by trying to resist obstructions from the environment that may adversely affect getting close to the target state: goal-directedness regulates perturbation. By setting specific sonic features as its own purpose, an audio feedback system can adapt toward them and this implies the possibility of exterior/guided intentional control. For our purposes, this requires real-time feature extraction of the feedback sound to measure present state and its deviation from a target state.

We investigated feature extraction methods from several improvisation systems in which a single or multiple agents interact with external performers. For example, Murray-Rust et al. [10] and Wulhorst et al. [11] present artificial intelligence based music compositions, which use real-time acoustic feature extraction for the purpose of transmitting information to internal agents. These mostly focused on rhythmic and harmonic information from MIDI signals. Van Nort et al. [12] recognizes sonic gestures simultaneously by parallel operation of gestural spaces in different time scales, such as variety, brightness and pitch in short gestures and phrases in long gestures. Hsu [13] measures loudness, tempo and timbre from pitch/amplitude envelope and auditory roughness (interference between partials in a complex tone) of saxophone sounds. Ciufo [14] uses control methods based on both high-level and low-level audio analysis.

A difference between improvisation systems and audio feedback systems is that the former typically receive an external sound, such as instrument or voice, while the latter receive acoustic reflections and diffusions of their own sound. Since feedback sound is essentially different from instrumental sounds, note-based musical analysis is less comprehensive and candidates for target sonic properties must be broadened to encompass timbral characteristics. We selected the following sonic characteristics and corresponding measurement methods:

- Average pitch: average fundamental frequency
- Vibrato: standard deviation of the fundamental frequency curve
- Tremolo: standard deviation of the amplitude curve
- Spectral tonality (distinction between tone-like and noise-like signal): spectral flatness
- Brightness: spectral centroid.

Fundamental frequency is measured using a YIN algorithm [15], a popular pitch detection method based on a cumulative mean normalized difference function. Amplitude curve is then measured by local maximum points, positive zero deviation points of a waveform.

3.2 Second-Order Feedback Structure

The system must search for digital signal processing algorithms having the capacity to achieve target sonic properties within unknown and possibly ever-changing environmental conditions. We suspect that no single, compact signal processing

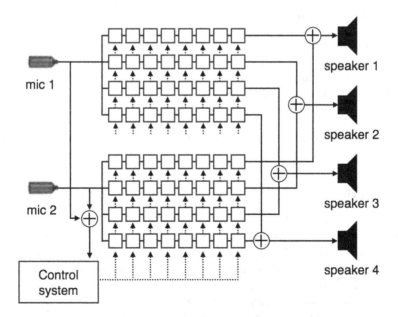

Fig. 2. The second-order structure connecting two microphones and four loudspeakers via each line consisting of eight DSP components organized by a controller

algorithm will satisfy this criteria, however a modular approach can be an effective alternative. Defined as a mechanism in which a live algorithm is not fixed and can be replaced by another, the modular approach facilitates creativity by providing the basis for combinatoric search through a vast space of possibilities [16].

In the self-organized music model [17] the interpretation of the audio input (denoted P) continually provides information (denoted F) about the acoustic environment. Neural network and decision tree systems were used to derive F, and internal processing activities then provide behavioral options that can be instantly substituted for each other, using a modular mechanism [16]. Neuman [18] allows composers to generate musical structures in real-time by stochastic rewriting rules. Ciufo [14] presents an improvisation system pursuing flexibility through a modular matrix mixing technique. All signal processing modules such as ring modulation (RM), resonant filtering, and memory are connected to a two-dimensional signal matrix, enabling links between any input and any output.

We also applied a modular approach in our system to support switching of internal structure, types, and parameters of signal processing components, in order to grant greater dynamics and variety in shaping the feedback. As Fig. 2 shows, the system connects microphones and loudspeakers via lines consisting of several signal-processing components, organized by a controller. Currently ten component types are possible, each with specific parameter ranges as follows:

- Lowpass Filter: 600~1200 Hz (cutoff frequency)
- Bandstop Filter: 600~900 and 3600~5400 Hz (lower/upper cutoff frequencies)
- Bandpass Filter: 30~200 and 430~600 Hz (lower/upper cutoff frequencies)
- Amplifier: 3~100 (amplification degree)
- Frequency Shifter: −300~300 Hz
- Delay Line: 3~1000 samples
- Sinewave Generator: 100~600 Hz
- Feedback: 0.5~3 (amplification degree)
- Feedforward: 0.5~3 (amplification degree)
- Bypass (no operation).

Each component also includes an amplifier for gain control, which is smoothly ramped through zero to avoid clicks when a DSP structure is switched.

3.3   Evolutionary Process for Second-Order Structure Control

Our system uses an evolutionary process to design the second-order feedback structure. Evolutionary algorithms are a well-established method to explore huge parameter spaces, including tasks in music composition and sound synthesis [19]. In [16,20] genotypes correspond to continuous-time recurrent neural networks (CTRNNs), which improvise through interactions with live performers. A CTRNN is a network of simple artificial neurons in which each neuron interconnected via weighted synapses and processes a floating-point value or maintains a state. The fitness of each genotype is measured by the absolute difference between corresponding pairs of values in input and output sequences; repeated sequences receive zero score. Individuals of high fitness values in a population are chosen to generate individuals in the next population, with mutation. In [20] each network controls parameters for sound playing, such as parameters for a FM synthesizer and playback position for a granular sample player. Fastbreeder [21] is a genetic programming synthesizer. It grows code for sound synthesis by choosing from automatically generated functions. Syntaxis [22] is an example using a genetic algorithm in an invariable structure of a feedback system: individuals in a population correspond to bandpass filters and the fitness is measured by their deviations from resonant frequencies of the feedback sound. Filter banks thereby gradually evolve to fit the resonant peaks. Use of such genetic algorithms produces musically interesting results in which target behaviors and other behaviors not specified by the goals coexist.

Our genotypes consist of pairs of genes to specify the types and parameters of signal-processing components. The manifestation of these genotypes as phenotypes forms a signal-processing algorithm. Eight genotypes in a present generation are manifested, and the sound generated as a result of each genotype re-enters the system via microphones after being diffused and reflected in a room. The controller evaluates the fitness of each genotype through a function measuring deviation of features of the incoming sound from the currently chosen target conditions. Individuals in subsequent generations are determined according to the fitness criteria of previous generations, with small mutations, so that the feedback sound gradually evolves toward the objective.

Reproduction incorporates the possibility of mutations in the parameters or type of a component. Based on informal experimentation we began with default mutation rates of 0.08 for the parameter change and 0.05 for the component change in each gene. Accordingly, the parameter change happens rather frequently, but this responds to a necessary condition of the task. Our system is subject to real-time/real-space bottleneck: the population size is limited because the evaluation of each individual must take place in real-space over a reasonable duration. It is analogous to the *fitness bottleneck* familiar to aesthetic selection and interactive evolution [23,24], yet different in that it is not the human that is a limiting evaluation factor. Nevertheless, an interactive installation for an audience may need to privilege fast adaptation over stability and accuracy, suggesting the use of higher mutation rates.

4   Results

We implemented this design as software authored using openFrameworks for the analyzer and controller (Fig. 3) and Max/MSP for the second-order DSP structure (Fig. 4). In an installation, four ESI nEar05 monitor speakers were installed at each corner of a room, and SM57 and SM58 microphones were placed in the middle facing toward the floor to avoid direct sound paths.

This installation was evaluated to show how sonic behavior of the system would change according to the target conditions. For example, Fig. 5 presents flatness states (spectral centroid values) when the minimum or maximum spectral flatness was selected as the target condition, which respectively drives the

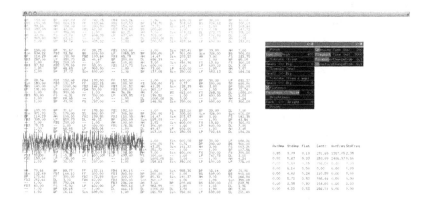

Fig. 3. The analyzer and the controller, authored with openFrameworks. Each 8 by 8 block represents a genotype of the present generation. Reading across the row gives the path from one of the microphones to one of the loudspeakers; with two microphones and four loudspeakers this makes 8 rows. The current best candidate is shown in pink at the top. The user can select target conditions and control system parameters using the black panels at the right-hand side. Numerical values resulting from the evaluations are given in the bottom-right corner (Color figure online).

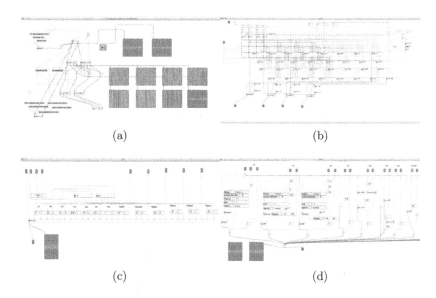

Fig. 4. (a) Main patch for the second-order signal processing structure, authored with Max/MSP, and (b) subpatches for operating branch lines between the microphones and the loudspeakers, (c) designating each DSP component and parameter from every candidate based on genetic information and (d) operating the DSP algorithms and linking the feedback loop.

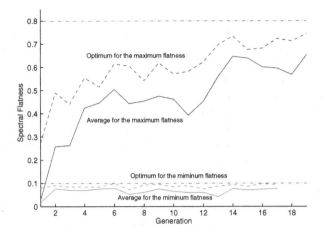

Fig. 5. Average (solid lines) and optimal flatness values (dotted lines) of individuals in each generation when the maximum or minimum flatness is selected as a target condition, which is represented as a green dash-dotted line. Red and blue lines are measured when the target state is set as maximum and minimum value, and target states are described as dashed lines (Color figure online).

Table 1. Comparisons of the sonic features of the feedback sounds in the first population and 15th population

	Target condition	Initial population		15th population	
		Mean	Optimum	Mean	Optimum
Average fundamental frequency (average pitch)	1000 (Hz)	167	472	528	845
	100 (Hz)	279	128	121	100
SD of fundamental frequency (vibrato)	1.2	0.25	0.70	0.91	1.09
	0	0.34	0.08	0.12	0.07
SD of local maximum amplitude (tremolo)	40	5.1	17.8	24.4	30
	0	17.8	8.3	10	7.3
Spectral flatness (spectral tonality)	0.8	0.03	0.27	0.64	0.68
	0.1	0.02	0.08	0.07	0.1
Spectral centroid (brightness)	1300 (Hz)	10	351	769	1030
	0 (Hz)	281	129	116	75

sound to a pure tone or a white noise. Dash-dotted lines represent the target conditions: spectral flatness is measured as 0.8 and 0.1 on average when the system plays a white noise and a pure tone instead of the feedback sound. Both cases start at below 0.1, but we can observe that it increases to almost 0.8 with some fluctuations when targeting noise sound (high flatness). Similarly, Table 1 compares the average and optimal values of individuals at the first and 15th population (after approximately 4 minutes), when one of the five sonic properties is chosen to be a target condition. Even though variations of the features are limited to certain ranges, we could find that the features of the feedback sound could be driven to a certain degree by these target conditions with the evolutionary process to design the second-order structure. These sounds samples are available at http://sites.google.com/site/asuramk88/research/feedbackevocontrol.

Figure 6 presents the sonic behaviors when the target condition changes during performance. We could observe adaptation of sonic behavior toward the current target condition as the sound tends to be brighter since the 15th generation, which is about eight generations after changing the target condition to high brightness (7th generation). One might expect the possibility of an installation in which the feedback sound is controlled by the audience who can set and change the target conditions in real-time.

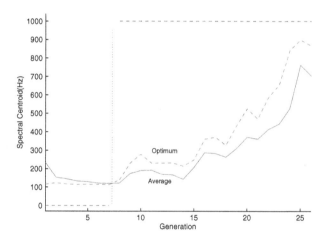

Fig. 6. Average (solid lines) and optimal centroid values (dotted lines) of individuals when a target condition is selected as minimum brightness until the 7th generation, and changed to high brightness as 1000 Hz spectral centroid.

5   Conclusion

This work presents a system for high-level intentional control of audio feedback, which uses a second-order structure in which the internal signal processing algorithms are developed according to an evolutionary process. Users control the system by selecting and changing feature objectives in real-time. A prototype was implemented and evaluated to observe changes of sonic behaviors depending on the target conditions. The results show the possibility of intentional control, which could result in enhancement of interactivity in the overall sonic behaviors of feedback systems and lead to sound/music applications which feature a balance between nonlinear emergence from the relations between low-level components and regulation over the overall sonic shape.

The target features are currently closely-tied direct audio analysis features, however in a broader motivation we hope to extend our system to support higher-level target features of sound streams that may have more readily musical application, such as stability, continuity, tension, and contrast. We noted that varying the mutation rates according to purpose follows a trade-off of the real-time/real-space bottleneck, such as increasing rates for interactive installation or decreasing for sound library generation. However we are also keen to investigate whether varying rates at per-gene or per-operator level, possibly also adaptively, may improve adaptation. Finally, analysis of the timbre space occupied by a second-order signal processing structure may also enhance intentional control.

Acknowledgments. This work was supported by the BK21 plus program through the National Research Foundation (NRF) funded by the Ministry of Education of Korea.

References

1. Di Scipio, A.: 'Sound is the interface': from interactive to ecosystemic signal processing. Organised Sound **8**(3), 269–277 (2004)
2. Kim, S., Yeo, W.S.: Musical control of a pipe based on acoustic resonance. In: Proceedings of the Internation Conference on New Interfaces for Musical Expression, pp. 217–219 (2011)
3. Kim, S., Yeo, W.S.: Electronic pipe organ using audio feedback. In: Proceedings of the Sound and Music Computing, pp. 75–78 (2012)
4. Kollias, P.A.: Ephemeron: control of self-organised music. Hz Music J. **14**, 138–146 (2009)
5. Sanfilippo, D.: Turning perturbation into emergent sound, and sound into perturbation, pp. 1–16 (2013). interferencejournal.com
6. Di Scipio, A.: Listening to yourself through the otherself: on background noise study and other works. Organised Sound **16**(2), 97–108 (2011)
7. Mitchell, M.: Complex systems: network thinking. Artif. Intell. **170**(18), 1194–1212 (2006)
8. Kollias, P.A.: The self-organising work of music. Organised Sound **16**(2), 192–199 (2011)
9. Heylighen, F., Joslyn, C.: Cybernetics and second order cybernetics. Encycl. Phys. Sci. Technol. **4**, 155–170 (2001)
10. Murray-Rust, D., Smaill, A., Maya, M.C.: VirtualLatin-towards a musical multi-agent system. In: Proceedings of the International Conference on Computational Intelligence and Multimedia Applications, pp. 17–22 (2005)
11. Wulfhorst, R.D., Nakayama, L., Vicari, R.M.: A multiagent approach for musical interactive systems. In: Proceedings of the Second International Joint Conference on Autonomous Agents and Multiagent Systems, pp. 584–591 (2003)
12. Van Nort, D., Braasch, J., Oliveros, P.: A system for musical improvisation combining sonic gesture recognition and genetic algorithms. In: Proceedings of the 6th Sound and Music Computing Conference, pp. 131–136 (2009)
13. Hsu, W.: Strategies for managing timbre and interaction in automatic improvisation systems. Leonardo Music J. **20**, 33–39 (2010)

14. Ciufo, T.: Beginner's mind: an environment for sonic improvisation. In: Proceedings of the International Computer Music Conference, pp. 781–784 (2005)
15. De Cheveigné, A., Kawahara, H.: Yin, a fundamental frequency estimator for speech and music. J. Acoust. Soc. Am. **111**(4), 1917–1930 (2002)
16. Bown, O.: Experiments in modular design for the creative composition of live algorithms. Comput. Music J. **35**(3), 73–85 (2011)
17. Blackwell, T., Young, M.: Self-organised music. Organised Sound **9**(2), 123–136 (2004)
18. Neuman, I.: Generative tools for interactive composition: real-time musical structures based on schaeffer's tartyp and on klumpenhouwer networks. Comput. Music J. **38**(2), 63–77 (2014)
19. Dahlstedt, P.: A mutasynth in parameter space: interactive composition through evolution. Organised Sound **6**(2), 121–124 (2001)
20. Bown, O., Lexer, S.: Continuous-time recurrent neural networks for generative and interactive musical performance. In: Rothlauf, F., Branke, J., Cagnoni, S., Costa, E., Cotta, C., Drechsler, R., Lutton, E., Machado, P., Moore, J.H., Romero, J., Smith, G.D., Squillero, G., Takagi, H. (eds.) EvoWorkshops 2006. LNCS, vol. 3907, pp. 652–663. Springer, Heidelberg (2006)
21. Griffiths, D.: Fastbreeder
22. Scamarcio, M.: Space as an evolution strategy: Sketch of a generative ecosystemic structure of sound. In: Proceedings of the Sound and Music Computing Conference, pp. 95–99 (2008)
23. Biles, J.: GenJam: a genetic algorithm for generating jazz solos. In: Proceedings of the International Computer Music Conference, pp. 131–131 (1994)
24. Biles, J.A.: Evolutionary computation for musical tasks. In: Miranda, E.R., Biles, J.A. (eds.) Evolutionary Computer Music, pp. 28–51. Springer, London (2007)

Echo

Christoph Klemmt[1,2(✉)] and Rajat Sodhi[3]

[1] Zaha Hadid Architects, London, UK
[2] University of Applied Arts Vienna, Vienna, Austria
christoph@orproject.com
[3] Orproject, New Delhi India
rajat@orproject.com

Abstract. This paper is interested in the artistic possibilities of systematic translations of sound or music into three-dimensional form. The generation of static two and three-dimensional form based on music or sound has been used by various artists, architects, scientists and technicians.

The time-based attributes of a sound can be directly transformed into spatial dimensions of the generated form. A two-dimensional example is the visualisation of a sound wave in which the time of the sound is recorded from left to right, while the frequency, another time-based attribute of the sound, is recorded in the vertical direction.

Many attempts in generating systematic three-dimensional translations are taking the form of single-surface morphologies, due to most data which can be extracted from a sound being dependent variables for any given time-frequency coordinate. We are proposing a system of analysing reassigned sound data within a variable time frame as a tool to extract multiple consecutive layers of information, which in their combination have the potential to form non-surface morphologies.

The artistic possibilities of the morphologies as an architectural geometry has been tested with the design of an exhibition for Design Shanghai 2013.

Keywords: Architecture · Sound · Data · Form · Reassignment · Echo

1 Introduction

The creation of static form based on sound has been used by both scientists and artists (Brand 2014; Chladni 1787; Davies and Walters 2008; Kanach 2008; Klanten et al. 2008; Klemmt 2012; Lieser 2010). Attempts to create three-dimensional form based on sound data spectrograms is often resulting in deformed single-surface morphologies, due to the spectrogram producing a single output for each time-frequency coordinate.

We are proposing to use the Kaiser window (Kaiser 1966) as used in reassigned sound data analysis as a third independent variable to create non-surface morphologies based on sound data.

The resulting three-dimensional geometries can be used as an acoustic representation and analysis tool. Its application as an architectural geometry has been tested with the exhibition design Echo for Design Shanghai 2013 (Fig. 1).

© Springer International Publishing Switzerland 2015
C. Johnson et al. (Eds.): EvoMUSART 2015, LNCS 9027, pp. 125–135, 2015.
DOI: 10.1007/978-3-319-16498-4_12

Fig. 1. Construction of echo.

2   Related Work

Artists as well as scientists have used various ways to create form from sound. In acoustics, the generation of two-dimensional diagrams and images of sounds is a widely used representation and analysis tool. The commonly used sound spectrogram maps the time dimension of a sound horizontally and the frequency in the vertical direction. The amplitude of a certain frequency occurring at a certain time is then mapped by a lightness or colour gradient (Flanagan 1972).

Many visual artists use sound as the driver for imagery. This can be done by visualising how acoustic vibrations influence or travel through a medium, resulting in distortions or interference patterns, as in the work of Ernst Chladni (Chladni 1787) or Linden Gledhill. Various programs such as audio players use the currently playing sound for the generation of visual representations.

Artist Jorinde Voigt states that she uses the visualisation of sound in principle like psycho-acoustics scientist Brigitte Schulte-Fortkamp, but not that precisely (Brand 2014).

Architect-composer Iannis Xenakis has applied the same concept of linearly connecting two different states of sound or spatial arrangement, in the Phillips Pavilion which he designed for Le Corbusier and his compositions Metastaseis (Kanach 2008).

2.1   Systematic Translations into 3-dimensional form

Different sculptors have used two- and three-dimensional spectrograms where the time of the sound or music piece is mapped in one spatial direction, while the frequency and the amplitude at which it occurs are mapped into the other two dimensions. The lightness or colour gradient of the two-dimensional graphic spectrogram has been used to define the third coordinate in volumetric terms. Examples of this are the works Reflection, Reflection 2, Spectral Density Estimation and other by Andreas Nicolas Fischer and Benjamin Maus (Klanten et al. 2008), or A Frozen Sound by Orproject (Klemmt 2012).

A spectrogram or other diagram which maps intensity attributes of a sound based on the time and frequency can be described as a mathematical function: for each variable of time and frequency, one specific intensity can be extracted (Flanagan 1972; Allen 1977). The resulting three-dimensional spectrogram is therefore always a surface, which is warped according to the sound data.

In order to generate more complex geometries, artists and designers have explored different ways of distorting the original surface geometry. Daniel Widrig and Shajay Bhooshan with their work Binaural distorted the base surface towards its peaks in sideways directions (Lieser 2010). Both Juan Manuel Escalante with Microsonic Landscapes as well as Andy Huntington with the Cylinder series use a circular or spiral mapping of the time and frequency values to create revolving geometries. Katie Davies and Peter Walters used a spherical mapping to create the piece Sound Form (Davies and Walters 2008).

3   Sound Data Reassignment

3.1   Topologic Constraints of Multi-dimensional Mathematical Functions

Although the above mentioned artists have managed to create geometries based on sound spectrogram data which are more complex than warped surfaces, in all the projects it is still apparent that the forms are based on surface data, and the resulting morphologies are limited accordingly.

This is caused by the fact that the extracted information has the form of a discrete mathematical function of two variables, plotted into three-dimensional space (Allen 1977). In the above cases, the two variables are the time and frequency values, and for each pair of those there is a defined dependent variable, the amplitude of the certain frequency, which is mapped in the third direction.

Sound data is recorded linearly during time as varying pressure values of the air. Those recordings can be represented as a sound wave, a one-dimensional signal based on time (Allen 1977). As digital recordings are based on discreet time steps, the representations of it are often pixel or voxel based. The signal can be described by the formula

$$s = x\,(t)$$

with s being the strength of the signal and t being time.

A mathematical technique called the Fourier transform is used to extract both time and frequency information from the signal and to map it to a two-dimensional spectrogram (Allen 1977). The formula for this is

$$s = X\,(t, \omega)$$

with t being the time and ω the frequency.

Every time–frequency coordinate has exactly one defined value s, the dependent variable, which results in the generation of the surface morphologies. At the same time, however, a certain intensity value of s may occur at various values for both of the independent variables time and frequency. The same is the case for other attributes which may be extracted from the sound sample other than the frequency. While there is a dependent variable for the other two independent variables, the geometry will result in a surface.

In order to explore possible non-surface morphologies that may be extracted from a sound, a further independent variable needs to be introduced which can have different values assigned for any combination of the time and frequency values. The formula then takes the form of

$$s = f(t, \omega, a)$$

with a being the additional independent variable. It is then possible to set the amplitude to any fixed value in order to achieve a relationship between the three remaining variables. For s in a range of $0 < s < 1$, it may be set for example to 0.5:

$$s = 0.5$$

$$0.5 = f(t, \omega, a)$$

Depending on the choice of the independent variable a, this can result in complex three-dimensional diagrams with the time, the frequency and the new variable as the three spatial coordinates. If variable a is also discreet, the resulting geometry will be layered or voxelised.

(This process can also be described as the surface function of the spectrogram extended into a hyper-surface in four-dimensional space, plotted along the axes of time, frequency, a and the amplitude. Of this hypersurface, a three dimensional section is cut across a value for s. As it is cut across the direction of the dependent variable, the resulting three-dimensional section can then take on a geometry which is not a surface.)

3.2   Scientific Sound Data Reassignment in Two Dimensions

For this research, we have used an analysis technique for time-frequency data to provide this additional variable.

As a frequency needs to occur for a certain duration in order to be identifiable, the Fourier transformation results in a blurred representation. The time, the frequency or both are blurred during the process (Hainsworth 2003).

In order to sharpen this information, it is possible to remap the data to their closest peak. This is done within a certain time frame, the Kaiser window (Kaiser 1966). Depending on the length of the Kaiser window, which may be in the range of 10–100 ms for an audio analysis, the remapping of the data will focus more on the harmonic or the pulse aspects of a sound (Fulop and Fitz 2006).

3.3   Form Based on Reassigned Time-Frequency Spectrograms

Reassigned spectrograms have been used for the generation of the sculpture and concept geometries Chuan and Lattice by the authors. In essence the geometries are still surface-based, however openings in this surfaces occur where there are voids in the reassigned data sets (Klemmt 2012) (Fig. 2).

Fig. 2. Chuan. Marble.

3.4   Sound Data Reassignment in Three Dimensions

For the generation of three-dimensional representations of sound as described above, the Kaiser window can be used as the third independent variable, which forms the third spatial coordinate. When the signal intensity is fixed, a certain combination of time and frequency values has the potential to occur during multiple values for the Kaiser window. The system therefore has the potential to generate complex three-dimensional morphologies other than surfaces, while at the same time extracting multiple refined information layers from the sound, i.e. information about its harmonic as well as pulse based structure.

The amplitude is mapped as a gradient for the frequencies and time of a sound. A set of these mappings are generated for the same sound data using Kaiser windows at regular intervals, and each mapping is stacked discreetly in an adjacent manner. To create geometry, the gradient in each map is filtered using a median value. This results in discreet voxel formation which is used to create the solid geometry.

Those three-dimensional spectrograms can be utilised as scientific tools for analysis and representation, while at the same time providing new geometries for artists and designers with an interest in acoustic form generation (Fig. 3).

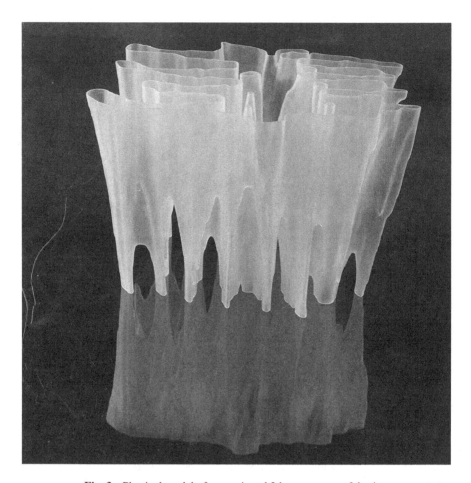

Fig. 3. Physical model of a reassigned 3d spectrogram. 3d print.

4   Echo

In order to evaluate the architectural potential of the generated morphologies, the tool has been applied for the design of an exhibition for Design Shanghai 2013 at the Power Station of Art in Shanghai (Design Shanghai Organising Committee 2013).

4.1   City of Interface

The exhibition, titled "City of Interface", has been curated by Degeng Li. It forms a collection of fragments of the city: designed elements such as signage, building facades or other urban visual information. The exhibits in the museum can be compared to windows into the world which surrounds us, and they connect with each other in the real world to form the whole (Design Shanghai Organising Committee 2013).

4.2   Design Concept

With Echo, the display installation which presents those fragments, the architects created a structure which connects those windows into the city with a continuous volume. Digital acoustic analysis techniques as described above were used to turn the sound of the city, which constantly surrounds us, into a physical volume. The resulting structure forms the backdrop of the exhibition just as the sound forms the back-drop to the city. It connects adjacent exhibits with each other, but it also forms connections between objects at other ends of the exhibition. It makes the visitor aware of how the city is built up of various layers of objects, structures and information (Fig. 4).

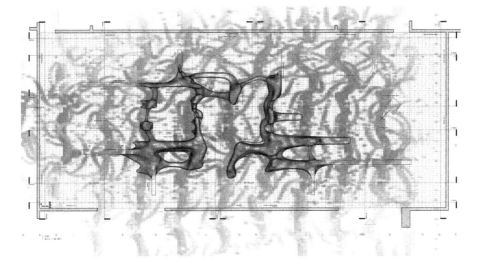

Fig. 4. Echo. Plan.

4.3   Design Development

A sound sample was analysed and processed using a custom written algorithm to transform the frequency from the recordings and to create a stacking of the mappings for a value range of the Kaiser window. These mappings were translated into voxels to generate the three dimensional form. Since sound is scaleless, the resulting morphology was scaled in relation to the dimensions of the exhibition space and programmatic requirements from the curatorial team. Relatively flatter areas were carved and adjusted to create niches for the accommodation of the exhibits, while the maximum height of the geometry was limited to 3600 mm.

4.4   Construction

The form of Echo was materialised using Polyurethane foam. Each layer of foam is 50 mm thick and 72 layers are stacked to reach the peak points at 3600 mm height. Using

Fig. 5. Echo.

Fig. 6. Echo.

a CNC process, all of the 24000 pieces were cut, numbered and assembled into panels that were 18 stacks high. Each layer of foam then responds to one specific value of the Kaiser window (Fig. 5).

4.5 Evaluation

Echo is a manifestation of the sounds of the city. The custom written algorithms are successfully able to convert sound into three dimensional form, which was scaled and appropriated to accommodate the exhibition. As the exhibition was well received and fulfilled all the curatorial requirements, it is viewed as a success in being able to build sound as a three dimensional morphology and departure from the surface based geometries.

The translation from analogue sound to digital geometry to built form using CNC machining techniques is also seen as a seamless method of converting sound to form (Fig. 6).

5 Conclusions

5.1 Three-dimensional Reassigned Spectrograms

Two-dimensional analysis and representations of reassigned spectrograms have previously proven a successful tool for sound analysis. The generation of three-dimensional representations does so even more, as it allows for a direct comparison of different Kaiser windows at the same time, within the same geometric assembly.

The often very complex harmonic and pulse based relationships of a sound can be reflected and studied in one single model, as opposed to a series of two-dimensional diagrams with different Kaiser windows.

The use in sound analysis may have its main application as a digital 3d model of the sound, which can be explored and analysed three dimensionally.

5.2 Artistic Form Generation

The process described appears to have a great potential as a tool for an artistic form generation, which should be tested through further implementations. The three-dimensional geometries generated in this way show a complexity while still having a strong visual coherence and dynamism. This can be explained by the fact that the origin of the geometries are sounds, in the examples of this paper natural sounds, which have an inherent physical logic based on the way they are created and they propagate.

The proposed transformation of sound to form is an abstraction which does not carry on any meanings which the original sound may have held. It does instead manifest the structural logic from which the sound is build up.

5.3 Application in Architecture and Design

The geometries have only been applied and realised for one project so far, the exhibition design Echo. The design of the exhibition was well received. As neighbouring exhibits were placed within the same object, even uninitiated visitors were able to read the exhibits as fragments of an overall unified entity.

The qualities of the morphology of generating parallel yet interconnected strata was very well suited for the application as it created sets of parallel walls which could be used to present the exhibits. Various design decisions which did not directly relate to the original sound had to be taken in order to turn the geometry into a useful structure. Any meaning of the original sound was not recognisable anymore in the exhibition, neither was the fact that the geometry originated from a sound. However the characteristics of the structure of the sound, which were represented in the morphology, could be used qualitatively for this application in spatial design (Fig. 7).

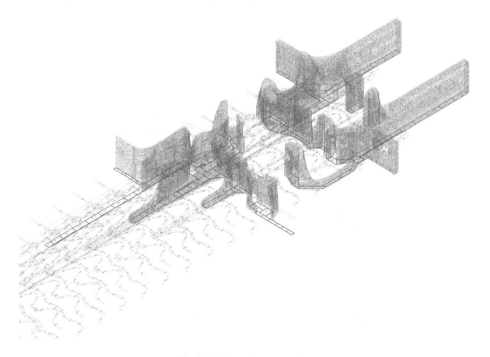

Fig. 7. Echo. Axonometric.

References

Brand, A.: Klangwelten. (video) Frankfurter Allgemeine Zeitung, 07 November 2014
Chladni, E.F.F.: Entdeckungen Über Die Theorie Des Klanges. Weidmanns Erben Und Reich. Leipzig (1787)

Davies, K., Walters, P.: Artist case study - sound form. University of the West of England, Bristol (2008).   http://www.uwe.ac.uk/sca/research/cfpr/research/3D/Artists/soundform/soundform.pdf

Kanach, S. (ed.) Music and Architecture by YannisXenakis. Pendragon Press, New York (2008)

Klanten, R., Bourquin, N., Ehmann, S., van Heerden, F., Tissot, T. (ed.) DATA FLOW Visualising Information in Graphic Design. Gestalten, Berlin. ISBN 978-3-89955-217-1 (2008)

Klemmt, C.: Anisotropia - morphological sound analysis. In: Costa, X., Thorne, M. (eds) Change, Architecture, Education, Practices – Proceedings of the International ACSA Conference, Barcelona, Spain, 20–22 June 2012. (ISBN 978-0-935502-83-1) (2012)

Lieser, W.: The World of Digital Art. Ullmann Publishing, Potsdam (2010)

Kaiser, J.F.: Digital filters. In: Kuo, F.F., Kaiser, J.F. (eds.) System Analysis by Digital Computer, Chap. 7. Wiley, New York (1966)

Flanagan, J.L.: Speech Analysis, Synthesis and Perception. Springer, New York (1972)

Allen, J.B.: Short time spectral analysis, synthesis, and modification by discrete fourier transform. IEEE Trans. Acoust. Speech Sig. Process. **ASSP-25**(3), 235–238 (1977)

Hainsworth, S.: Chapter 3: Reassignment methods. Techniques for the Automated Analysis of Musical Audio (Ph.D.). University of Cambridge (2003)

Fulop, S.A., Fitz, K.: Algorithms for computing the time-corrected instantaneous frequency (reassigned) spectrogram, with applications. J. Acoust. Soc. Am. **119**, 360–371 (2006)

Design Shanghai Organising Committee: Design Shanghai 2013 - Aesthetics City. Shanghai People's Fine Art Publishing House, China (2013)

Evotype: Evolutionary Type Design

Tiago Martins[✉], João Correia,
Ernesto Costa, and Penousal Machado

CISUC, Department of Informatics Engineering,
University of Coimbra, 3030 Coimbra, Portugal
{tiagofm,jncor,ernesto,machado}@dei.uc.pt

Abstract. An evolutionary generative system for type design, Evotype, is described. The system uses a Genetic Algorithm to evolve a set of individuals composed of line segments, each encoding the shape of a specific character, i.e. a glyph. To simultaneously evolve glyphs for the entire alphabet, an island model is adopted. To assign fitness we resort to a scheme based on Optical Character Recognition. We study the evolvability of the proposed approach as well as the impact of the migration in the evolutionary process. The migration mechanism is explored through three experimental setups: fitness guided migration, random migration, and no migration. We analyse the experimental results in terms of fitness, migration paths, and appearance of the glyphs. The results show the ability of the system to find suitable glyphs and the impact of the migration strategy in the evolutionary process.

Keywords: Type design · Evolutionary design · Island model

1 Introduction

Although conventional computational design tools are effective for precise design tasks during the later phases of the design process, they offer insufficient support to design exploration during the earliest, essentially conceptual, stages of the design process.

We present an evolutionary system for type design — Evotype. Although it is still a work in progress, the system is already able to automatically generate alternative designs for glyphs from scratch. A glyph consists in a specific graphic expression of a given readable character. For the purposes of this article, we focus in the evolution of glyphs for letters of the Roman alphabet.

The main contribution presented herein is a functional prototype of a generative system capable of creating consistent glyphs. Other contributions include: (i) a Genetic Algorithm (GA) with a generic representation wherein individuals are composed by line segments encoded as sequence of numeric values; (ii) a fully autonomous evolutionary approach for the evolution of glyphs; (iii) the use of an island model and the study of the impact of migration on evolution; and (iv) the use of a Machine Learning (ML) approach to guide the evolution and the migration process.

C. Johnson et al. (Eds.): EvoMUSART 2015, LNCS 9027, pp. 136–147, 2015.
DOI: 10.1007/978-3-319-16498-4_13

The paper is organised as follows: Sect. 2 presents related work, considering applications of evolutionary techniques in the domain of glyphs design; Sect. 3 thoroughly describes the GA of the proposed system; Sect. 4 describes the experimental setup; Sect. 5 presents the analysis of the experimental results; finally, conclusions and future work is presented in Sect. 6.

2   Related Work

Designers, engineers, artists, and scientists have been using evolution-based techniques to support the creative process and evolve innovative artefacts. Although evolutionary glyph design is a relatively unexplored area, some applications exist.

Butterfield and Lewis [1] employ Interactive Evolutionary Computation (IEC) to explore the creation of fonts. More specifically, they evolve deformations, i.e. the letters of a specific typeface are deformed by a set of implicit surface primitives, which are encoded in the genotypes. Lund [2] also uses IEC to evolve the settings of a parametric typeface system. Each parameter controls the appearance of a given characteristic of the font. Unemi and Soda [3] propose an IEC system for the design of Japanese Katakana glyphs. Schmitz [4] presents the interactive program *genoTyp*, which allows the user to create new fonts through the breeding of existing ones, according to genetic rules and manual manipulation of their genes. The possibility of recombining famous typefaces is exciting, however, the limitations of the representation hinder the quality of the results. Levin et al. [5] use IEC to implement the *Alphabet Synthesis Machine*, a system which allows the creation and evolution of abstract letter forms.

Despite evolutionary systems for glyph design exist, as far as we know all of them rely on user evaluation. Thus, the user interactively iterates a cyclic process of selection and generation until an acceptable solution is obtained. As such, all suffer from the well-known limitations of IEC systems, namely user-fatigue and inconsistency in evaluation. Additionally, they require the creation of a parametric typeface (e.g., [2]), or pre-existing typefaces or skeletons (e.g., [4] and [1], respectively), and are conditioned by these requirements.

3   The Approach

Evotype evolves glyph designs for various characters in a parallel and autonomous way. To achieve this, a GA [6] is implemented to evolve different populations of candidate glyph designs. Each individual is a glyph design. Each population lives in its own island and is composed of individuals that represent a specific character. Thus, to evolve glyphs for 26 characters we use 26 populations in 26 islands. The different islands can communicate with each other, allowing the migration of glyphs among them.

The system is schematically represented in Fig. 1 and behaves as follows. The evolutionary process begins with the initialisation of all populations with randomly created glyphs. The individuals are evaluated and then selected for mating according to their fitness. Recombination and mutation operators are

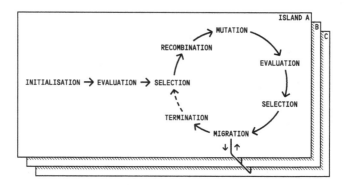

Fig. 1. Overview of Evotype.

applied to generate offspring. The selection stage follows, determining which individuals proceed to the next generation. The next step is migration, where individuals may be moved to or received from other islands. As depicted in Fig. 1 the process is cyclically repeated. The termination criterion is based on the number of generations. In the following subsections we detail the genetic mechanisms employed in Evotype.

3.1   Representation

The genotype consists of a sequence of genes encoding a glyph. Each gene codifies a two-dimensional line segment that is composed by a sequence of five numbers, wherein the first four are the coordinates of its end points and last one correspond to its thickness (see Fig. 2). The genotype' length may vary from individual to individual, thus different individuals can be composed of different number of line segments.

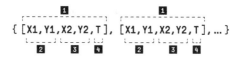

Fig. 2. Encoding of the genotype, composed of genes that codify line segments (1) defined by their end points (2 and 3) their thickness (4).

A mapping mechanism, normally referred to as *embryogenesis*, is in charge for the expression of the genotype into a perceptible artefact—the phenotype. The phenotype consists in a graphical representation of the genotype, i.e. a glyph created from the encoded parameters. The expression process consists in the drawing of dark line segments, defined by the genotype, on a white canvas, as illustrated in Fig. 3.

The dimension of the search space is reduced through the use of a rectangular grid that constraints the coordinates of the line segments' end points,

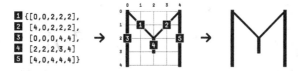

Fig. 3. Mapping process from genotype to phenotype. On the left, the genotype; On the middle, an intermediate representation depicting the grid and the correspondence between genes and line segments; On the right, the phenotype.

which must adhere to the grid points. The density of the grid is configured by the user.The representation ensures high locality. Neighbouring genotypes are mapped to similar phenotypes, meaning that small modifications of the genetic code induce small changes in the phenotypic space.

3.2 Initialisation

The initial populations are seeded with randomly generated glyphs. Each glyph of the first population is composed of a single line segment, with all the gene values set by uniform random selection over the admissible interval for each parameter. All islands receive identical initial populations. This initialisation setup provides equality and simplicity among all initial populations, enabling us to access the ability of the system to evolve glyphs for different characters, starting from the same set of random glyphs.

3.3 Crossover

The crossover operation consists in the exchange of line segments between parents. Crossover operates on gene boundaries, preserving the integrity of line segments. The operator proceeds as follows: randomly select a rectangular area of the grid; determine, for both parents, the line segments whose middle points are inside the rectangle; exchange those line segments between parents. As illustrated in Fig. 4, crossover may be asymmetric, in the sense that the number of line segments a genotype "receives" may be different from the one it "donates".

3.4 Mutation

Mutation also operates on a gene basis. Thus, the mutation of a gene implies changing one of its five parameters by a value of one, as illustrated in Fig. 5. At the phenotype level, this variation results in the minimum translation of one of the end points of the line segment in one of the four possible directions—up, down, left, or right—or the minimum variation of its thickness. The impact of this change at the phenotype level depends on the density of the grid. A denser grid allows smaller visual variations. The probability of mutation is defined per gene, meaning that multiple genes may be mutated.

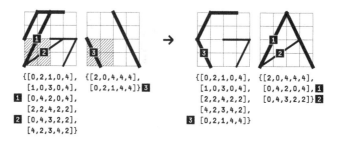

Fig. 4. Crossover process. On the left, two parents, the corresponding genotypes, and a randomly selected rectangular area (shaded region). The selected area determines the line segments that will be exchanged (1, 2, and 3). On the right, the results of the crossover operation at the genotype and phenotype level.

Fig. 5. Mutation process. On the left, the original genotype and phenotype; On the right, the results of the mutation operator.

A second type of mutation exists, gene deletion and insertion, allowing the variation of the size of the genotype. There is a probability of deleting a randomly selecting gene and inserting a randomly created one.

Unfeasible variations are prevented during the mutation, including translations of coordinates that (i) go beyond the grid limits, (ii) create line segments with null length, or (iii) generate two line segments which are defined by the same end points.

3.5   Evaluation

As previously mentioned, each population (i.e. each island) is composed of individuals that are candidate graphic representations of a specific character. As such, the fitness of an individual depends on the environment, i.e. the island were it lives. In the scope of this paper we use Optical Character Recognition (OCR) to assign fitness. The details of the fitness assignment scheme are described in Sect. 4.1.

3.6   Migration

Migration can occur once per each island in each generation. The probability of occurrence is determined by the migration rate. To study the influence of migration in the evolutionary process we considered three migration mechanisms:

No Migration – As the name indicates, no migration is used. The islands are isolated.

Random – When migration occurs, each island selects one random individual among the ones living on different islands. A copy of the individual is added to the population of the island, replacing the individual with worst fitness.

Fitness Guided – When migration occurs, each island evaluates all its individuals according to the environment of the other islands. A copy of the individual that attains the highest fitness is added to the queue of that destination island. When this process is completed for all islands, each island checks its immigration queue, which may be empty, and selects the fittest individual. This individual is added to the population of the island, replacing the individual with worst fitness.

It is important to remember that in Evotype fitness is local. Therefore, the fitness of an individual depends on the environment (i.e. the character it is trying to represent graphically) and each island corresponds to a different character.

3.7   Visualisation

Evotype is able to fluidly show the evolutionary process through a simple graphic user interface, conceived to allow the user to visualise the different evolving glyphs of all islands (see Fig. 6). Islands (each corresponding to a character) are arranged horizontally in different columns, in alphabetical order from left to right. The individuals (glyphs) of the current generation of each island are depicted vertically, in descending order of fitness. At any moment of the evolutionary process, the user can export the evolved glyphs as vectors files to make further design refinements.

The glyphs' fitness is visualised through a simple graphic approach. The fitness value of each individual is represented through a horizontal line that overlays the corresponding column, and is vertically positioned according to the mapped value

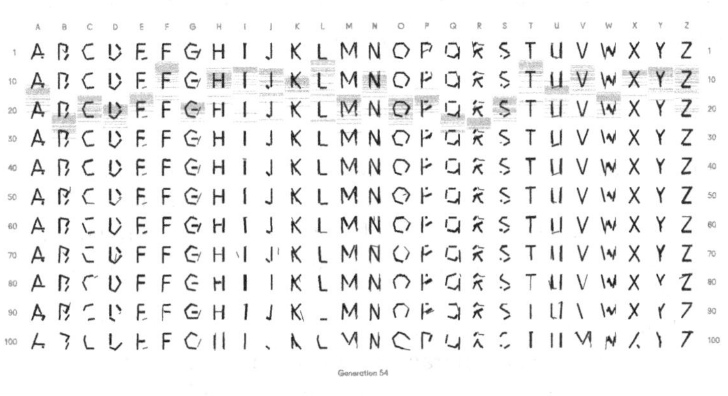

Fig. 6. Screenshot of the graphic user interface of Evotype. A demo video can be seen on http://cdv.dei.uc.pt/2015/evotype.mov.

<table>
<tr><td colspan="2">Table 1. Evolutionary system</td></tr>
</table>

Parameter	Setting
Number of runs	30
Number of generations	100
Population size	100
Crossover rate	0.8
Delete gene mutation rate	0.075
Insert gene mutation rate	0.075
Change gene mutation rate	0.3
Selection method	Tournament
Tournament size	3
Elite size	1
Glyph grid size	40×40

Table 2. Classifier

Parameter	Setting
Input image size	48×48
Quantized colours	5
Threshold (θ)	200
Promotion (α)	1.005
Demotion (β)	0.995
Initial weights values	2
Training iterations	1000
Examples per island	78

of the fitness value to the height of the interface (higher fitness values on top). We consider this fitness visualisation technique functional for the purposes of this work, in the sense that we are not particularly interested in seeing the specific fitness values. Instead, we wish to visualise the distribution and convergence of fitness over time, and the comparison of fitness values among islands.

4   Experimental Setup

In this work, we evolve glyphs for all the uppercase letters of the Roman alphabet, so a total of 26 islands are considered. We conduct experiments to assess the adequacy of the engine for the evolution of glyphs. Furthermore, we study the impact of the migration policy (see Sect. 3.6) in evolution.

The experimental parameters used in the course of the experiments described in this paper are summarised in Tables 1 and 2. In the following subsections we detail the fitness assignment scheme for the experiments.

4.1   Fitness

In this work, we have 26 islands, each one evolving towards a different objective, so we need to provide a proper fitness function to guide evolution for each island. We consider that interactive evolution of all these islands' populations would be an hard and tedious task. For that reason, we sought to use an automatic fitness assignment scheme.

We are dealing with the evolution of character glyphs. Certainly, one of the preconditions of a visual character representation is its recognisability. As such, we evolve images that are recognised automatically as specific characters. We choose an OCR ML approach to automatically assign fitness. Although the use of ML to assign fitness is not novel (refer to, e.g., [7–9]).

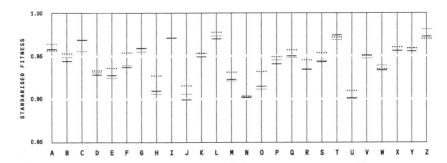

Fig. 7. Standardised fitness of the best individual of the last generation of each island. With a solid line, the *no migration*; dashed line, the *random* migration; and dotted line, the *fitness guided* migration. The visualised results are averages of 30 runs.

Each individual is processed as a bit map image by an OCR system, and the intermediary values from OCR process are used to assign fitness. Based on the work of Burry et al. [10] we use Sparse Network of Winnow (SNoW) [11], a sparse network of linear units, as the classifier system for the OCR approach. The SNoW classifier is characterised as having two layers, the input layer and n target nodes, which are linked through weighted edges. To perform OCR, we train, offline and per character, 26 different classifiers. The input examples consist of bitmap images corresponding to the characters of 78 different typefaces. These are pre-processed to extract features, which are used in training/classification. The process and decisions made for the feature extraction are based on the work of Burry et al. [10]. Table 2 summarises the overall OCR system parameters.

To deal with the OCR multi-class classification problem we use a *one versus all* strategy for training and classification. We train each classifier by treating all the instances of the character as the positive class and all instances of all other characters as the negative class. Thus, each classifier has two target nodes, one for the positive class (i.e. the character in question) one for the negative class (i.e. all the remaining characters). The activations of the nodes indicates the degree of membership of the input image to the respective class.

To assign fitness each input image is mapped to a $2D$ space where the x coordinate corresponds to the activation value of the positive class node of the classifier, and the y coordinate corresponds to the activation value of the negative class node. Thus, the ideal scenario would be maximising x while minimising y. Unfortunately, this is typically not possible since the letters share characteristics among them. For instance, the input pattern that maximizes the x coordinate for Q, will, necessarily, yield a high y value due to the presence of examples of the letter O in the negative class. Therefore, as is often the case multi-objective optimization problems, a compromise between x and y is necessary to obtain good results.

As such, we adopted the following procedure, establish a *target* activation point empirically. We begin by calculating the input pattern that minimises the y coordinate, the activation value of the output node corresponding to the negative

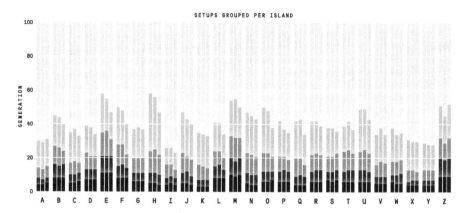

Fig. 8. Progression of the fitness of the fittest individual of each island over 100 generations. The results are grouped per island from left to right in the following order: *no migration, random* migration and *fitness guided* migration. Each graphic bar represents the variation of the standardise fitness of the best individual from 0 to 1 across the generations, divided in 5 different intervals of equal size (0.2). These intervals are represented by different shades of grey which change from darker to lighter according to its fitness value (from lower to higher). The visualised results are averages of 30 runs.

class for this pattern becomes y_t. Then, also analytically, we determine the input pattern for which the absolute difference between the activation values between x and y is minimal. Such input, typically, has the features necessary for the image to be classified as a member of the positive class, but still possesses features that are common with other characters. The activation value of the output node corresponding to the positive class for this pattern becomes x_t. Finally the fitness of a new input image is based on the following formula: $dist(x) = \|(x_t, y_t) - (x_i, y_i)\|$, where x_i, y_i are the activation values of the output nodes associated with the input image, and results in the euclidean distance between these two points. Since we wish to minimise the distance to this point, fitness becomes: $fitness(x) = 1/(1 + dist(x))$.

5   Experimental Results

We begin the analysis of the experimental results by focusing on the fitness values obtained by the 3 migration strategies. Figure 7 summarizes these results by presenting the average fitness of the best individual of the last generation. For the purposes of readability the fitness values have been normalized to [0, 1], by dividing the raw fitness scores by the maximum fitness score obtained for each character in the course of the 90 runs (30 per migration strategy). A brief perusal of the results indicates that fitness based migration outperforms the other two strategies, attaining higher fitness values for 20 out of the 26 islands. There are two "ties" among strategies, namely for islands I and N. *Random* migration outperforms the other methods for three islands (A, W, and Z), while *no migration* obtains the best results for island T.

Fig. 9. Best individuals of each island for different generations from a typical run using *fitness guided* migration.

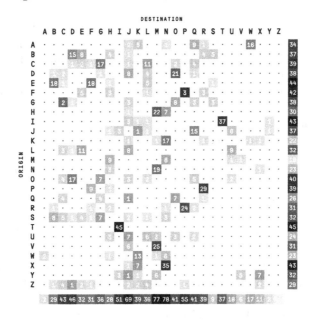

Fig. 10. Visualisation of the average number of migrations between the different islands when using *fitness guided* migration. Origin islands are positioned horizontally and the destiny islands vertically. High numbers of migrations are highlighted by darker squares. The results are averages of 30 runs.

To better understand the dynamics of the evolutionary process we summarise in Fig. 8 the evolution of fitness over time. The results suggest that the use of migration (*fitness guided* or *random*) promotes a faster convergence for maximum fitness values. To illustrate how the evolution of fitness is reflected in the graphic appearance of the glyphs, Fig. 9 depicts the glyphs evolved through time in a typical run using fitness based migration.

Regarding the speed of convergence to maximum fitness values, *fitness guided* is the first approach to attain high fitness values in 22 of 26 islands, with the

A B C D E F G H I J K L M N O P Q R S T U V W X Y Z
A B C D E F G H I J K L M N O P Q R S T U V W X Y Z
A B C D E F G H I J K L M N O P Q R S T U V W X Y Z
A B C D E F G H I J K L M N O P Q R S T U V W X Y Z
A B C D E F G H I J K L M N O P Q R S T U V W X Y Z

Fig. 11. Some examples of glyphs evolved in different runs.

exceptions being the letters A, V, W, and Z. These exceptions can be justified by the analysis of the migration paths along the evolutionary process. Figure 10 depicts the average number of migrations among islands for *fitness guided* migration.

The results in these islands can be justified as follows. For the letter Z, the migration paths indicate that the island does not receive immigrants from other islands, as such the performance of the *no migration* and *fitness guided* migration should be, and is, comparable. The same justification explains the results obtained for island A and V. The explanation for the behaviour observed in island W is harder to explain, in this *fitness guided* case migration appears to be detrimental to the evolutionary process, the migration of individuals from island A to island W, although helpful in the beginning of the run, leads to premature convergence to sub-optimal solutions.

Figure 10 also shows that islands corresponding to visually similar characters migrate more individuals among them. Some examples of these migration paths are the following: A→W; B→D; E→B,F; F→P; K,X→N; L→E; H,N,V→M; C⇌G; D⇌O; I⇌T; and P⇌R.

Although the analysis of the evolutionary process is valuable, from an evolutionary design point of view, the analysis of the visual output of the system is also important. The visual results presented in Fig. 11 highlight the diversity of the glyphs evolved in different runs. Additionally, and although this is difficult to measure objectively, migration appears promotes the visual coherence among the characters of different islands, which is important from a typeface design point of view. These outputs may be provided to a type designer as alternative sources of inspiration, thus arguably assisting creation of glyphs during the conceptual phase of the creative process. The analysis of the impact of these suggestions is outside the scope of the paper, and will be left for a future opportunity.

6 Conclusions and Future Work

We have presented Evotype, an evolutionary approach for the automatic generation of character glyphs with an automatic fitness assignment scheme based on an OCR approach. The approach adopts an island model where the glyphs corresponding to each character populate each island. The experimental results shows that migration of individuals among islands is beneficial, provided that the fitness in the destination environment is taken into consideration. More importantly, the experimental results show that Evotype provides an efficient architecture to evolve and explore alternatives for glyph design.

Future work will focus on: (i) the extension of the genetic representation to allow a wider range of graphic primitives; (ii) the exploration of different migration policies and topologies; (iii) the exploration of other fitness assignment schemes, which may promote the diversity, aesthetic appeal, and creative potential of the glyphs; and (iv) the further development of the system as tool for supporting the creativity of the designer.

Acknowledgments. This research is partially funded by: iCIS project (CENTRO-07-ST24-FEDER-002003), which is co-financed by QREN, in the scope of the Mais Centro Program and European Union's FEDER; Fundação para a Ciência e Tecnologia (FCT), Portugal, under the grants SFRH/BD/90968/2012 and SFRH/BD/105506/2014; project ConCreTe. The project ConCreTe acknowledges the financial support of the Future and Emerging Technologies (FET) programme within the Seventh Framework Programme for Research of the European Commission, under FET grant number 611733.

References

1. Butterfield, I., Lewis, M.: Evolving fonts (2000). Consulted in http://accad.osu.edu/~mlewis/AED/Fonts/, October 2014
2. Lund, A.: Evolving the shape of things to come: A comparison of direct manipulation and interactive evolutionary design. In: International Conference on Generative Art. Domus Argenia, Rome, Italy (2000)
3. Unemi, T., Soda, M.: An iec-based support system for font design. In: Proceedings of the IEEE International Conference on Systems, Man & Cybernetics, Washington, D.C., USA, 5–8 October, pp. 968–973 (2003)
4. Schmitz, M.: Genotyp, an experiment about genetic typography. Presented at Generative Art Conference 2004 (2004)
5. Levin, G., Feinberg, J., Curtis, C.: The alphabet synthesis machine (2006). Consulted in http://www.alphabetsynthesis.com, October 2014
6. Holland, J.H.: Adaptation in Natural and Artificial Systems. University of Michigan Press, Ann Arbor (1975)
7. Baluja, S., Pomerlau, D., Todd, J.: Towards automated artificial evolution for computer-generated images. Connection Sci. **6**(2), 325–354 (1994)
8. Machado, P., Romero, J., Manaris, B.: Experiments in computational aesthetics: An iterative approach to stylistic change in evolutionary art. In: Romero, J., Machado, P. (eds.) The Art of Artificial Evolution: A Handbook on Evolutionary Art and Music, pp. 381–415. Springer, Berlin Heidelberg (2007)
9. Machado, P., Correia, J., Romero, J.: Expression-based evolution of faces. In: Machado, P., Romero, J., Carballal, A. (eds.) EvoMUSART 2012. LNCS, vol. 7247, pp. 187–198. Springer, Heidelberg (2012)
10. Artan, Y., Burry, A., Kozitsky, V., Paul, P.: Efficient smqt features for snow-based classification on face detection and character recognition tasks. In: 2012 Western New York Image Processing Workshop (WNYIPW), pp. 45–48, Nov 2012
11. Carlson, A., Cumby, C., Rosen, J., Roth, D.: The snow learning architecture. Technical report UIUCDCS-R-99-2101, UIUC Computer Science Department, May 1999

Interior Illumination Design
Using Genetic Programming

Kelly Moylan and Brian J. Ross$^{(\boxtimes)}$

Department of Computer Science, Brock University,
500 Glenridge Avenue, St. Catharines, ON L2S 3A1, Canada
{km07ok,bross}@brocku.ca
http://www.cosc.brocku.ca/

Abstract. Interior illumination is a complex problem involving numerous interacting factors. This research applies genetic programming towards problems in illumination design. The Radiance system is used for performing accurate illumination simulations. Radiance accounts for a number of important environmental factors, which we exploit during fitness evaluation. Illumination requirements include local illumination intensity from natural and artificial sources, colour, and uniformity. Evolved solutions incorporate design elements such as artificial lights, room materials, windows, and glass properties. A number of case studies are examined, including a many-objective problem involving 6 illumination requirements, the design of a decorative wall of lights, and the creation of a stained-glass window for a large public space. Our results show the technical and creative possibilities of applying genetic programming to illumination design.

Keywords: Illumination · Genetic programming · Radiance · Many-objective optimization

1 Introduction

The illumination design of interior spaces is a challenging task. Within any space, the efficient use of both natural and artificial light sources is required, as rooms are often occupied during both day and night. Light reflects off of walls, floor, furniture, and other objects, and the degree of reflection depends on their geometry and material composition. Although large windows can fill an environment with sunlight, designers must ensure that occupants are also protected from harsh brightness and glare. These same rooms can then be illuminated during the night, with artificial lighting designed to create completely different moods and settings. Although the aesthetic nature of this task is difficult to formally model, technical requirements such as illumination levels, colours, material effects, and others, are more easily quantified.

This paper explores evolutionary design problems in illumination using genetic programming (GP) [1].[1] We use the Radiance system for evaluating aspects

---

[1] See http://www.cosc.brocku.ca/~bross/IllumGP/ for more details about this research.

© Springer International Publishing Switzerland 2015
C. Johnson et al. (Eds.): EvoMUSART 2015, LNCS 9027, pp. 148–160, 2015.
DOI: 10.1007/978-3-319-16498-4_14

of illumination in an environment [2,3]. Radiance uses a sophisticated simulation of illumination, which lets it accurately account for a wide range of relevant factors. By using Radiance, the GP system can consider a variety of factors for artificial and natural (solar) illumination. Since multiple and often conflicting instances of lighting specifications can be used, the problem is multi-objective in nature. By using the "many objective" technique of sum of rank (or average rank), we consider problems using up to 6 factors. The GP language addresses a host of factors relevant to illumination design, including artificial lighting (location, intensity, colour), windows (size, locations, colour), and room materials (walls, floors, ceiling).

Another contribution made is the application of GP to some innovative problems in illumination design. First, we design a decorative "wall of lights", comprising a variable-sized grid of coloured lights. In another problem, an enormous stained-glass window is generated for a public space. In both these problems, we exploit GP's ability to evolved mathematical expressions for generating the colour of lights and windows, essentially evolving procedural textures to solve the problems. The evolution of procedural textures has an established history in evolutionary design [4,5].

The paper is organized as follows. Section 2 reviews some relevant concepts in illumination design, and discusses the Radiance illumination modeling system. We discuss the implementation of our system architecture in Sect. 3. Experiments and results are reported in Sect. 4, including a many-objective room illumination problem, a decorative wall of lights, and a stained glass wall. Concluding discussions are in Sect. 5.

2   Background

2.1   Illumination Design

Illumination is a topic of specialization within architecture and interior design [6]. The inverse illumination problem involves finding of potential lighting options for a pre-defined interior space [7]. It takes into account the desired lighting requirements in various locations in the space, and looks for optimal positions, kinds, and number of light sources. This allows a degree of freedom and creativity to solve illumination problems, given the many feasible solutions possible. Energy efficiency are often considered as well, since passive solar illumination can be used for both illumination requirements and energy saving (artificial light reduction, room heating).

The challenges of illumination design makes it an interesting problem for computer automation and computational intelligence. Fernandez [8] used a heuristic search to recreate an initial lighting scene. The program was tasked with finding placements of skylights to illuminate a pre-made building layout. Tena [7] used an interactive genetic algorithm to find solutions for inverse illumination problems. Castro [9] used a number of different heuristic and evolutionary based approaches, which searched for a desired illumination solution using optimally minimum emission power. Caldas [10] investigated energy efficiency concerns

involving illumination, using a multi-objective genetic algorithm. Another approach to the problem is to design a building model incorporating specific illumination characteristics – and especially in regards to solar illumination [11,12].

2.2 Radiance

Radiance is a well known open-source illumination simulation tool for designers
and architects [2,3]. It implements a physically-based backward raytracer rendering algorithm that accounts for a number of important environmental factors,
including light intensity, materials, geographic location, time, date, and others.

To use Radiance, one first defines a 3D model of the environment. For a
room, this will be the obvious room walls, ceiling, floors, and windows. Material
definitions specifying colours and reflectivity are also defined. The room can be
filled with objects, such as furniture and decoration, and materials are similarly
supplied. Artificial lighting is defined, and involves locations, colours, and intensities. The geographic location, time, and date are then supplied, in order to
simulate natural sunlight accurately.

Once the environment is defined, Radiance performs an illumination simulation. A number of outputs can be obtained. Individual lighting measurements
can be sampled at locations of interest. Lighting characteristics such as glare can
be measured. An overall rendering of the scene can be generated. This can be a
photorealistic image, or a colour-coded illuminosity map.

3 System Design

3.1 Genetic Programming Language

A strongly-typed GP language [13] is used (Table 1). Types designate specific
design tasks within the environment. This defines GP trees similar to those used
in grammar-guided GP [14]. For example, W is a type denoting the generation of
windows and skylight for a room, and the *Windows* operator fulfills that design
task. Numeric types include float (F), integer (I), and tree float (TF). Some of
functions used are:

- *Materials(...)* assigns materials for the 4 walls, ceiling, and floor. If not used,
  pre-defined materials are assigned.
- *North_Wall_Center(I,a,b,c,d)* creates windows for the north wall. "*I*" is converted to a value between 0 and 30, and is the number of wall panels or sections
  to create for windows. The a, b, and c arguments use the fraction portion of
  the float value. They scale the windows, as shown in Fig. 1(a). All the windows on a wall's panels will have the same scale. The d argument determined
  whether a window is to be created on a panel. Its floating point expression is
  given the panel coordinates. If the value is positive, a window is defined on
  that panel. Otherwise no window is created.

Table 1. Language

Type	Function Name	Description
R	Root(W,MM,LM,...)	Creates the scene. Parameters vary according to design task
LM	Top_Light(LB)	Creates the artificial lighting
W	Windows(C,NW,SW,EW,NW)	Creates walls and windows
MM	Materials(M,M,M,M,M,M)	Creates materials
M	(F,F,F,F,F)	Material defn: R, G, B, reflection, roughness
C	SkyLight(F,F,F,F)	Skylight window on the ceiling. Args define coords for 2 opposite corners
NW	North_Wall_Center(I,F,F,F,TF)	Evenly patterns the wall of the
SW	South_Wall_Center(I,F,F,F,TF)	room based on percentage
EW	East_Wall_Center(I,F,F,F,TF)	measures for window size and
NW	West_Wall_Center(I,F,F,F,TF)	location on wall section
LM	Top_Light(LB)	Creates artificial lighting
LB	Light_Filler(LB,LB)	Branches the light creation tree
LB	Basic_Light(F,F)	Light source of fixed white intensity. Args define location
LW	Light_Wall(I,I,TF,TF,TF)	Grid of lights on a wall. TF expressions compute RGB of each light
SG	Stained_Glass(I,I,TF,TF,TF)	Grid of stained glass on wall
TF	Add(TF[2..4])	Add op for colour expressions. Between 2 to 4 arguments
TF	-, *, /, neg, sin, cos, log	Other math operators
TF	X, Y	Grid coordinates
TF	ERCTF	Ephemeral TF $(-1.0 \leq TF < 1.0)$
F	ERCFloat	Ephemeral float $(0.0 \leq F < 100.0)$
I	ERCInt	Ephemeral integer $(0 \leq I < 100)$

- *Basic_Light(...)*: Create a fixed intensity white light. A minimum distance of 0.5 metres between lights is enforced.
- *Light_Wall(I,J,R,G,B)* generates a K-by-L grid of lights. I and J are integers converted to values between $3 \leq K \leq 10$ and $3 \leq L \leq 36$. Each light's grid coordinate is accessible to the colour channel expressions.
- *Stained_Glass(I,J,R,G,B)* creates a grid of square stained glass windows on a wall. It works much like *Light_Wall(I,J,R,G,B)*. One difference is that we project each glass element's coordinate to the range $-1.0 \leq x, y \leq 1.0$. This range can be altered as desired.

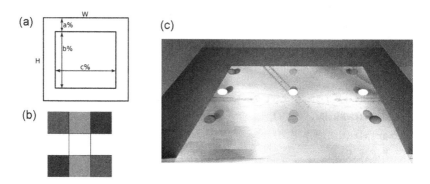

Fig. 1. (a) Window sizing parameters. (b) Colour map for wall of lights and stained glass. (c) Colour mapping in stained glass room. Spheres locations and colours show where matching done. Example uses solution in Fig. 6(a).

3.2   Fitness Evaluation

Fitness evaluation is performed on designated illumination readings of interest within the environment. These measurements are requested from Radiance to compute, at specific locations and directions. Illumination features used as fitness criteria are measured at desired locations in a room. They are as follows:

1. *Illumination intensity (or illumination)*: This is a measure of brightness. Measurements are performed in units of lux, a measurement of luminous flux per unit area. It is equal to one lumen per square metre. Lumens measure the total illumination power emitted from a light source. Lux readings are matched in the scene against corresponding target values, and the absolute difference between them is measured. Often multiple sample points are measured and averaged.
2. *Colour sampling*: Radiance's illumination model denotes light values using a high dynamic range (HDR) data type. This makes it difficult for specifying exact colours to match, as can be done with a more constrained RGB colour scheme. We therefore denote colour matching using ratios between colour channels:

$$Value1 = RedChannel \div GreenChannel$$
$$Value2 = RedChannel \div BlueChannel$$
$$Value3 = GreenChannel \div BlueChannel$$

This permits a range of colours having a similar hue, based on the relationship of channel values in a target colour. The sum of errors between the measured and target colour ratios is calculated. Low scores are preferred.
3. *Uniformity (evenness)*: Uniformity promotes gradual illumination changes. Typically some K number of illumination readings are sampled from an area. Then uniformity is:

$$Uniformity = L_{min}/L_{avg}$$

where L_{min} and L_{avg} are the minimum and average lux readings from the samples. We use the sum of 3 separate test areas for uniformity scores, giving a target value of 3.

Next, the absolute error differences between the measured values described above and the targets are placed in a feature vector. This vector denotes the multi-objective scores for the GP individual being assessed. Lower error values are better scores. Once all the population is assessed, the sum of ranks fitness score is determined for the population. This is a multi-objective scoring strategy for high-dimensional multi-objective problems [15]. Given a feature vector of size n, a population member k has a raw objective vector $(f_1^k, ..., f_n^k)$. Each objective f is separately ranked for the population, resulting in a rank vector $(r_1^k, ..., r_n^k)$. The sum of ranks score is calculated:

$$Fitness_k = \sum_{i=1}^{n} \frac{r_i^k}{max_i}$$

where max_j is the maximum rank value for objective j. The scaling by each objective's maximum rank is a normalization step that balances the contribution of each objective to the overall score.

3.3   GP Parameters

We use RobGP – a C++ based GP system [16]. It was chosen for its ease of integration with Radiance. Typical GP parameters used are shown in Table 2, and are common in the literature [1].

Table 2. GP Parameters

Parameter	Value
Runs/experiment	20
Generations	50
Population size	250
Initialization	Ramped half-and-half
Init. tree depth range	4–6
Max tree depth	11
Tournament size	3
Crossover rate	90 %
Mutation rate	10 %
Mut. grow tree depth range	2–4

Table 3. Room parameters

Parameter	Value
Room width	20 m
Room length	60 m
Ceiling height	6 m
Wall material	Plastic(0.309,0.051,0.051,0,0)
Ceiling material	Plastic(0.8,0.8,0.8,0,0)
Floor material	Radiance library wood floor
Glass definition	Glass(0.96,0.96,0.96)
Light size	0.125 m
Daylight date, time	Sept 23, 12:00EDT
Location	43.12 N, 79.25 W

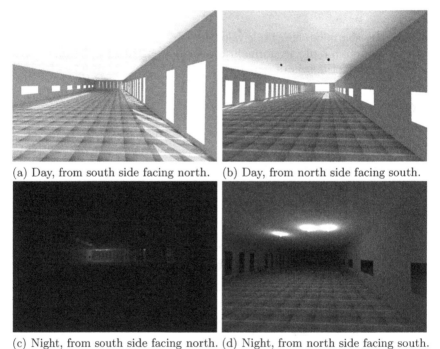

(a) Day, from south side facing north. (b) Day, from north side facing south.

(c) Night, from south side facing north. (d) Night, from north side facing south.

Fig. 2. Day/night illumination best solution.

4   Results

4.1   Illuminated Room: Day and Night

We consider the illumination of a rectangular room having a north-south orientation, with long walls facing east and west. Two variations of the problem are

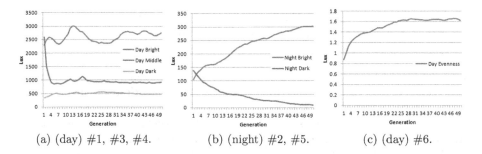

(a) (day) #1, #3, #4.   (b) (night) #2, #5.   (c) (day) #6.

Fig. 3. Population fitness plots for day/night illumination (avg 20 runs). See text for target values for these objectives.

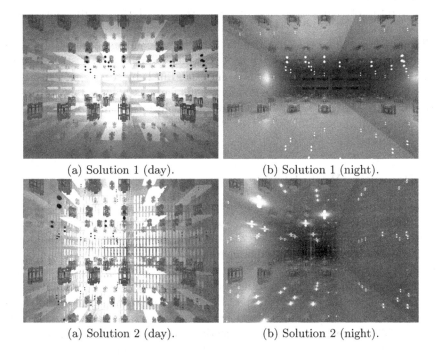

(a) Solution 1 (day).   (b) Solution 1 (night).

(a) Solution 2 (day).   (b) Solution 2 (night).

Fig. 4. Day/night illumination with materials evolution.

considered. In the first, we supply material definitions for the room (Table 3). The second experiment discards the predefined materials, and uses GP to evolve them. In both cases, we use GP to define artificial lights and a sky light on the ceiling, and optional windows on all 4 walls. The room is divided into 3 equal areas – north, middle, and south. Measurements are performed twice during the day – at noon, and during a moonless night. The objectives are:

#1 (day) South area having an illuminance of 4000 lux.
#2 (night) South area having an illuminance of 500 lux.

#3 (day) Middle area having an illuminance of 1000 lux.
#4, #5 (day, night) North having an illuminance of 0 lux.
#6 (day) Uniformity value of 3.

This represents a many-objective optimization problem. Illumination is sampled and averaged over 16 evenly distributed measurement locations in each section. Lights are turned off during the day.

Figure 2 shows the best scoring solution. The south sides (facing north) are made brighter by artificial lighting (day and night) and a skylight during the day. The middle and north sides are darker. The uniformity test encourages the even distributions of lights and windows. Figure 3 shows the population performance of the predefined material runs, averaged over 20 runs. Plots show the raw measurements of the factors. Most plots show a general convergence towards the desired target values. However, objective #4 (day dark) had difficulty reaching the target of 0.

Figure 4 shows two selected results from the second experiment. In both, side windows were ignored, and reflective walls were used to distribute light in the room. Whereas the predefined materials in Table 3 had no reflectivity, the evolved wall materials had reflection coefficients as high as 0.86 (a perfect mirror is 1.0). Analysis showed that material evolution resulted in statistically significant improvements in objectives #3 and 4, while the pre-defined material runs were superior in #5 and 6.[2]

4.2   Decorative Wall of Lights

The task is to define a wall of coloured lights at one side of the room. The Light_Wall function is used to do this, and treats light colouring as a procedural texture. The resolution of the light grid can be evolved to range between 3×3 to 10×36. We require a minimum distance of 0.5 m between neighbouring lights. A total of 9 lights in a 3×3 square pattern are selected from the whole light grid for colour sampling. The goal is to have these selected lights evolve colours that match those in the target colour map of Fig. 1(b). The colour score computes the sum of ratio errors of the 9 sampled lights and respective target colours (see Sect. 3.2). Therefore, this is a single-objective problem. Note that the lights not measured are more free to emit any colour (although overly bright lights may influence nearby colour measurements). This should result in interesting patterns of colours that are still somewhat constrained by the colour map. The integer grid coordinates of lights are used by the colour expressions.

Figure 5 shows 4 selected results from different runs. Figure 5(a) has the best score. The low resolution light grid produces different styles of images compared to high resolution bitmaps [5]. Also, direct colour matching is difficult for GP [17]. Therefore, typically 6 of the 9 colour targets might be satisfied at best.

---

[2] Two-tailed unpaired t-test with unequal variance, $p = 0.05\%$.

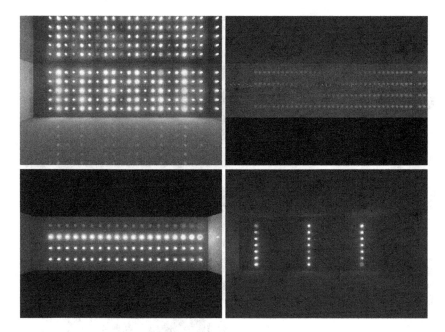

Fig. 5. Examples of light wall results.

4.3   Stained-Glass Windows

An enormous wall encompassing a stained glass window is to be created for a large public space. We use the *Stained_Glass* function to generate this windowed wall. The evolvable grid resolution resides between 50×50 to 100×100 (i.e. between 2500 and 10000 glass panels). We used a coordinate system of $-1.0 \leq x, y \leq 1.0$, with the origin (0,0) centered on the window.

To make this experiment different from the wall of lights problem, a new approach to colour analysis is used. Although somewhat contrived, the scheme is interesting and challenging, and must rely on Radiance's rendering abilities. Colour measurement is done at mid-day, when the southern Sun shining through the window maximally illuminates the interior floor. Although the window colours vary during the day as the Sun's direction changes, this mid-day illumination is used for fitness evaluation. Colour matching again uses the colour map in Fig. 1(b). We use 9 evenly-spaced sample points on the floor, from where projected window colours are sampled as they are seen by a viewer looking downward at the floor at a 45 degree direction. Thus colour is measured indirectly, and relies on the stained glass illuminating the sample positions on the floor that match the target colour map colour. The view from the window looking towards these locations is shown in Fig. 1(c). As before, a sum of colour ratio errors is used for colour scoring.

Figure 6 shows 2 interesting results. The window encompasses the entire far wall, and a vaulted ceiling slopes downwards on each side to the height indicated by the dark bands on each side of the window. Each image shows the window

(a) Solution 1, noon.   (b) Solution 1, late day.

(c) Solution 2, noon.   (d) Solution 2, late day.

Fig. 6. Example stained glass results.

illuminating the empty room at two times during the day. The evolved pattern is centered on the window, showing the effect of the projected texture coordinate space on the evolved colour expression [18]. Note how the window's colour changes substantially during the day.

5   Conclusion

This paper makes a number of contributions in evolutionary illumination design. The Radiance system allowed us to accurately consider a number of illumination factors. By treating illumination design as a many-objective problem, we considered up to 6 objectives. Elsewhere, we used up to 8 objectives, concluding factors such as glare. Although all fitness strategies introduce particular search biases, we feel that the sum of ranks is less prone to the immediate influences of poorly designed weighted sum formulae. It also handles higher-dimensional problems than Pareto ranking, without generating outlier solutions.

We also considered two innovative problems – a decorative wall of lights, and a stained-glass window. The success of these problems was due to GP's well known proficiency in evolving procedural textures. In both cases, rather than compute pixel colours on a bitmap, we defined the colour of lights and stained glass. Being able to apply procedural textures to these alternative problems was due to Radiance's illumination abilities.

There are many directions for future work. One obvious extension is to include energy-efficiency considerations, as done by Caldas [10], Marin *et al.* [12] and others. Although we considered the illumination of pre-existing structures, it is possible to integrate floorplan and 3D model design with illumination. We have only scratched the surface of using procedural textures for decorative illumination. By including texture operators that use noise and entropy [18], and employing aesthetic fitness evaluation techniques [19], many exciting results in illumination design are waiting to be discovered.

References

1. Koza, J.: Genetic Programming: On the Programming of Computers by Means of Natural Selection. MIT Press, Cambridge (1992)
2. Larson, G.W., Shakespeare, R., Ehrlich, C., Mardaljevic, J., Phillips, E., Apian-Bennewitz, P.: Rendering with Radiance: The Art and Science of Lighting Visualization. Morgan Kaufmann, San Francisco (1998)
3. Fuller, D., McNeil, A.: Radiance, http://www.radiance-online.org/
4. Sims, K.: Interactive evolution of equations for procedural models. Vis. Comput. **9**, 466–476 (1993)
5. Graf, J., Banzhaf, W.: Interactive Evolution of Images. In: Proceedings of International Conference on Evolutionary Programming, pp. 53–65 (1995)
6. Russell, S.: The Architecture of Light: Architectural Lighting Design Concepts and Techniques. Conceptnine, San Diego (2008)
7. Tena, J.E., Rudomin, I., Eugenio, A., Sada, G., Gordo, C.: An interactive system for solving inverse illumination problems using genetic algorithms. In: Proceedings of Computación Visual (1997)
8. Fernández, E., Besuievsky, G.: Inverse lighting design for interior buildings integrating natural and artificial sources. Comput. Graph. **36**, 1096–1108 (2012)
9. Castro, F., del Acebo, E., Sbert, M.: Energy-saving light positioning using heuristic search. Eng. Appl. Artif. Intell. **25**(3), 566–582 (2012)
10. Caldas, L.: Generation of energy-efficient architecture solutions applying gene_arch: an evolution-based generative design system. Adv. Eng. Inform. **22**(1), 59–70 (2008)
11. Watanabe, M.S.: Induction Design: A Method for Evolutionary Design. Birkhauser, Basel (2002)
12. Marin, P., Bignon, J.C., Lequay, H.: Generative exploration of architectural envelope responding to solar passive qualities. In: Design & Decision Support Systems in Architecture and Urban Planning. Eindhoven U of Tech (2008)
13. Montana, D.: Strongly typed genetic programming. Evol. Comput. **3**(2), 199–230 (1995)
14. McKay, R., Hoai, N., Whigham, P., Shan, Y., O'Neill, M.: Grammar-based genetic programming: a survey. GPEM **11**, 365–396 (2010)
15. Corne, D., Knowles, J.: Techniques for highly multiobjective optimisation: some nondominated points are better than others. In: Proceedings of GECCO 2007, pp. 773–780. ACM Press (2007)
16. Flack, R.: Robgp - robust object based genetic programming system, September 2009. http://sourceforge.net/projects/robgp/
17. Wiens, A., Ross, B.: Gentropy: evolutionary 2D texture generation. Comput. Graph. J. **26**(1), 75–88 (2002)

18. Ebert, D., Musgrave, F., Peachey, D., Perlin, K., Worley, S.: Texturing and Modeling: A Procedural Approach, 2nd edn. Academic Press, New York (1998)
19. den Heijer, E., Eiben, A.: Comparing aesthetic measures for evolutionary art. Applications of Evolutionary Computation. LNCS, vol. 6025, pp. 311–320. Springer, Heidelberg (2010)

Lichtsuchende: Exploring the Emergence of a Cybernetic Society

Dave Murray-Rust[1](✉) and Rocio von Jungenfeld[2]

[1] School of Informatics, University of Edinburgh, Edinburgh, UK
dmrust@inf.ed.ac.uk
[2] School of Design, University of Edinburgh, Edinburgh, UK
rocio.von-jungenfeld@ed.ac.uk

Abstract. In this paper, we describe *Lichtsuchende*, an interactive installation, built using a society of biologically inspired, cybernetic creatures who exchange light as a source of energy and a means of communication. Visitors are invited to engage with the installation using torches to influence and interact with the phototropic robots. As well as describing the finished piece, we explore some of the issues around creating works based on biologically inspired robots. We present an account of the development of the creatures in order to highlight the gulfs between conceptual ideas of how to allow emergent behaviours and the manners in which they are implemented. We also expose the interrelations and tensions between the needs of the creatures as they emerge and the needs of the creators, to understand the duet between the cyber-organisms and their initiators. Finally, we look at the ways in which creators, robots and visitors are enrolled to perform their functions, so that the network of activity can be woven between all parties.

1 Introduction

In this paper, we are concerned with systems inspired by biology (and to some extent evolution), and those seeking to produce artworks with a sense of agency and autonomy. The autonomy present in some artworks inspired by biological systems has the potential of being experienced by visitors and creators alike as the systems having some kind of life of their own. This leads to a web of needs, whose interplay must be navigated in the creation of the work. There are needs common to most artistic practice: the artist's need for expression and fulfilment of aesthetic goals and the creation of work that can be parsed by visitors. However, as the creations edge ever closer towards creaturehood—or eventually, some form of personhood—additional needs arise. There may be a need to stay, in some sense 'true' to the creatures, to allow their narratives to develop alongside their implementation. When people experience digital algorithms associated with the physical structures of artificial creatures, there is a tendency to anthropomorphise, to project ideas of emotion and behaviour, and to empathise with them.

Thanks to the Innovative Initiative Fund of the University of Edinburgh.

C. Johnson et al. (Eds.): EvoMUSART 2015, LNCS 9027, pp. 161–174, 2015.
DOI: 10.1007/978-3-319-16498-4_15

Hence, there may also be a need to support the public's understanding of the piece in a manner which correlates with the experience of the creatures, to sculpt the anthropomorphisation to be consistent with the internal mechanics of the cyber entities.

2   Background and Related Work

In this paper we will discuss a particular project which the authors carried out, but it is important to connect this into a diverse collection of existing work.

There is a vibrant history of swarm behaviour and artificial life within the world of computational art, many of which have influenced this project. To pick a few examples from many, Blackwell's SwarmMusic [1] paired a digital swarm with a skilled human improviser to create musical duets; rAndom International's *Audience* piece works with the idea of static robot swarm directing their attention to visitors which they find in some sense 'interesting'[1]; Miranda created a series of digital societies where autonomous communicative agents developed repertoires of sounds [2]; finally, there is a clear relation to Ihnatowicz's seminal *Sound Activated Mobile*[2], one of the earliest cybernetic kinetic sculptures.

Part of our project engages with the relation between embodied algorithms and emotional responses, the ways in which we may socialise with robots [3]. Here, we are interested in the ways in which internal state is performed and understood, how activity is organised, and what gives rise to the underlying dynamics of action and response. In animal behavioural theory, we find the concept of modal action patterns—recognisable behaviours with clear preconditions underpinning theories of animal communication [4]. For instance, many animals have a zone around them, the transgression of which will provoke agonistic behaviour or a readiness to flee. For human psychology, Maslow's hierarchy of needs [5] gives a common sense account of the underpinnings of human behaviour, based on the idea that human needs can be organised into a hierarchy, with each level of needs being dependent on the one below. There is hence the requirement to satisfy base needs before more rarefied desires are considered.

Analogies have been drawn between this hierarchy of needs and Brooks' subsumption architecture for robotics [6]: multiple states exist with preconditions for activation, and the highest priority state which can activate at any point in time is given control of the robot's actuators. This connection has not gone unnoticed, and forms the basis for several intelligent multi-agent systems e.g. [7,8].

Another area of interest is the relation between digital creatures and their environment. Cybernetic organisms tend to have a different range of sensory and processing apparatus from humans, and this is reflected in their experience of their environment. Uexküll introduces the idea of *Umwelt*—the perceptual

---

[1]   http://www.chrisoshea.org/audience.
[2]   http://www.senster.com/ihnatowicz/SAM/sam.htm.

life-world which gives rise to the creatures' biosemantic view of their environment: "Every subject spins out, like the spiders threads, its relations to certain qualities of things and weaves them into a solid web, which carries its existence" [9, p. 53]. The environments in which these creatures exist, however, are often created alongside their inhabitants, developed in dialogue with the ways in which the creatures practise and perform their behavioural routines. This creates a symbiotic relation, where the environment and its organisms shape and influence each other [10, p. 20], an ecosystemic network between the emerging lifeforms, their creators, and their visitors.

3   Description of the Work

Lichtsuchende is an interactive installation, comprising a society of cybernetic creatures. The creatures base their interaction on the exchange of light, using it both as a source of energy and a means of communication. Visitors to the installation can interact with the creatures using torches to influence their behaviour (Fig. 1). A video showing a pre-installation version of the robots can be found here: http://bit.ly/1HF0od8[3].

Fig. 1. Lichtsuchende installed in Vault 13 at Hidden Door Festival, Edinburgh, April 2014. Photo credit Chris Scott @chrisdonia

---

[3] The work won the 3rd place Public Choice Award at the 2014 New Technological Art Awards (http://www.ntaa.be/2014/).

The creatures resemble sunflowers to some extent: they are fixed to the floor, and rotate their heads to track light. They have a relatively curtailed set of basic capabilities for sensing and affecting their environment (Fig. 2):

– Two actuators allow them to control the orientation of their head horizontally and vertically, covering most of a hemisphere. This both focuses their attention in a specific direction, and conveys a sense of focus.
– 5 isotropic ambient light sensors arranged in a cross allow them to sense the intensity of the light field in the direction of attention, along with gradients in intensity from top to bottom and left to right.
– A cluster of superbright LEDs emit a strong, narrow beam of light in the direction that they are facing, with variable intensity.
– Additional LEDs allow them to illuminate their stems as a means of conveying internal state.

This means their *Umwelt* is built on an extremely pared down set of basic inputs: they know which direction they are looking in, and they have access to a tiny slice of the structure of illumination surrounding them. A central aesthetic of this piece is to work outwards from this minimal set of capabilities to produce a rich and engaging experience.

The basic principle of action is the flowers' tendency to turn their attention towards sources of light, and to project light in the direction of their attention as a means of engaging. This connects their inner world to that of their fellows and any visitors in the installation environment.

We describe the piece along four axes: the thematic elements which inform its construction; the technical and material components which constitute the robotic creatures' physical presence; the implementation of the conceptual elements which

Fig. 2. Robot component detail showing (a) the electronic components mounted on the main circuit board (note that the CPU is obscured by the wireless networking module) and (b) the board mounted on an armature composed of transparent acrylic and servo motors.

give rise to the robot's behaviours; and the aesthetic and situational concerns relating to displaying the robots within an exhibition context.

3.1 Thematic Motivations

As presented, the artwork draws on three broad themes, relating to the anthropomorphisation of embodied algorithms, the role of needs and desires in creating complex behaviour, and the emergence of socialisation both with a collection of robots and between robots and humans. In Sect. 3.4 we will unravel the emergence of some of these themes, but initially, we present them as a *fait accompli*.

Embodiment and Interpretation. One of the motivations behind this work is the relationship between simple specification and the perception of complex behaviour and state. This is especially apparent when the behaviours are embodied in a physical system that people can engage with. The key behaviour of the robots is tracking light by navigating the intensity gradient of the light field in front of them. This navigation is implemented as a purposefully crude and brutally simplistic algorithm, simply moving towards brighter light. However, the exigencies of the physical and digital incarnation of algorithms inevitably lead to idiosyncrasies, which are open to anthropomorphic interpretation. Slightly different algorithms and parameterisations give rise to patterns of movement which can be interpreted as curious, nervous, excitable, graceful and so on. Some physical behaviour is unplanned, resulting from their embodiment and situation: if a person reaches out to touch a flower which is tracking light, their hand casts a shadow on the sensor, and the robot will turn away. This can happen abruptly, and has been interpreted as shyness, or a nervous reaction. We are interested in the reactions which these algorithms provoke, and which responses are due to intentional design parameters versus idiosyncrasies of implementation.

Navigating Internal State. Ihnatowicz's cybernetic 'Senster' has a single behaviour—to track continuous sounds. There is a lot of nuance within this behaviour, such as the ways in which different sounds trigger movement, but ultimately it is a direct, immediate response to input. In order to enrich the possibilities for action, we draw on: (i) Maslow's hierarchy for an organisation of internal states; (ii) Brooks' subsumption architecture for a computational implementation of these states; and (iii) Barlow's modal action patterns as a means to enact and display these states (see Fig. 3). The states derived correspond to physical and emotional concepts, a sense of desires, and the means to satisfy them. We are interested firstly in how the robots' internal state can be communicated to visitors, the relation between display and interpretation and matching conceptual ideas to anthropomorphic readings. Secondly, how can the network of states be constructed to give rise to pathways of behaviour that are understandable and plausible in the context of creaturehood.

Emergent Behaviour, Interactivity and Socialisation. The behaviours above provide a link between the individual and the social, and these interrelationships provide fertile ground for emergent behaviour. At one level, there are the effects of having several autonomous, embodied entities sharing a space: communication may occur or not; if it does, it may be subject to misinterpretation, or interrupted by the actions of others. There is the possibility of cascades of behaviour change throughout the space, a positive feedback as each robot activates others, spreading excitation. The system may become stuck in one overall global state, such as all of the robots deactivated and unable to initiate movement. There may be local patterns, where some of the robots become locked into enmeshed repetitive behaviours. We are interested in the question of what it takes to design an 'interesting' robot society, which exhibits a range of behaviour, which reacts to visitors but has its own internal dynamics, and which doesn't exhibit pathological complete failure modes.

3.2   Internal States and Their Implementation

As previously noted, the central characteristic of the creatures is their fascination with light, their immediate enrapturement and constant alignment with any source of photons. However, this is only one of their possible behavioural states (Fig. 3), which are arranged in a rough parallel with Maslow's hierarchy of needs [5]. The basis for moving between the behaviours is the sensory input available to the creature, combined with internal variables to representing energy level, the time spent tracking a source and so on. Taken in increasing priority, the states, their conditions and the associated observable activities are as follows:

Sleeping occurs when a flower lacks energy. The head is pointed downwards, and the base pulses slowly with light, intended to evoke the calm breathing of a sleeping animal. While the flower sleeps, its energy level gradually increments.

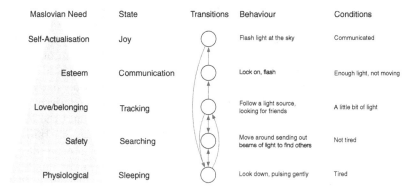

Fig. 3. Behavioural states of the robots with their activation conditions, and a relation to the Maslovian hierarchy of needs.

Searching occurs when a flower has some energy, but there is no strong light source present. It will move by a small, random amount, and then send out a slow pulse of light in that direction to see if anything responds. This enables the flowers to maintain their society in the absence of any human intervention.

Tracking is the response to any sufficiently bright light source. The flower will turn towards the sensor(s) giving the highest reading. This is a simple, cybernetically inspired approach, with differences in intensity between opposed sensors driving acceleration in each axis[4]. When tracking, the robot outputs a strong beam of light, to allow itself to be tracked by whatever is producing the light. Tracking consumes a lot of energy, meaning that often the flower will go to sleep if the light source is lost.

Communication is enabled when a robot has seen a bright light, for a certain amount of time, with minimal movement. This indicates that it has enough evidence that the light source is a fellow flower, and discourse can begin. The physical effect is that the robot freezes in place, and flashes rapidly, as a placeholder for exchange of information.

Joy occurs when communication is successfully completed: the flower points at the sky, emits a few bright flashes of light. It then points down towards the ground with the base pulsing rapidly to indicate brief exhaustion, from which it cannot be interrupted. At the end of this behaviour, the flower goes back to sleep.

3.3 Aesthetic and Interactive Considerations

In addition to the ideas of state, action and behaviour outlined above, since the endeavour was to create an interactive art installation, we had some aesthetic principles to guide construction and deployment of the robots:

- The work should be immediately accessible, and give a broad range of visitors a direct way to engage, yet rich enough to support some degree of prolonged investigation.
- Nothing should be hidden: all of the electronics, cables, motors, circuits and sensors are clearly visible. There are no coverings or casings to hide the skeleton and nervous system of the creatures. The only parts which are hidden are the egregiously ugly computer power supplies used.
- The work should be minimal, so colour has been avoided, using only black, white and transparent materials. No additional sound has been added, leaving just the susurrus of 60 servo motors to create the sonic environment.
- The creatures should be part of the space in which they are situated. This generally means finding spaces with character in which to show them, and finding some kind of locally relevant material to connect the plastic and electronic entities with their surroundings.

---

[4] Roughly: $d\theta_{lr}/dt \sim i_l - i_r$ where θ_{lr} is the pan or horizontal alignment of the head, and i_l and i_r are the intensities of the left and right sensors respectively, with a similar relation holding for the vertical (tilt) orientation. However, tweaks have been made to stabilise this in an effort to improve the interactivity.

3.4   An Account of the Emergence of Embodied Identity

The account given so far presents a certain picture of the piece, in a relatively resolved, finished form. Of course, as with any project, the realities of development are far messier and more complex than the polished presentation given above. In many pieces of work, this developmental process would be taken as a given: ideas are refined as they are tried and executed, design becomes iterative as it meets reality. However, this piece involves robots which are working their way towards creaturehood. As such, development needs to take into account several different communities, their reasons for being part of the process. As usual, we must consider the web of relations between the artists and creators of the work, and the audience of the work, but here we must also consider the community of creatures which form the body of the work: what are their needs, their reasons for enrolling in the cyber-society and initiating dialogue with the visitors. There is a parallel here to Callon's seminal work on translation in Actor Network Theory, where the organisms under scrutiny—scallops—are taken as actors within the system [11]. The development of the piece must balance the emerging identity of the digital creatures against the artist's original intention and the presentational necessities related to exhibiting art for an audience.

In order to engage with this, we present a shared account, teasing apart how the conceptual development was informed by the coalescence of the infant creatures' character.

Initial Experiments. The initial seed of development had nothing to do with artificial life, or biologically inspired robotics. The germ of the project was a pure electronics experiment: we wanted to construct a very simple mechanism which moved a servo motor from side to side in response to changes in light. This was an undirected act of construction: at this point, we had no strong idea of a piece in mind, or conceptual framework for constructing one. Using scrap circuit boards, glue and toothpicks, we put together a slightly enhanced version of the original idea which used four sensors and two servos to track bright lights. A video of this setup can be found here: http://bit.ly/1vkdMy6. As soon as we played with this, the potential for anthropomorphisation was apparent: the movements seemed eager, straining. Overshoot and positive feedback gave it a bit of a twitch, a nervous tick. Suddenly, it felt alive, and the idea formed to use this as the basis for creating a society of creatures.

Reactions to Embodiment. Based on this, we set out to construct several robots, and look at their potential for interaction. To do this, the robots needed to produce light, so we added LEDs, and created three prototypes. A video of this can be found here: http://bit.ly/1rq758A. As Anderson said, "More is different" [12]: the interrelationships and structures which emerged from having several robots interacting fundamentally changed the way in which we viewed them. They transitioned from being assemblages of components to—approximately, metaphorically—living beings. There were several specific events which brought this about:

- As previously noted we found that reaching out to touch one of the robots often makes it jerk away. Intellectually, this is just a reaction to the shadow cast by a hand; however, this was clearly interpretable as shyness, retreating from unfamiliar touch. This was not a behaviour we has planned or anticipated, yet it felt very much in line with the character we were starting to imagine.
- When two robots came face to face when they are very close together, they begin jerking around wildly—this can be seen at 00:58 in the video above. As their creators, we knew that this is simply an artefact of the implementation: quantized time and position representations coupled with a crude algorithm lead to overshoot, positive feedback and instability. However, it was difficult to shake our gut reaction, that this was a communication, a territorial display, a reaction to the invasion of their space.
- One of the prototypes—now proto-creatures—lost a sensor. This threw out it's tracking algorithm, and it ended up systematically smashing itself to pieces on the post next to it. This was surprisingly distressing to watch, conjoring images of mental illness and self harm. Again, it was hard, on a personal level, to separate knowledge of the algorithmic causes from our emotional response to the enacted movements.

Taken together, the existence of unplanned behaviour, the emergence of needs and communication and the potential for pathological behaviour made it impossible to ignore the growing identity, autonomy and socialisation of these creatures.

Inner Lives. The next point of engagement was to try and add some variation to the behaviour: it felt incomplete that the creatures would only ever reactively track light, without purpose, boredom or communication; there needed to be some teleological context for that behaviour. We started to think about what existence was like for these robots, what would motivate their movements and actions, and how their limited *umwelt* could be parsed into states which we consistent with both their life narratives and our interpretations of what they were doing. It was at this point that we invoked the mechanics of Brooks' subsumption architecture coupled with Maslow's hierarchy as a way to develop the psychology of the individuals.

The final set of states are given in Sect. 3.2, but this doesn't relate to their development. It is one thing to have a clear conceptual idea of what the creator would like the states to be, and another to implement them in a digital creature. We had to experiment with different ideas, abandoning some—such as transmitting serial bitstrings by flashing their lights—due to time constraints or technical difficulties, and others as they did not ring true with the emerging character of the robots.

A large part of the process was developing the biosemiotics relating to the different states and their human interpretation. We can say that there is a behaviour called 'sleeping', but that requires definition in terms of both sensor outputs and state variables, and the code which comprises the active behaviour. This is a

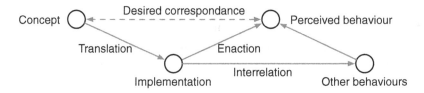

Fig. 4. Relationships between ideas, implementation and perception for the behavioural states of the robots

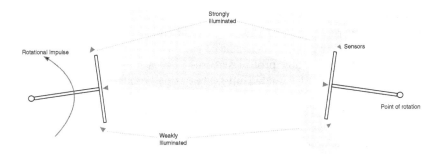

Fig. 5. Illustration of the way in which the robots experience and react to slightly off-axis alignment with others. For both robots, the brightest part of the beam intersects with the topmost sensor, so the intensity gradient increases towards the top of the diagram, giving a rotational impulse *away* from alignment rather than towards.

process of translation, of ideas into code (Fig. 4); the translation involves parameterisation, which is often a poorly constrained process in these situations. It is also a process of alignment with perception, correlating the performance of behaviours with human interpretation. Initial versions of the way in which 'sleeping' was performed presented as either too sparse, feeling more like malfunction or coma, or too active, loosing their tranquil, reflective aspect. Similarly, the transitions needed management: a robot going to sleep in the middle of an interaction with a human can leave them disappointed or frustrated.

There were conflicts here which needed to be resolved between our intentions as artists, and what came naturally to the flowers, avoiding doing violence to their autonomy. This is in contrast to other projects we have carried out, where there is some phenomenon or concept we wish to articulate using technological means, and development is fundamentally about making that elucidation as clear as possible. Here, we had to work within the needs and idiosyncrasies of the community we were creating, and acknowledge the gulf between clean conceptual ideas and their implementation in a messy, limited sphere.

Come Find Me - Search and Reaction. Once a reasonable set of behaviours were in place, we could concentrate our effort on one of the core ideas, that of the flowers managing to connect with each other and transmit information. Conceptually, this felt like it should be straightforward: as a human with a torch it was intuitive and easy to make a flower point in any direction, so they should be able to find each other. However, this showed up the differences between our *umwelt* and that of the flowers. We are situated in three dimensional space, with powerful sensory apparatuses, and can resolve the position of distant objects. The robots sensors are isotropic across a half sphere, so they do not resolve the source of light—they are only sensitive to how the beam intersects their sensors, not its origin (Fig. 5).

In order to understand this issue, we needed to imagine what it is like to be one of the robots [13], to try to internalise their nascent biosemantics. It became clear that there was not a clean, implementable analytic solution to the problem of two robots aligning themselves, and that some form of memory and negotiation was needed. In response, we built a modified, collaborative version of a simplex search [14] into the robots. If one thought it might be near to connecting with something, it would sweep out a cross pattern, recording light intensity. Depending on the maximum value, it would adjust the cross to grow or shrink in either dimension[5]. It would then freeze in the centre of its cross for a random amount of time, and emit light in proportion to how much it was receiving. This allowed the objective function to be based on how much light was reaching the *other* robot, using collaboration to make up for limitations in the sensory apparatus, and pairs of flowers would gradually converge on each other's locations.

However, this caused a disconnect: the flowers could now find each other relatively well, but the motion they used to do so was inaccessible to humans. While it was visually reminiscent of mating dances and other codified animal behaviour, it was an abrupt difference to the smooth tracking motion, and more importantly, it was an activity which humans could not participate in due to their different capabilities. In the interests of interactivity, we settled for tweaking the existing behaviours, modifying the tracking algorithm to move less if it is close to a connection, and to allow the robots to be more promiscuous with their connections.

Presentation and Aesthetics. At this point the identities of the robots were well resolved: they could sometimes connect with each other, and had autonomous lives and interactions with or without human presence. In order to make a compelling installation, we then needed to adjust the parameterisation and setup of the robots to create the right feeling. In early tests, there was a lot of activity, fast movement and flashing, which felt at odds with the way the creatures wanted to be: it was a byproduct of moving from exploring with a group of two or three to suddenly having a larger society. In response, we looked for ways to balance out their activity, letting them sleep for longer, move more

---

[5] The modification to the general simplex algorithm is largely to cover the idea that moving to a new point to sample it is expensive, while actually evaluating the objective function is cheap.

slowly and pulse more gently. Given the time demands, we did this by adjusting parameter settings; a more sensitive technique would be to give the robots control of their own activity levels, so they could respond to a changing societal context.

In the end, we found a range of interactions between the robots, some of which were intentional, some which were emergent, and most of which were accessible to people we tested them with. This included:

Wake up: the beam of one flower grazes the sensors of another and wakes it up, but the connection is lost before anything further can develop.

Brushing: one flower grazes another, and there is a weak connection, where their movements align briefly, a small moment of choreography, which then dissipates.

Negotiating: two flowers find each other and interact for a period of time, circling around alignment. However, they are not able to settle, lock and satify each other, and their attention is taken either down into sleep, or out to another source of light.

Connecting: two flowers find each other and start negotiating, then go further and actually manage to settle and lock with one another, flashing sequences of light at each other.

Repetition: a group of flowers become enmeshed in a cycle of incomplete connections, passing animus back and forth, with one missed connection brushing another flower into life. Conversational groupings emerge, with similar motions and negotiation, and occasional moments of connection.

This range felt appropriate: there was richness, and emergence, but an observer could parse the choreography, make sense of the links, and interfere at will.

3.5   Actors and Networks

It would be helpful in this situation to have a framework for looking at the competing demands of the various entities engaged in this process. Minimally, this means the robots, their creators and any visitors, but this can extend to the gallery and funding agencies which permit the creation and exhibition of the work.

Latour included non-human actors within Actor Network Theory, starting with the anthrax bacterium [15]. This allowed an analysis of the power relationships between various people and the bacterium. This is also evident in Callon's analysis of the networks between scientists, fishermen and the scallops which they fish. As well as giving a framework for considering the different needs and characteristics of the actor groups, this view looks at *interessement*, the means by which the various actors are enrolled to perform within the network: "... physical violence (against the predators), seduction, transaction, consent without discussion" [11]. Within this setup, we find several devices of *interessement*.

Multiple aspects of the space and context conspire in the *interessment* of the robots. Their consent to be present is assumed without discussion, as they are disassembled, shipped and re-assembled in situ. By their positioning, they are seduced into engaging with others, fulfilling their societal roles, and by the addition of torches they can be seduced into interacting with human visitors. Physical structures are used to keep the visitors from damaging the flowers, maintaining the flowers' survival, their ability to act and to enroll in their society.

Similarly, the architecture of gallery and exhibition spaces is set up to enroll people to perform as visitors. In this, additionally, having a curtain to pass through and a disconnected space further lock visitors into their roles. The picking up and using of a torch further *interesses* visitors into the cyber-society, setting up the context for their interaction with the robots.

Finally at all points, there is the negotiation around: does power move towards the creators, altering the creatures without consent towards an imagined ideal? does power move towards the visitors, subjugating the behaviour and conceptual underpinnings of the creatures to provide an engaging or entertaining experience? or does power flow towards the creatures, pushing their creators and visitors to align themselves with the creatures modes of being?

4   Conclusion

In this paper, we have looked at the development of a biologically inspired robot swarm. We have taken a viewpoint which touchs on:

- The gulf between clean, presentable specifications of desired behaviour and the implementations which allow a rich, emergent set of responses.
- How the biosemantics of the lifeforms under development may be non-intuitive, and hence the need for a translational imagining of their experience as part of their development.
- The need, when creating artificial life, to carry out a continual negotiation between the needs of the nascent lifeforms, their creators and imagined or actual visitors. In particular, the manner in which the creators engage in a duet with creatures which do not yet exist, in order to allow their identity to emerge.

As a potential framework for dealing with these tensions, we have sketched some of the compontents of an Actor Network Theory approach to analysing the situtation, which provides insight into the devices used to engage people and robots in the interactions, and a model for understanding their competing needs.

Acknowledgments. This work is supported under SOCIAM: The Theory and Practice of Social Machines, a programme funded by the UK Engineering and Physical Sciences Research Council (EPSRC) under grant number EP/J017728/1, and a collaboration between the Universities of Edinburgh, Oxford, and Southampton.

References

1. Blackwell, T.: Swarm music: improvised music with multi-swarms. In: 2003 AISB symposium on AI and Creativity in Arts and Science, pp. 41–49 (2003)

2. Miranda, E.R.: On the evolution of music in a society of self-taught digital creatures. Digital Creativity **14**(1), 29–42 (2003)
3. Fong, T., Nourbakhsh, I., Dautenhahn, K.: A survey of socially interactive robots. Rob. Autonom. Syst. **42**(3), 143–166 (2003)
4. Barlow, G.W.: Modal action patterns. In: Sebeok, T.A. (ed.) How Animals Communicate, pp. 98–136. Indiana University Press, Bloomington (1977)
5. Maslow, A.H.: A theory of human motivation. Psychol. Rev. **50**(4), 370–396 (1943)
6. Brooks, R.A.: A robust layered control system for a mobile robot. Rob. Autom. **2**(1), 14–23 (1986)
7. Moffat, D., Frijda, N.H.: Where there's a will there's an agent. In: Wooldridge, M.J., Jennings, N.R. (eds.) ECAI-94. LNCS, vol. 890, pp. 245–260. Springer, Heidelberg (1995)
8. Merrick, K.E., Maher, M.L.: Towards the future. In: Merrick, K.E., Maher, M.L. (eds.) Motivated Reinforcement Learning, pp. 193–199. Springer, Heidelberg (2009)
9. Von Uexküll, J.: A Foray into the Worlds of Animals and Humans. University of Minnesota Press (2010)
10. Ingold, T.: The Perception of the Environment: Essays on Livelyhood, Dwelling and Skill. Routledge, London (2000)
11. Callon, M.: Some elements of a sociology of translation: domestication of the scallops and the fishermen of St Brieuc Bay. In: Law, J. (ed.) Power, Action, and Belief: A New Sociology of Knowledge?, pp. 196–223. Routledge & Kegan, London (1986)
12. Anderson, P.W.: More is different. Science **177**(4047), 393–396 (1972)
13. Nagel, T.: What is it like to be a bat? Philos. Rev. **83**, 435–450 (1974)
14. Nelder, J.A., Mead, R.: A simplex method for function minimization. Comput. J. **7**(4), 308–313 (1965)
15. Latour, B.: Give me a laboratory and I will raise the world. In: Biagioli, M. (ed.) The Science Studies Reader, pp. 258–275. Routledge, New York (1999)

Automatic Generation of Chord Progressions with an Artificial Immune System

María Navarro[1(✉)], Marcelo Caetano[3], Gilberto Bernardes[3],
Leandro Nunes de Castro[2], and Juan Manuel Corchado[1]

[1] Department of Computer Science, University of Salamanca,
Plaza de la Merced S/n, 37008 Salamanca, Spain
{maria90,corchado}@usal.es
[2] Natural Computing Laboratory, Graduate Program in Computing and Electrical
Engineering, Mackenzie Presbyterian University, São Paulo, SP, Brazil
lnunes@mackenzie.br
[3] INESC Porto, Rua Doutor Roberto Frias 378, 4200-465 Porto, Portugal
{mcaetano,gba}@inesctec.pt

Abstract. Chord progressions are widely used in music. The automatic generation of chord progressions can be challenging because it depends on many factors, such as the musical context, personal preference, and aesthetic choices. In this work, we propose a penalty function that encodes musical rules to automatically generate chord progressions. Then we use an artificial immune system (AIS) to minimize the penalty function when proposing candidates for the next chord in a sequence. The AIS is capable of finding multiple optima in parallel, resulting in several different chords as appropriate candidates. We performed a listening test to evaluate the chords subjectively and validate the penalty function. We found that chords with a low penalty value were considered better candidates than chords with higher penalty values.

Keywords: Artificial immune systems · Chord progressions · Harmony · Consonance

1 Introduction

Harmony plays a central role in Western tonal music. Simply put, harmony refers to the simultaneity of pitch (i.e., chords) and their progressions, known as chord progressions. Chord construction and chord progression are governed by implicit and explicit principles which are central in the study of harmony. Schönberg [1], Lerdahl [2], Riemann [3], and Schenker [4], among many others, have discussed these principles extensively and proposed rules to create optimal chord progressions according to the principles considered.

In music composition, creating chord progressions commonly requires knowledge usually acquired after years of music training. Not surprisingly, chord progressions have been a central topic in algorithmic composition given the challenging aspect of encoding the principles to generate a desired result. There have

© Springer International Publishing Switzerland 2015
C. Johnson et al. (Eds.): EvoMUSART 2015, LNCS 9027, pp. 175–186, 2015.
DOI: 10.1007/978-3-319-16498-4_16

been several proposals to automatically generate chord progressions following different paradigms [5], including grammars, learning, biological principles, and rules (*a priori* knowledge). CHORAL [6] is a system that harmonizes chorales in the style of Johann Sebastian Bach. The system is based on grammars and contains about 350 rules representing musical knowledge from multiple viewpoints of the chorale, such as the chord skeleton, the melodic lines of the individual parts, and Schenkerian voice leading. Steedman [7] presents a small number of rules to generate chord sequences using generative grammars. Eigenfeldt [8] proposes the generation of harmonic progressions by learning using case-based analysis of an existing material and employing a variable-order Markov model. Moroni [9] has developed a system called Vox Populi, based on evolutionary computation techniques for interactive algorithmic composition. In Vox Populi, a population of chords evolves through the application of a genetic algorithm to maximize a fitness criterion based on musically relevant factors. Anders [10] developed a computational model that creates chord progression following the rules that Schönberg proposed in his harmony treatise [1]. Paiement [11] adopts a probabilistic approach to model chord progressions. Fukumoto [12] generates chord progressions suited for user's feeling by using genetic algorithms.

In this work, we describe a method to automatically generate chord progressions with an artificial immune system (AIS). We propose a penalty function that encodes rules about chord construction as vertical constraints and chord progression as horizontal constraints. Then we use an AIS to find chords that minimize the penalty function and propose the next chord in a sequence as a minimum-penalty chord given the sequence as input. The AIS used is opt-aiNet [13], an algorithm inspired by the immune network theory for function optimization. Opt-aiNet is capable of finding multiple optima in parallel upon convergence, resulting in several chords as candidates for the next in the sequence. Thus we performed a listening test to evaluate the candidate chords and validate the penalty function.

In the next section, we describe how the penalty function encodes the rules we use to automatically generate chord progressions as vertical and horizontal constraints. Section 4 explains how to encode the chords and the constraints, followed by how to find minima of the penalty function with the AIS. The last section shows some results of the system, a discussion about evaluation of these new chords, chord progressions obtained and future work proposed.

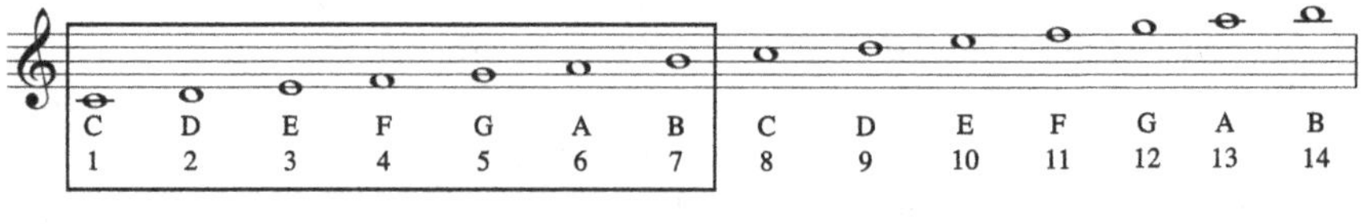

Fig. 1. Encoding diatonic scales. The figure shows the musical notation for the notes with letter names and the corresponding codification in the algorithm below each note. The C major scale is highlighted in the image.

2   Representing Individual Chords and Progressions

The aim of this work is to generate chord progressions as sequences of three-note chords. Each chord X is represented as a vector with three integers $X = \begin{bmatrix} x_1 \\ x_2 \\ x_3 \end{bmatrix}$, where $[x_1, x_2, x_3]$ define each note in the chord. Figure 1 shows the two octaves of the diatonic (C major) scale used to construct the chords, where each note is encoded as an integer. For example, C major gives $X_n = \begin{bmatrix} 1 \\ 3 \\ 5 \end{bmatrix}$. Notice that the system can easily work with any other major or minor scale by simply adapting the representation. A sequence of chords is thus represented as $[X_1, X_2, \ldots, X_n]$, where the subscript is the position in the sequence and n is the current position.

3   Evaluating Chord Progressions with a Penalty Function

The aim of the penalty function P is to automatically evaluate a chord X_n given a sequence of p previous chords $[X_{n-1}, X_{n-2}, \ldots, X_{n-p}]$. For $p = 3$, the penalty function becomes $P(X_n / X_{n-1}, X_{n-2})$, interpreted as penalty of chord X_n following $[X_{n-1}, X_{n-2}]$. The penalty function $P(X_n / X_{n-1}, X_{n-2})$ shown in Eq. (1) encodes rules about chord construction as vertical constraints $V(X_n)$ and chord progression as horizontal constraints $H(X_n / X_{n-1}, X_{n-2})$. In turn, $V(X_n)$ and $H(X_n / X_{n-1}, X_{n-2})$ penalize chords by adding a different penalty value depending on the rules encoded. The final value of $P(X_n / X_{n-1}, X_{n-2})$ is the sum of all penalties and thus represents how appropriate chord X_n is as a candidate to follow $[X_{n-1}, X_{n-2}]$. As such, the aim is to find chords that minimize the penalty function $P(X, Y)$. Next we explain the vertical and horizontal constraints and how to assign penalties to chords using $V(X_n)$ and $H(X_n / X_{n-1}, X_{n-2})$.

$$P(X_n / X_{n-1}, X_{n-2}) = V(X_n) + H(X_n / X_{n-1}, X_{n-2}) \qquad (1)$$

3.1   Vertical Constraints

The vertical constraints $V(X_n)$ are related to chord construction, so they only are applied to notes that belong to the candidate chord X_n. The aim of the vertical constraints is to minimize both chord dissonance and balance the distance between the notes in the chord. The measure of consonance is based on the Pythagorean [14] theory, which orders complementary intervals as listed below.

1. Unison and octave
2. Perfect fourth and perfect fifth
3. Major third and minor sixth
4. Minor third and major sixth
5. Minor second and major seventh
6. Augmented fourth and diminished fifth.

   The vertical constraints are the following:

- V1: Maximize chord consonance
- V2: Favor triad chords to reinforce progression consonance.

3.2 Enconding the Vertical Constraints in $V(X_n)$

$V(X_n)$ encodes the vertical constraints (See Eq. 2). This function consists of two parts, $V_1(X_n)$ encodes rule V1 and $V_2(X_n)$ encodes rule V2.

$$V(X_n) = V_1(X_n) + V_2(X_n) \tag{2}$$

$V_1(X_n)$ measures the level of consonance of each chord as

$$V_1(X) = ln \left[\sum_{i=2}^{N} k\left[d\left(x_1, x_i\right)\right] \right] \tag{3}$$

where, N is the number of notes in the present chord (in this case $N = 3$, x_1 is the first note in the present chord, x_i is the i-note in the present chord, $d(x_1, x_i)$ is the distance between first and i-note of the chord in half-steps, and $k[d(x_1, x_i)]$ is the dissonance between x_1 and x_2 as proposed by Euler [15] to evaluate the consonance of intervals using Pythagoras theory. The distance k takes the product of the numerator and denominator of the rates shown in Table 1.

Table 1. Table showing dissonances between n1 and n2

$d(x_1 - x_j)$	1	2	3	4	5	6	7	8	9	10	11	12
Interval	m2	M2	m3	M3	P4	dim5	P5	m6	M6	m7	M7	P8
Pythagorean Ratio	$\frac{16}{15}$	$\frac{9}{8}$	$\frac{6}{5}$	$\frac{5}{4}$	$\frac{4}{3}$	$\frac{7}{5}$	$\frac{3}{2}$	$\frac{8}{5}$	$\frac{5}{3}$	$\frac{7}{4}$	$\frac{15}{8}$	$\frac{2}{1}$
$k[d(x_1, x_i)]$	240	72	30	20	12	35	6	40	15	28	120	2

As an example, we consider the chord of C major $X = \begin{bmatrix} 1 \\ 3 \\ 5 \end{bmatrix}$. The intervals considered are always the intervals obtained from the fundamental to the rest of the notes. In this case, the consonance measure is calculated as follows in the Eq. 4.

$$V_1(X) = ln(k(d(x_1 - x_2)) + k(d(x_1 - x_3))) = ln(k(d(1 - 3)) + k(d(1 - 5))) =$$
$$= ln(k(d(2)) + k(d(4))) = ln(k(4) + k(7)) = ln(20 + 6) = ln(26) = 3.26 \tag{4}$$

Likewise, $V_2(X_n)$ checks if the chord is part of a triad-chord (three-note chords) family [1]. $TRIAD\_SET$ is a set with the triad chords in major mode, where n is the number of elements of X_n contained in $TRIAD\_SET$.

$$V_2(X) = 2 * n(X \subseteq TRIAD\_SET) \tag{5}$$

For example, $V_2\left(\begin{bmatrix} 1 \\ 3 \\ 5 \end{bmatrix}\right) = 0$ because C major belongs to the triad-chord.

3.3   Horizontal Constraints

The horizontal constraints are related to chord progressions, so they compare the candidate chord X_n with previous chords $[X_{n-1}, X_{n-2}]$ taking into account functional (tonal) harmony and voice leading. Following the works of Schönberg [1] and Riemann [3], we considered the following horizontal constraints.

- H1: Reward pre-determined harmonic progression
- H2: Avoid chord repetition
- H3: Avoid constant use of *superstrong* progression
- H4: Minimize distance between voices
- H5: Resolve leading-note
- H6: Avoid parallel fifths and octaves.

H1, H2 and H3 are related to harmonic functions or the role a chord has within the context of a specific key. In the context of this work, we reward pre-determined harmonic progressions based on the functional theory of Riemann [3]. Figure 2 illustrates the harmonic progressions according to Riemann's functional harmony. Thus the rules we adopt reward the progression Tonic-Subdominant-Dominant-Tonic (H1) and penalize the repetition of the same chord (H2). Finally, H3 was inspired by Schönberg's [1] harmonic treatise.

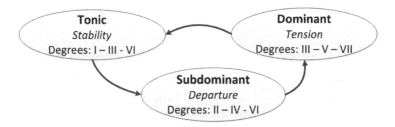

Fig. 2. Shows the relationship between the three main harmonic functions in a tonality. Each ellipse gives information about the name and the meaning of each function. Additionally the degrees corresponding to each function are shown. It is noteworthy that some chords have different function depending on its previous chord in the progression

H4, H5, and H6 are related to voice leading, namely, the horizontal progression of the individual voices. In this work, the voices are the notes in the chord. The guiding principle aims to minimize the distance between consecutive voices (H4). We further stress the importance of resolving the leading tone in H5 and avoiding parallel fifths and octaves in H5. The leading-note creates a temporary instability that requires melodic resolution to a stable tone [16]. For example, in C major, the seventh scale degree (B) has a strong melodic tendency towards the first degree (C) [17]. We chose to additionally penalize parallel fifths and octaves because, according to traditional Western musical practice, they result in weak relative motion between chords.

3.4   Encoding the Horizontal Constraints in $H\left(X_n/X_{n-1}, X_{n-2}\right)$

Equation (6) shows that $H\left(X_n/X_{n-1}, X_{n-2}\right)$ encodes the horizontal constraints in six terms, each corresponding to one Rule H.

$$H\left(X_n/X_{n-1}, X_{n-2}\right) = H_1\left(X_n/X_{n-1}, X_{n-2}\right) + H_2\left(X_n/X_{n-1}, X_{n-2}\right) + \\ + H_3\left(X_n/X_{n-1}\right) + H_4\left(X_n/X_{n-1}\right) + H_5\left(X_n/X_{n-1}\right) + H_6\left(X_n/X_{n-1}\right) \tag{6}$$

Notice that H_1 and H_2 depend on both X_{n-1}, X_{n-2} whereas the others depend only on X_{n-1}. $H_1\left(X_n/X_{n-1}, X_{n-2}\right)$ measures how the progression is adapted to a harmonic function structure predefined. In this case, we need X_{n-1} and X_{n-2}, the two last chords of the sequence given as the input. We are trying to follow the structure: Tonic-Subdominant-Dominant-Tonic. The weights proposed are shown in the Table 2.

Table 2. Table showing the values of $H_1\left(X_n/X_{n-1}, X_{n-2}\right)$. First Row reflects the function of the previous chord, whereas first column represents the function of the evaluating chord X_n.

	Tonic	Subdominant	Dominant
Tonic	2	0	5
Subdominant	5	2	0
Dominant	0	5	2

In that case, if we consider an input of $X_{n-1} = \begin{bmatrix} 1 \\ 3 \\ 5 \end{bmatrix}$ (tonic) and the system proposes the chord $X_n = \begin{bmatrix} 2 \\ 4 \\ 6 \end{bmatrix}$ (subdominant), this chord obtains a punctuation of 0 points, because tonic must be followed by a subdominant chord.

We consider that a chord repetition deserves a penalization of 2 points for each consecutive repetition of the chord along the time, as we can see in Eq. 7. In particular, only the last two chords of the progression are considered to apply Eq. 7.

$$H_2\left(X_n/X_{n-1}, X_{n-2}\right) = 2 \quad \text{if } X = Y \\ H_2\left(X_n/X_{n-1}, X_{n-2}\right) = 0 \quad \text{otherwise} \tag{7}$$

In the previous sample, the input $X_{n-1} = \begin{bmatrix} 1 \\ 3 \\ 5 \end{bmatrix}$ followed by the same chord $X_n = \begin{bmatrix} 1 \\ 3 \\ 5 \end{bmatrix}$ is penalised with two points.

Inspired by Schönberg treatise [1], the *superstrong* progression occurs when the root of the second chord is a second step up or down. This kind of progression is not frequently used, but this does not mean the progression should be avoided. For this reason, we punctuate the appearing of this progression with a half point (Eq. 8). X_n is the present chord and X_{n-1} is the last chord of the input progression.

$$H_3\left(X_n/X_{n-1}\right) = 0.5 \quad \text{if } X_n \cap X_{n-1} = \emptyset \\ H_3\left(X_n/X_{n-1}\right) = 0 \quad \text{otherwise} \tag{8}$$

In the study case, considering input $X_{n-1} = \begin{bmatrix} 1 \\ 3 \\ 5 \end{bmatrix}$, a superstrong cadence appears if the next chord has not any common notes with it, i.e., $X_n = \begin{bmatrix} 2 \\ 4 \\ 6 \end{bmatrix}$.

$H_4\left(X_n/X_{n-1}\right)$ is the distance between the X_n array and the previous chord X_{n-1} in the progression. This is related to rule H4, and measures the "voice leading" of the progression.

We were looking for a way to penalize larger intervals against shorter intervals when comparing one chord option with another in the same input progression. For this reason, we used an exponential function. In order to smooth the value obtained, a logarithmic function was added, as we can see in Eq. (9).

$$H_4\left(X_n/X_{n-1}\right) = \ln\left(\sum_{i=1}^{p} 4^{\left|\left(x_{ij}-x_{i(j-1)}\right)\right|} \right) \tag{9}$$

where i refers to the note of a given chord, j refers the element of the chord sequence, and p is the maximum number of voices (in this particular case, $p = 3$).

In the sample given, the input $X_{n-1} = \begin{bmatrix} 1 \\ 3 \\ 5 \end{bmatrix}$ followed by $X_n = \begin{bmatrix} 2 \\ 4 \\ 6 \end{bmatrix}$ has the following distance measure:

$$\begin{aligned} H_4(X_n/X_{n-1}) &= \ln(4^{|x_{12}-x_{11}|} + 4^{|x_{22}-y_{21}|} + 4^{|x_{32}-y_{31}|} = \\ \ln(4^{|1-2|} &+ 4^{|3-4|} + 4^{|5-6|}) = \ln(4+4+4) = \ln(12) \end{aligned} \tag{10}$$

$H_5\left(X_n/X_{n-1}\right)$ is a melody penalty that considers the parallel fifths and octaves (rule H5). If a parallel fifth or octave appears, we weighted this rule with a 3 (See Eq. (11)).

$$\begin{aligned} H_5\left(X_n/X_{n-1}\right) = 3 \quad &\text{if } |x_{ij} - x_{(i-1)j}| + 1 = 5 \wedge |x_{(i(j-1)} - x_{(i-1)(j-1)}| + 1 = 5 \\ H_5\left(X_n/X_{n-1}\right) = 3 \quad &\text{if } |x_{ij} - x_{(i-1)(j-1)}| + 1 = 8 \wedge |x_{(i(j-1)} - y_{(i-1)(j-1)}| + 1 = 8 \\ H_5\left(X_n/X_{n-1}\right) = 0 \quad &\text{otherwise} \end{aligned} \tag{11}$$

Between $X_{n-1} = \begin{bmatrix} 1 \\ 3 \\ 5 \end{bmatrix}$ and $X_n = \begin{bmatrix} 2 \\ 4 \\ 6 \end{bmatrix}$ exists a parallel fifth, because $|x_{32}-x_{22}| + 1 = |1-5|+1 = 4+1 = 5$ and $x_{31} - x_{21} + 1 = |2-6|+1 = 4+1 = 5$. For this reason, the last chord obtains a score of 3 points.

Finally, the last element in Eq. (6), $H_6\left(X_n/X_{n-1}\right)$, is a melody penalty that takes into account the leading-tone resolution (H6). If the leading-note resolution rule is not accomplished, the penalty is of 2.5. (See Eq. (12)).

$$\begin{aligned} H_6\left(X_n/X_{n-1}\right) = 2.5 \quad &\text{if } hf\left(X_n\right) = Tonic \wedge x_{(i(j-1)} = 7 \wedge x_{ij} \neq 8 \\ H_6\left(X_n/X_{n-1}\right) = 0 \quad &\text{otherwise} \end{aligned} \tag{12}$$

where x_{ij} represents the i-note of the j-chord in the sequence X. $hf\left(X_n\right)$ calculates the harmonic function that the chord X_n represents in the moment j. $hf\left(X\right)$ can take three values: *Tonic*, *Subdominant* and *Dominant*.

It is important to remark that each weight proposed in functions H_5 and H_6 has been obtained empirically.

4   Chord Progressions as Minima of the Penalty Function

Given a sequence of two previous chords as reference, it is possible to associate a penalty value to any three-note chord representable by a vector of three integers between 1 and 16. For instance, the chord $X_n = \begin{bmatrix} 1 \\ 3 \\ 5 \end{bmatrix}$ preceded by $X_{n-1} \begin{bmatrix} 2 & 1 \\ 3 & 5 \\ 7 & 8 \end{bmatrix}$ has a penalty of 12.79. Thus $P(X_n/X_{n-1})$ can be used to propose the next chord in a sequence using the penalty value as measure. According to the vertical and horizontal constraints encoded in the penalty function, chords with low penalty values should be better candidates to follow a given sequence of two chords than chords with higher penalty values. Thus the problem of automatically proposing the next chord in a given chord sequence $[X, X_1, \ldots, X_n]$ becomes simply finding the chords that correspond to the minima of the penalty function with $[X, X_1, \ldots, X_n]$ as input. The method can be iteratively applied to add a new chord to the sequence at each iteration, such that the automatic generation of chord progressions becomes the search for the minima of the penalty function.

Finding chords with low penalty values can be a difficult problem. An exhaustive (or brute-force) search would require testing every possible three-note chord representable to determine which has the lowest penalty value. Thus we use an optimization method to search for a minimum of the penalty function at each iteration. Similarly to the approach adopted in Vox Populi [9], the generation of chord progressions can be considered as a search problem in which the constraints must be followed so as to explore the conceptual space of possible solutions. However, the penalty function can potentially have several minima, each corresponding to a different chord. These minima will have different penalty values associated, such that the global minimum of the penalty function might not be the best candidate in a particular musical context. Therefore, we use opt-Ainet [18] to minimize the penalty function due to its ability to find several minima in parallel.

This algorithm, inspired in natural immune systems [19], assumes a randomly initialized set of immune cells or antibodies (in our particular case, each antibody is a three-note chord) in the network. Their affinity is determined using a distance metric, in this case, the penalty function. Some high affinity antibodies are selected and reproduced based on their affinity: the higher the affinity, the higher the number of clones and vice-versa. The clones generated suffer a mutation inversely proportional to their affinity. Those antibodies whose affinity is less than a given threshold are eliminated from the network. Finally, a number of newly generated antibodies are incorporated into the network.

As an example, we created a short sequence of two chords in C major as input, and we had the AIS generate multiple options for the third chord in the sequence. The input chords sequence is [1 3 5]([60 64 67] in MIDI mode). After convergence, 42 chords were presented as candidates to follow the input sequence. Each of these chords corresponds to a minimum of the penalty function, but they all have different penalty values associated. In our implementation, we have observed that the AIS typically results in over 30 chords with penalty values ranging from 8 to 22. It is impractical to listen to so many chords every time we want to add a new chord to a given sequence. Thus we decided to investigate if the penalty values can be used to further inform us about the quality of the chords to follow the sequence.

5 Evaluation

We conducted a preliminary study into the relationship between the penalty function and the subjective evaluation of chords in a sequence. The evaluation aims to investigate if chords with low penalty values are judged more appropriate to follow a given chord sequence than chords with higher penalty values.

We created a short sequence of two chords in C major as input, and we had the AIS to generate multiple options for the third chord in the sequence. The input chords sequence is [60 64 67, 62 67 71] After convergence, 35 chords were presented as candidates to follow the input sequence, with penalty values ranging from 8.32 to 22.26. We ranked the chords by penalty values and selected 17 chords to represent the whole range of values between the minimum and the maximum. We asked participants to listen to the three-chord progressions and evaluate how well the third chord follows the first and second using the following scale: very good (1 point), good (0.75 points), fair (0.5 points), bad (0.25 points), or very bad (0 points). The listening test can be found here: http://goo.gl/forms/flTb4PbZY6.

We expected chords with low penalty values to be considered better candidates to follow the input sequence than chords with higher penalty values. In total, 24 people took the test, among which 8 declared no musical training, 7 considered themselves amateurs, and 9 professional musicians. In Fig. 3 we see the subjective evaluation as a function of the penalty value for each third chord that they listened.

The aim of the evaluation is twofold, we would like to validate the penalty function and investigate if there is a threshold value that can be used as decision boundary for chord quality. The validation of the penalty function involves investigating whether chords with low penalty are considered better candidates to follow a given sequence than chords with higher penalty values. We also want to automatically determine the quality of a chord as candidate to follow a sequence. Ideally, we want to be able to use the penalty value as decision boundary. Thus chords with penalty value lower than a certain threshold would correspond to good candidates.

Figure 3 shows the result of the listening test as the subjective evaluation of the penalty function. In Fig. 3, we see the mean and standard deviation of the subjective rating for each candidate chord plotted against the corresponding penalty value. The horizontal lines labeled *very bad*, *bad*, *fair*, *good* and *very good* can be used as reference to interpret the figure. The chords with lower penalty value were indeed rated better chords with lower penalty values. Using the line labeled *fair* as decision boundary, we can associate penalty values lower than 0.5 with chords that were rated positively.

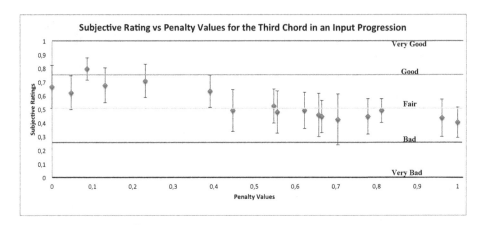

Fig. 3. It shows a plot of the subjective evaluation as a function of the penalty value. Each point (X, Y) represents the evaluation of the third chord created by the system, considering the chord progression given as the input. x is the penalty value normalized and y is the mean of the scores the listeners made. The standard deviation is shown for each point by using vertical bars. The lines labeled shows the rate corresponding to "very good","good","fair","bad" and "very bad" values in the listening test. As we can see, good values in the subjective test corresponds to good values in the penalty function.

6 Discussion

The main goal of the evaluation is to validate the penalty function proposed to to create a compositional aid application. The penalties associated with vertical and horizontal constraints are selected empirically, testing the system to balance all the rules. The penalty values seem to be inversely proportional to how well people judged the chords proposed by the AIS follow a given sequence. This indicates that we might be able to determine suitable chords using the penalty function. However, the threshold depends on the penalties associated with the constraints and changing these would probably change the threshold values.

More importantly, the listening test asked participants to evaluate how well a given chord proposed by the AIS follows two others in a sequence. This question does not specify whether to consider vertical or horizontal aspects. In other words, a chord proposed by the system might be rated *very good* because it is very pleasant independently of the two previous chords heard. Some participants reported using different criteria to rate how well the chords follow the sequence. This question seems important to pursue in future work.

7 Conclusions

In this work, we proposed a penalty function using rules about chord construction and chord progression. These constraints apply rules from tonal Western music and functional harmony as vertical and horizontal constraints. Then we apply an artificial immune system (AIS) to automatically generate the next chord in a sequence taking two previous chords as input. The AIS is capable of finding multiple optima in parallel, resulting in different chords as appropriate candidates.

We performed a listening test to evaluate the chords subjectively and validate the penalty function. We found that chords with a low penalty value were considered better candidates than chords with higher penalty values.

According to the results obtained, we can conclude it exists a threshold in the fitness function to divide the chords the system proposes. Chords obtained above this threshold value are considered as good chords that fit with the previous chord progression. On the contrary, chords below this value are not suitable to be the next chord in the given progression.

Future work can integrate the system into an application to assist users in composing chord progressions. In addition, we can develop a Markov Model to decide the harmonic function of the chord that we can propose, so that the system will be capable of automatically composing a chord progression given only one initial chord. It would also be good to improve chord codification into a MIDI encoding in order to enable the integration of several musical systems.

Acknowledgements. This work has been partially supported by the Spanish Government through the project iHAS (grant TIN2012-36586-C01/C02/C03), the Media Arts and Technologies project (MAT), NORTE-07-0124-FEDER-000061, financed by the North Portugal Regional Operational Programme (ON.2 ? O Novo Norte), under the National Strategic Reference Framework (NSRF), through the European Regional Development Fund (ERDF), and by national funds, through the Portuguese funding agency, Fundação para a Ciência e a Tecnologia (FCT), and the Mackenzie University, Mackpesquisa, CNPq, Capes (Proc. n. 9315/13-6) and FAPESP.

References

1. Schoenberg, S.: The Musical Idea and the Logic, Technique and Art of its Presentation. Indiana University Press, Bloomington (2006)
2. Lerdahl, F.: Tonal pitch space. Music Percept. **5**, 315–349 (1998)
3. Agmon, E.: Functional harmony revisited: a prototype-theoretic approach. Music Theory Spectrum **17**(2), 196–214 (1995)
4. Stock, J.: The application of schenkerian analysis to ethnomusicology: problems and possibilities. Music Anal. **12**, 215–240 (1993)
5. Papadopoulos, G., Wiggins, G.: AI methods for algorithmic composition: a survey, a critical view and future prospects. In: AISB Symposium on Musical Creativity, pp. 110–117 Edinburgh, UK (1999)
6. Ebciouglu, K.: An expert system for harmonizing chorales in the style of js bach. J. Log. Program. **8**(1), 145–185 (1990)
7. Steedman, M.J.: A generative grammar for jazz chord sequences. Music Percept. **2**(1), 52–77 (1984)
8. Eigenfeldt, A., Pasquier, P.: Realtime generation of harmonic progressions using controlled markov selection. In: Proceedings of 1st International Conference on Computational Creativity, pp. 16–25 (2010)

9. Moroni, A., Manzolli, J., Von Zuben, F., Gudwin, R.: Vox populi: an interactive evolutionary system for algorithmic music composition. Leonardo Music J. **10**, 49–54 (2000)

10. Anders, T., Miranda, E.R.: A computational model that generalises schoenberg's guidelines for favourable chord progressions. In: 6th Sound and Music Computing Conference, Porto, Portugal (2009)

11. Paiement, J.F., Eck, D., Bengio, S.: A probabilistic model for chord progressions. In: Proceedings of International Conference on Music Information Retrieval, pp. 312–319 (2005)

12. Fukumoto, M.: Creation of music chord progression suited for user's feelings based on interactive genetic algorithm. In: 2014 IIAI 3rd International Conference on Advanced Applied Informatics (IIAIAAI), pp. 757–762. IEEE (2014)

13. De Castro, L.N., Timmis, J.: Artificial Immune Systems: A New Computational Intelligence Approach. Springer, Heidelberg (2002)

14. Crocker, R.L.: Pythagorean mathematics and music. J. Aesthet. Art Crit. **22**, 325–335 (1964)

15. Knobloch, E.: Euler transgressing limits: the infinite and music theory. Quaderns d'història de l'enginyeria **9**, 9–24 (2008)

16. Babbitt, M.: The structure and function of musical theory: I. In: College Music Symposium, JSTOR 49–60 (1965)

17. Benward, B., Saker, M.: Music in Theory and Practice. McGraw-Hill, London (2003)

18. de Castro, L.N., Timmis, J.: An artificial immune network for multimodal function optimization. In: Proceedings of the 2002 Congress on Evolutionary Computation, CEC 2002, vol. 1, pp. 699–704. IEEE (2002)

19. Murphy, K.: Janeway's Immunobiology. Garland Science, New York (2011)

Evolving Diverse Design Populations Using Fitness Sharing and Random Forest Based Fitness Approximation

Kate Reed$^{(\boxtimes)}$ and Duncan F. Gillies

Department of Computing, Imperial College London,
South Kensington, London SW7 2AZ, UK
k.reed12@imperial.ac.uk

Abstract. A large, diverse design space will contain many non-viable designs. To locate the viable designs we need to have a method of testing the designs and a way to navigate the space. We have shown that using machine learning on artificial data can accurately predict the viability of chairs based on a range of ergonomic considerations. We have also shown that the design space can be explored using an evolutionary algorithm with the predicted viability as a fitness function. We find that this method in conjunction with a fitness sharing technique can maintain a diverse population with many potential viable designs.

Keywords: Chair design · Generative design · Fitness sharing · Multi-model evolutionary algorithms

1 Introduction

In the field of creative design, function is at least as important as aesthetics. If we wish to study the aesthetics of an object we must also consider the function, as placing hard constraints on the design space to ensure a functional product can inadvertently rule out novel functional designs. A designer can explore these areas, drawing on previous experience of functions as a designer and user. Machine learning can be used to find similar conditional constraints based on a dataset of good and bad designs [1]. We propose to use a simulation of the ergonomics of a chair to categorise potential designs, as it will be able to generate the large amounts of data we need for machine learning. We use a chair as a case study as chairs have a wide range of styles but a relatively simple function.

Once we can estimate how a design will function we can generate new designs for a specific brief. To do this we will use an evolutionary algorithm with a fitness function based on our learned estimates. We wish to evolve a wide range of styles, therefore we will use fitness sharing to maintain the diversity of the population. We will also use the knowledge of significant parameters learned from the simulation to help guide the evolution.

© Springer International Publishing Switzerland 2015
C. Johnson et al. (Eds.): EvoMUSART 2015, LNCS 9027, pp. 187–199, 2015.
DOI: 10.1007/978-3-319-16498-4_17

1.1   Maintaining Diversity in Evolutionary Design

Using automated measures can result in loss of diversity [2]. This is caused by the optimization aspect of evolutionary design - we are aiming for the design with the highest score. However in many aspects of creative design the concept of 'best' is difficult to define; it may depend on personal preference for example. In these cases it is beneficial to find a range of solutions that fit the brief, which can then be assessed manually. The benefits of multimodal search is not just limited to areas with subjective assessments; having a range of possible solutions is also beneficial in cases where there may be unexpected reasons why the best solution is no longer viable, such as planning a spacecraft launch [3].

Despite their apparent drawbacks, evolutionary algorithms are actually well suited to the task of finding diverse populations as they are capable of developing many designs in parallel [4]. Within evolutionary computing a wide number of methods have been developed. A good overview of these can be found in [5]. Although many of these are designed to provide high diversity early in the evolutionary process to prevent convergence to local minima, many can also be used to maintain diverse populations in the later stages.

Previous work has also explored ways of creating large diverse sets of 3D designs both with [6] and without [7] an evolutionary component. These both use sets of existing models to synthesise new designs. Xu et al. [6] (designing lamps and chairs among others) have two components to their fitness function, automatically assigned viability and a manually assigned user preference component. They also use a diversity control method where original designs that are suitably different from the current population are reintroduced in later stages of the evolution.

1.2   Learning Automated Measures

When evolving 3D products our options for evaluating fitness are limited. Although the rapid development of 3D printing technologies could eventually make physical testing of the evolving products a viable part of the process [8], this is not currently possible with large complex products such as chairs. Here we must rely on simulation to test the designs. However simulation comes with its own set of drawbacks such as large calculation times. One solution to this is to learn a fitness measure, using either real or simulated data [9]. Thus a design space can be mapped once and used repeatedly. This is particularly advantageous if we wish to run the algorithm multiple times.

We propose to test the physical properties of chairs by simulating a user sitting. We can then test properties of the simulation to gather information about the ergonomics of the design. Dabbeeru and Mukerjee [1] describe a similar method of mapping a design space using machine learning. Their design space (of a padlock design) has 2 variables and they reduce this based on the strength and clearance of the bolt. They showed that it was possible to learn viable subspaces of the design space in this way and we take their simple model as evidence that our more complex, discontinuous space may be viable. In the creative domain similar methods have been used to learn design spaces in areas such as music [10] and door handle design [11].

2   Background Work

2.1   Chairmaker

To study chair forms a generator was built in SketchUp [12] that could create possible designs parametrically. The parametric structure can create a wide variety of original chairs and also allows us to see the effect of changing individual parameters. A chair is constructed by positioning a number of cross–sections. These are then lofted together and finished with a texture. Some of the parameters control the proportions such as heights and widths (by changing the size and position of the cross–sections); these are continuous. Others select the cross–sections and textures from a predefined set; these are discrete. In total there are 38 parameters.

A set of 3 handmade (i.e. choosing the parameters manually, based on famous designs) and 5 random chairs generated by the chairmaker is shown in Fig. 1. As we see, the design space for the chairmaker is very large and contains both good and bad designs. We hypothesise that many of the designs that look bad to our eyes appear this way as they are perceived to be uncomfortable or unstable. Before we can consider the aesthetics of the chairs we must remove the non-viable designs so the reviewers are not distracted by the physical problems.

By looking at the designs we observe some reasons for their issues. For example we see that there is a chair (far right) with a small but highly curved seat that is not suitable to sit on. We can make this seat viable by either flattening the seat or increasing the width. As we wish our design space to contain both narrow flat seats and wide curved seat we must find a way to remove the narrow curved seat without affecting these.

2.2   Ergonomic Measure

As we needed a large quantity of samples (both good and bad) to learn the function space, we decided that the best way to gather this data was to build a simulation of a user. Analysing real chairs would have taken much longer and would have only given us examples of viable chairs. There are existing ergonomic models available but they did not suit our purpose as we needed to collect large amounts of general data automatically from randomly generated designs and the existing models are designed to collect very precise data from a small number of designs. The following simulator was build in Matlab [13].

Fig. 1. 3 handmade (left) and 5 randomly generated (right) chairs

We test each chair with a set of users with a range of different body sizes. These simplified human body models were built using proportion data from DINED [14], an anthropometric database from TU Delft, and body mass data from [15]. Examples of the seated users are shown in Fig. 2. We also build a simplified chair model which uses 25 of the 38 parameters. The missing parameters are those that control the leg style and will have little or no impact on the user.

The simulation first positions the user in the chair. The user sits at the back of the chair (not perching on the front). The legs are then positioned so that the height of the centre of mass of the leg is minimised. In the case of the seat being too long this causes the user to raise their knees to bend their leg. The back and neck are placed to minimise the effort required to stay in that position. If the back provides little support this results in the user sitting up, slouching slightly. If the back offers support for the shoulders then the user leans back into the seat but keeps their head vertical. If the slope of the back is too great for them to support their head they resume the slouched position. Finally if the back offers enough support for the head, the user sits against the back at any angle. We give examples of this movement in Fig. 2.

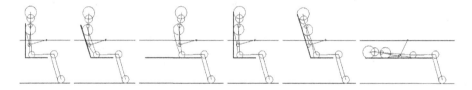

Fig. 2. Example of the movement of the skeleton as the back changes length and angle

Once the user is seated we can estimate the peak pressure of seat and back of the chair by finding the angles between the chair surface and a simplified body shape (e.g. a truncated cone for a leg). The pressure in each 1 mm square is then found using $f_0 sin^2(\theta)$ [16], where θ is the angle of contact and f_0 is the force normalised so that the sum of the squares add to the full force.

If the feet are resting on the floor then the mass of the lower legs is not used, likewise if the user is leaning against the back some of the torso and head weight is applied to the back instead of the seat. The highest value of the 1 mm square pressure points is taken as the peak pressure. To provide extra accuracy for the pressure map we focus the pressure under the hip bones. We do this by adding a second layer, so we transfer the weight of the upper body from the spherical hip bone to the leg surface before finding the pressure between the leg and seat. This method is very different from the usual method of finite element analysis (an early example being [17] with a good overview in [18]) but it gives a good approximation of the range and distribution of pressure found experimentally. It is less detailed than found by finite element analysis but much faster and therefore ideal for our purpose.

We find 10 physical measures of 10 traits from the seated user. These are given in Table 1. The first 3 measure how close the user is to the ideal working

Table 1. Physical Measures used in Fitness Function

No	Description of measure	Type
0	Angle of elbow and shoulder away from ideal	Practicality
1	Angle of eye line away from horizontal	Practicality
2	Height of foot above floor	Practicality
3	Pressure of body against back	Comfort
4	Pressure of body against seat	Comfort
5	Curvature of Spine	Comfort
6	Percentage of chair back that is unused	Efficiency
7	Width of chair beyond body	Efficiency
8	Full length of seated person	Efficiency
9	Angle between chair back and body	Efficiency

position (feet on the floor, eyes straight ahead and arms resting at desk height at 90°). Measures 3–5 give the comfort of a user and the final 4 measure how efficiently the chair achieves its purpose by recording the space it occupies and how much of the chair is surplus to requirements.

We generate test data for the chairs using 12000 random parameter sets, each tested by a set of 20 users. We then take the median of these 20 measure values for each chair and trait. This gives us our data set for learning the design space. The set of chairs took several days to test using the simulator. Preliminary testing showed that although the accuracy of the learning algorithm was improved by larger data sets, there was very little improvement after 12000 parameter sets.

2.3 Learning Algorithm

To find a fitness function we use random example chairs, tested by the ergonomic measure, to learn the generation parameters that will affect each physical trait. The learning algorithm we use is 'random forests', which computes the average of a set of decision trees. We use these as decision trees are good at coping with discrete variables such as those that dictate the cross-section shape. Decision trees also perform feature selection as part of their algorithm. This is likely to be important in our case as it is anticipated that some generating parameters will have no effect on certain physical traits. For example back shape will have no effect on feet height. We use the 'RandomForestClassifier' from the scikit learn Python library [19], with minimum leaf size 5.

This algorithm gives us values that indicate how important each generating parameter is for determining a trait. This is the total of the reduction of the gini impurity that is caused by a split using a particular parameter [20]. We use this later in the evolutionary algorithm.

Decision trees classify data into 2 or more bins. However we found that having only 2 bins, good and bad, increased the accuracy of the learning process,

Table 2. Measure cutoff values and values used to define dining chair

No	Unit	Best				Worst	Dining Chair	
		5	4	3	2	1	Target	Score
0	radians	0.4	0.6	0.8	1.0	1.2	0.6	4
1	radians	0.005	0.1	0.2	0.4	0.8	0.005	5
2	mm	80	120	200	330	480	80	5
3	kPa	20	25	30	35	40	30	3
4	kPa	20	40	60	80	100	60	3
5	N/A	1.00	1.25	1.50	1.75	2.00	1.25	4
6	% back	0.3	0.4	0.5	0.6	0.7	0.6	2
7	% shoulder	1.2	1.4	1.6	1.8	2.0	1.2	5
8	mm	600	700	800	900	1000	800	3
9	radians	0.01	0.02	0.03	0.04	0.05	0.02	4

particularly for the pressure traits. Using two bins gave very good accuracy, with 8 of the measures over 95 % accuracy and the other 2 over 85 % when you set the cutoff to the mean value. However, a consequence of this algorithm is that any evaluation of new test data will be the binary good/bad rather than a relative continuous score. We show how we convert this into a gradient fitness function in the next section.

3   Generation of New Designs

3.1   Fitness Function

Once we have a way to estimate the function measures of a chair we can use this as a fitness function. If our brief is a dining chair we can define target good values for all of our physical measures. These target values define a dining chair. We can then define any value less than or equal to this as 'good' and any value greater as 'bad'. To use an evolutionary algorithm however, we need a progression of fitness values to create a gradient for the algorithm to climb. The simplest gradient would be the number of physical traits that achieve this good value, giving a gradient from 0 to 10. We extend this so that we have 5 intermediate points for each trait; this is to accommodate different chair requirements. Thus we have a gradient from 0 to 50, where 0 is it fails all minimum cutoff criteria and 50 is it has passed all criteria. The cutoff value set is given in Table 2.

For our dining chair brief, we can choose our new cutoff values from the set. For a dining chair we require high practicality and moderate comfort. Efficiency is mixed as we need it to be very slim to fit diners in around a table but the back can be purely decorative. We therefore choose cutoff points that reflect these desired traits (also shown in Table 2). When evolving a dining chair we will not be able to score higher than these points; a dining chair can be more

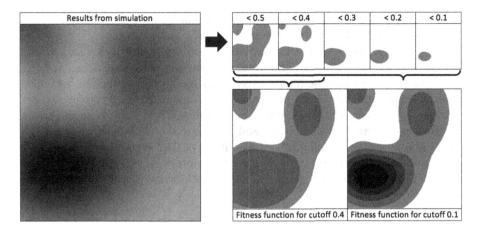

Fig. 3. Illustration of finding the fitness function from simulation results

comfortable than this value but its fitness score will be the same as one with moderate comfort.

Figure 3 illustrates this process using a model 2D function for clarity. The continuous values from the simulation data (left) are classified into 5 different 'good' and 'bad' sets using 5 cutoff values (top right). Then, depending on the desired target value, we can construct different fitness functions by adding the sets together. If our brief for this trait was quite flexible (e.g. moderate comfort) we could use 0.4 as our target, giving us 3 possible peaks and high diversity. If we needed the trait to be very strict (e.g. high practicality) we could use 0.1, giving us just one peak.

3.2   Exploring the Design Space

For the purposes of this paper we only considered the 25 parameters that are used in the ergonomic model, excluding the 13 parameters that have no effect on the ergonomics, such as colour and leg style. Therefore the representation of our design space is a list of 25 variables, all bounded by the maximum and minimum values from the test set. Some of these are continuous and others discrete (our cross-section parameters, given by an integer). During initial generation and after every mutation we checked that the numbers still fell within our bounds. Any that did not were replaced by the bound that they crossed. We allowed non-integer mutations of the discrete values but rounded to the nearest integer before any testing stage.

When we trained the decision trees we found the importance of each generating parameter for each trait. We then used this to guide the evolution of the chairs. When a chair has a low score we want to focus the changes on the parameters that will have the largest effect on its score. However, once the chair has reached the score plateau for a trait we want to focus the changes on the parameters that are unlikely to reduce its score but will increase the diversity of the population. This allowed the early mutations to explore the design space but ensured that the later mutations exploited the good areas.

The biases are given by Eq. 1, where C_j, F_j are the cutoff value and fitness score for trait j and M_{ij} is the importance value for parameter i and trait j. We subtract the mean of the importance values so the parameters with smaller importance and fitnesses with a perfect score become negative. Therefore we get a positive score when a parameter is either significant and there is an imperfect score or a parameter is insignificant and a perfect score. We sum over all the traits and only use positive biases. The addition of 0.02 is to allow a very small chance that other parameters can change; it also prevents excessive mutation in Eq. 2. P_i therefore gives the proportion of mutation that should be applied to parameter i.

$$P_i = max\left(\sum_{j=1}^{10}\left(((C_j - F_j) - mean_i(M_{ij}))(M_{ij} - mean_i(M_{ij}))\right), 0\right) + 0.02$$

$$(1)$$

$$Mutation_i = \frac{P_i}{\sum_1^{25} P_i}\sigma_i R_i f$$

$$(2)$$

Equation 2 gives the mutation value for a parameter i. Here we use normalised P_i, σ_i is the standard deviation of parameter i and R_i is a Gaussian random number with mean 0 and standard deviation 1. We also have f, a mutation factor. In each generation m children are produced with a range of values for f, giving us a set of new chairs with increasing differences from their parent.

To maintain diversity we use fitness sharing. This imagines that each niche has finite resources that will be shared with all individuals within a set radius [21]. Rather than sharing the main fitness value found by the fitness function we share a bonus fitness value between similar designs. We define similar as sharing a second generation parent, e.g. '1st cousins' and 'siblings' are all considered similar. This allow us to quickly and easily find distinct sets of chairs rather than having to calculate a radius of similarity around each chair, which saves calculation time. It also bypasses the question of defining visual similarity that we have no way of measuring automatically.

$$B_x = \frac{1}{n/3\sqrt{2\pi}}\exp\left(-\frac{x^2}{2(n/3)^2}\right) * (n + 10)$$

$$(3)$$

The bonus fitness is shared as shown in Eq. 3. This gives a Gaussian distribution of bonus scores for each cousin x in $0...n$, where the cousins are ordered highest to lowest scoring. By changing σ according to the number of cousins we change the height of the peak, and therefore the maximum bonus score. A unique cousin would get a bonus of $\sim$13.2 but the best cousin of 10 would get $\sim$2.4. In practice there will be multiples of m cousins, where m is the number of offspring from each parent.

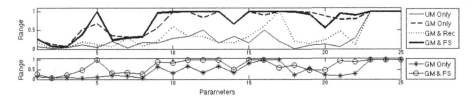

Fig. 4. Proportion of total parameter range used with different genetic operators. UM - Unguided Mutation, GM - Guided Mutation, Rec - Recombination, FS - Fitness Sharing. Top shows sample of 18 from 6 independent evolutionary runs for each method. Bottom shows 18 from a single run for each method.

The only genetic operator used in this process was the guided mutation. Experiments show that this could give us the largest diversity in the finished population. The top chart in Fig. 4 shows the percentage of the parameter range that was used in the final population with the first 3 designs sampled from 6 independent evolutionary runs (dining chair, 50 parents, 30 generations, 5 children per parent). We can see that unguided mutation (no parameter importance bias) and guided mutation with recombination both have low diversity. It was observed that this low diversity was also visible in the phenotypes for recombination, with the same chair type developed consistently throughout multiple evolutionary runs. The parameters where all methods have low diversity are ones which are restricted by the brief. For instance the first 3 parameters are seat height, seat length and back recline, which are going to be similar for all dining chairs.

Guided mutation and guided mutation with fitness sharing appear similar when considered over multiple runs but if we consider a single run (Fig. 4 bottom chart) we see that guided mutation cannot produce this diversity in one run without fitness sharing.

3.3 Results

To show the effect of the evolutionary process we use the dining chair measure as our example. We use this as the functional requirement is easily defined and observations of dining chairs on the market indicate that a wide range of designs can fulfill this brief. The target cutoff values are shown in Fig. 2 and are designed

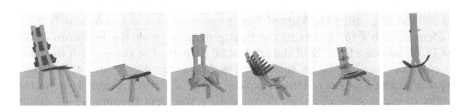

Fig. 5. Randomly generated parent chairs, numbers 42–47 (of 50) from left to right

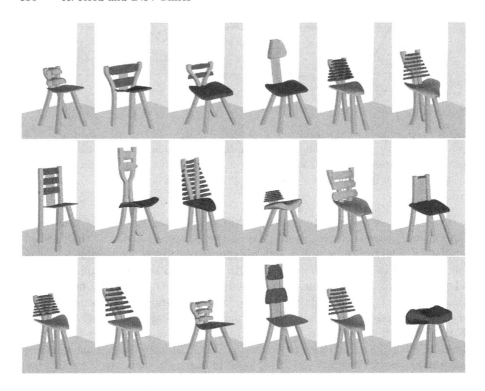

Fig. 6. Top scoring dining chairs

to give a practical and moderately comfortable chair. The maximum score for a chair is 38 (i.e. maximum of 4 for measure 1, 5 for measure 2 etc.). We will show a single run of the algorithm, with the difference between the first generation and the last, as well as the range that is present in the final generation.

In Fig. 5 we show a sample of randomly generated chairs which we used as the original parents. In this run we use a total of 50 parents. Factors that are not used in the ergonomic model are all set to a single value so we are not distracted by their changes. This includes the leg style and cross-section, as well as the textures, although a distinction is made between upholstered (purple) and solid (pale wood texture) finishes. We ran 30 generations to get this set of chairs and created 5 children per parent in a generation. This set of evolutionary parameters has in excess of 7500 fitness evaluations. Using the simulation directly this would take around 45 h; using the learned fitness function it takes approximately 2.5 s.

Figure 6 shows the chairs in the final generation with the full score of 38. The 18 chairs came from 12 of the original 50 parents. The parent with the most offspring was number 45, as shown in Fig. 5 (parents 42, 46 and 47 also had offspring in the final set). This is typical of the algorithm; Table 3 shows the number of top scoring chairs in 15 consecutive runs and the number of unique parents that created them. These 15 runs were done with the same set of original

Table 3. Number of top scoring children and unique parents in 15 consecutive runs

Run	1	2	3	4	5	6	7	8	9	10	11	12	13	14	15
No. Children	12	16	12	19	10	13	16	20	16	29	10	13	19	15	18
No. Unique Parents	10	9	7	5	8	6	8	11	6	13	5	7	12	7	9

parents. In total, across all the runs, 41 of the random set of 50 produced suitable offspring, including all of our example set in Fig. 5.

As we see from Fig. 6, evolving to this fitness function has had the desired effect. The chairs are consistently at a suitable height and have upright backs. They also have seats low enough to allow the user's feet to touch the floor and the seat and back are narrow enough to get the chairs around a table, but they have retained a wide variety of forms that could be later searched for desired aesthetic traits. They also use a wide proportion of each of the parameter ranges; Fig. 4 shows the range of this set as 'GM & FS'.

Figure 7 shows the effect of choosing different target values. Here we have increased the comfort requirement, but have relaxed the functional requirement. This creates a range of feature chairs.

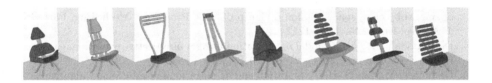

Fig. 7. Sample with target values [1.2, 0.8, 80, 25, 30, 1.25, 0.7, 2.0, 1000, 0.02]

4   Conclusions and Future Work

We have shown in this paper that it is possible to evolve a wide range of designs based on learned fitness functions, giving a large time saving over using a directly simulated fitness function. We have also shown that the ergonomics of a design can help reduce the design space by removing non-viable designs. Finally we have shown that we can use higher level information learned about the space (in this case the importance of different parameters) to guide the evolution.

We could have used the ergonomic model directly as a fitness function, however this would have vastly increased the calculation time (a single generative run of 50 designs and 30 generations would take nearly 2 days). Using random forests also allows us to gather information about the wider space that can be used as part of the evolutionary algorithm. It also stands as a case study to support our future work on learned fitness functions that cannot otherwise be simulated. We intend to consider style as our next task, which cannot be simulated in the same way.

We could also expand this work by using physical modeling and material properties to learn the viability of different leg styles given their materials. We do not intend to do this immediately as it will be of little interest beyond what we present here since similar work on viability and stability has already been done in other papers such as [22], but it will eventually allow us to maintain a large design space for the legs. Eventually we hope to combine all of the learned measures, in the way that we combine the 10 physical measures, to be able to evolve items to a desired type and style.

Ultimately we aim to demonstrate that it is possible to explore large design spaces and find a selection of designs that fit required criteria. Functionality of this type could be used to populate game environments, where an object type and style is known and a unique item is required for every instance.

References

1. Dabbeeru, M.M., Mukerjee, A.: Discovering implicit constraints in design. Artif. Intell. Eng. Des. Anal. Manuf. **25**, 57–75 (2011)
2. Reed, K.: Aesthetic measures for evolutionary vase design. In: Machado, P., McDermott, J., Carballal, S. (eds.) EvoMUSART 2013. LNCS, vol. 7834, pp. 59–71. Springer, Heidelberg (2013)
3. Schütze, O., et al.: On the detection of nearly optimal solutions in the context of single-objective space mission design problems. Proc. Inst. Mech. Eng. Part G: J. Aerosp. Eng. **225**, 1229–1242 (2011)
4. Deb, K., Saha, A.: Multimodal optimization using a bi-objective evolutionary algorithm. Evol. Comput. **20**(1), 27–62 (2012). MIT Press
5. Črepinšek, M., Liu, S.-H.: Exploration and exploitation in evolutionary algorithms: a survey. ACM Comput. Surv. **45**, 3 (2013)
6. Xu, K., Zhang, H., Cohen-Or, D., Chen, B.: Fit and diverse: set evolution for inspiring 3D shape galleries. ACM Trans. Graph. **31**(4), 57:1–57:10 (2012). Article 57
7. Kalogerakis, E., Chaudhuri, S., Koller, D., Koltun, V.: A probabilistic model for component-based shape synthesis. ACM Trans. Graph. **31**(4), 55:1–55:11 (2012). Article 55
8. Clune J., Lipson H.: Evolving three-dimensional objects with a generative encoding inspired by developmental biology. In: Proceedings of the European Conference on Artificial Life, pp 141–148 (2011)
9. Jin, Y.: A comprehensive survey of fitness approximation in evolutionary computation. Soft Comput. **9**(1), 3–12 (2005). Springer
10. Yüksel, A.Ç.: Automatic music generation using evolutionary algorithms and neural networks. In: 2011 International Symposium on Innovations in Intelligent Systems and Applications (INISTA), pp 354–358 (2011)
11. Hsiao, S.-W., Tsai, H.-C.: Applying a hybrid approach based on fuzzy neural network and genetic algorithm to product form design. Int. J. Ind. Ergon. **35**, 411–428 (2005)
12. Trimble SketchUp. http://www.sketchup.com
13. Mathworks Matlab. http://uk.mathworks.com/products/matlab/
14. TU Delft DINED Database. http://dined.io.tudelft.nl/dined/full

15. Winter, D.A.: Biomechanics and Motor Control of Human Movement, 4th edn. Wiley, New York (2009)
16. SolidWorks Bearing Load Distribution. http://help.solidworks.com/2015/english/ SolidWorks/cworks/c_Bearing_Load_Distribution.htm
17. Todd, B.A.: Three-dimensional computer model of the human buttocks in vivo. J Rehabil. Res. Dev. **31**(2), 111–119 (1994)
18. Zhu, H.: Modeling of pressure distribution of human body load on an office chair seat. Masters thesis. Department of Mechanical Engineering, Blekinge Institute of Technology (2013)
19. scikit-learn. http://scikit-learn.org/stable/index.html
20. Breiman, L., Cutler, A.: Random forests. http://www.stat.berkeley.edu/~breiman/ RandomForests/cc_home.htm
21. Yu, X., Gen, M.: Introduction to Evolutionary Algorithms. Decision Engineering. Springer, London (2012)
22. Umetani, N., Igarashi, T., Mitra, N.J.: Guided exploration of physically valid shapes for furniture design. ACM Trans. Graph. **31**(4), 86:1–86:11 (2012). Article 86

Moody Music Generator: Characterising Control Parameters Using Crowdsourcing

Marco Scirea[1](✉), Mark J. Nelson[2], and Julian Togelius[3]

[1] Center for Computer Games Research,
IT University of Copenhagen, Copenhagen, Denmark
msci@itu.dk
[2] Anadrome Research, Copenhagen, Denmark
mjn@anadrome.org
[3] Game Innovation Lab, New York University, Brooklyn, NY, USA
julian@togelius.com

Abstract. We characterise the expressive effects of a music generator capable of varying its moods through two control parameters. The two control parameters were constructed on the basis of existing work on valence and arousal in music, and intended to provide control over those two mood factors. In this paper we conduct a listener study to determine how people actually perceive the various moods the generator can produce. Rather than directly attempting to validate that our two control parameters represent arousal and valence, instead we conduct an open-ended study to crowd-source labels characterising different parts of this two-dimensional control space. Our aim is to characterise perception of the generator's expressive space, without constraining listeners' responses to labels specifically aimed at validating the original arousal/valence motivation. Subjects were asked to listen to clips of generated music over the Internet, and to describe the moods with free-text labels. We find that the arousal parameter does roughly map to perceived arousal, but that the nominal "valence" parameter has strong interaction with the arousal parameter, and produces different effects in different parts of the control space. We believe that the characterisation methodology described here is general and could be used to map the expressive range of other parameterisable generators.

1   Introduction

Music has the power to evoke moods and emotions—even music generated by an algorithm. In fact, in many cases the whole purpose of a music generation algorithm is to evoke a particular mood. This is particularly true of music generators that form part of highly interactive systems such as games, where a common goal of dynamic music systems is to elicit a particular mood from the user on demand, as suits the current state of the system. To take the example of a video game, the music generation could be seen as content within the experience-driven procedural content generation framework [1], where the game adaptation mechanism generates music with a particular mood in response to player actions.

© Springer International Publishing Switzerland 2015
C. Johnson et al. (Eds.): EvoMUSART 2015, LNCS 9027, pp. 200–211, 2015.
DOI: 10.1007/978-3-319-16498-4_18

To enable such a capability we need a music generator that can take mood-related parameters and output music that elicits moods that as closely as possible correspond to what was specified by the parameters. This, however, is not a trivial task. While there are a number of features of music that are known to elicit particular moods and that can be incorporated into a music generation, the interplay between these features is complex and it is not clear that any particular change of the generator parameter will have a particular effect.

This paper describes a music generator which is parameterisable in mood space, and a validation of this generator through crowdsourcing. The generator is parameterisable along the two axes of valence and arousal, and uses Pure Data and stochastic processes to produce music. The validation involves letting hundreds of subjects listen to music clips produced by the generator, and express the moods they perceive in the music. Subjects were allowed to express their experiences in free text, which was then preprocessed and plotted on chart to see how particular mood expressions are centred on different on parts of the intended valence–arousal axis. In the following, we will first situate this research with respect to other research on music generation and mood expression, and then describe the music generator and the validation methodology.

2   Background

2.1   Procedurally Generated Music

Procedural generation of music for games is a broad field. While a good number of games use some sort of procedural music structure, there are different approaches (or degrees), as suggested by Wooller *et al.*: *transformational* algorithms and *generative* algorithms [2].

Transformational algorithms act upon an already prepared structure, for example by having the music recorded in layers that can be added or subtracted at a specific time to change the feel of the music (e.g., *The Legend of Zelda: Ocarina of Time* is one of the earliest games that used this approach). Note that this is only an example and there are a great number of transformational approaches, but we won't discuss them in this paper.

Generative algorithms instead create the musical structure themselves, which leads to a higher degree of difficulty in having the music stay consistent with the game events and generally requires more computing power as the musical materials have to be created on the fly. An example of this approach can be found in *Spore*: the music written by Brian Eno was created with Pure Data in the form of many small samples that created the soundtrack in real time.

Adopting the latter approach, we present generative procedural music generation in games for emotional expression. While the topics of affect [3], semiotics [4] and mood-tagging [5] are also interesting and significant, our focus lies in the **real-time generation of background music able to express moods**.

2.2 Emotions and Moods

The topic of emotions has been extensively researched in the field of psychology, although their nature (and what constitutes the basic set of emotions) is still controversial. Lazarus argues that *"emotion is often associated and considered reciprocally influential with mood, temperament, personality, disposition, and motivation"* [6].

Affect is generally considered to be the experience of feeling or emotion. It is largely believed that affect is post-cognitive; emotion arises only after an amount of cognitive processing of information has been accomplished. With this assumption every affective reaction (e.g., pleasure, displeasure, liking, disliking) results from *"a prior cognitive process that makes a variety of content discriminations and identifies features, examines them to find value, and weighs them according to their contributions"* [7]. Another view is that affect can be both pre- and post-cognitive (notably Lerner and Keltner [8]); thoughts are created by an initial emotional response which then leads to producing affect.

Mood is an affective state. However, while an emotion generally has a specific object of focus, moods tends to be more unfocused and diffused [9]. Batson, Shaw, and Oleson say that mood *"involves tone and intensity and a structured set of beliefs about general expectations of a future experience of pleasure or pain, or of positive or negative affect in the future"* [10]. Another important difference between emotions and moods is that moods, being diffused and unfocused, can last much longer (as also remarked by Beedie *et al.* [11]).

In this paper, we focus on moods instead of emotions, for we expect that in games—where the player listens to the background music for a longer time duration than the duration that a particular emotion is experienced—moods are more likely to be remembered by the players after their gameplay. In addition, they are easier for game designers to integrate, since they represent longer-duration sentiment suitable for segments of game play.

2.3 Music Mood Taxonomy

The set of adjectives that describe music mood and emotional response is immense and there is no accepted standard. For example in the work by Katayose *et al.* [12], the emotional adjective set includes *Gloomy, Serious, Pathetic* and *Urbane*.

Russell [13] proposed a model of affect based on two bipolar dimensions: *pleasant-unpleasant* and *arousal-sleepy*, theorising that each affect word can be mapped into this bi-dimensional space by a combination of these two components. Thayer [14] applied Russell's model to music using as the dimensions of *stress* and *valence*; although the names of the dimensions are different from Russell's their meaning is the same. Also, we find different names in different research while the semantic meanings are identical. We will use the terms *valence* and *arousal*, as they are the most commonly used affective computing research.

Then the affect in music can be divided into the four clusters based on the dimensions of valence and arousal: **Anxious/Frantic** (Low Valence, High

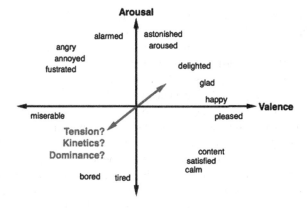

Fig. 1. The Valence-Arousal space, labelled by Russel's direct circular projection of adjectives [13]. Includes semantic of projected third affect dimensions: "tension", "kinetics", "dominance". In our study we haven't considered this third dimension as it's still not very defined.

Arousal), **Depression** (Low Valence, Low Arousal), **Contentment** (High Valence, Low Arousal) and **Exuberance** (High Valence, High Arousal). These four clusters have the advantage of being explicit and discriminable; also they are the basic music-induced moods [15,16] see Fig. 1.

3   The Generator

To generate music for our study we employed a real-time procedural music generator that we developed using the PD (Pure Data) programming language. Our music generation approach does not take into account chord sequences, leitmotifs, or improvisation. Instead, we aim to create a very minimalistic ambient music created by simple random number generators. This allows us to test our hypothesis of being able to display moods through only the manipulation of the mood defining features we consider.

3.1   Musical Mood Features

In order to generate mood-based music, we used four musical features intensity, timbre, rhythm, and dissonances, which are mainly inspired by Liu *et al.* [17]. While Liu et al.'s research focused on mood information extraction, we applied their approaches to generate music instead. This section extends our previous approach [18], introducing a new feature called dissonances.

Intensity. Intensity is defined by how strong the volume of the music is. It is an arousal-dependent feature: high arousal corresponds to high intensity; low arousal to low intensity. Intuitively the more stress is present in the music, the more it will have a high volume. Calm pieces of music, in a similar manner, have a lower one.

Timbre. Timbre is what we could call the brightness of the music, that is, how much of the audio signal is composed by bass frequencies. It is often associated with *"how pleasing to listeners"* it appears [19]. In previous literature audio features such as MFCC (Mel-Frequency Cepstral Coefficients) and spectral shape features have been used to analyse this timbral feature.

We associated this timbral feature with valence: the more positive the valence, the higher will the timbre be. The brightness of Exuberance music, for example, is generally higher than that of music in Depression, which will result in greater spectral energy in the high sub bands for Exuberance.

Generally, timbre is a factor that is very dependent on the instrumentation choice. In our case we acted on the synthesisers, our instruments, to generate brighter and darker sounds. In our generator we had three different sets of instruments (which are actually the same synthesisers with different settings to make them sound different) for high, low and neutral valence.

Rhythm. We included three features related to rhythm: strength, regularity and tempo [17].

- Rhythm strength: how prominent the rhythmic section is (drums and bass). This feature is arousal dependent.
- Regularity: how steady the rhythm is. This feature is valence dependent.
- Tempo: how fast the rhythm is. This feature is arousal dependent. In a high valence/high arousal piece of music, for instance, we can observe that the rhythm is strong and steady. In a low valence/low arousal, on the other hand, the tempo is slow and the rhythm cannot be as easily recognised.

We acted on these features in different ways. To influence rhythm strength, we changed how much the drums and the synthesiser which plays the bass are prominent in the music. Having the instruments play notes on the beat or the upbeat creates different feelings of regularity and irregularity. For example, in Contentment music, we favoured a steady rhythm with notes falling on the beats of the measure. In Depression music, on the other hand, we gave more space to upbeat notes. Finally, to influence the tempo we just acted on the BPMs (Beats Per Minute) of the music.

Dissonances. What we mean by dissonance is the juxtaposition of two notes very close to each other: for example C and C♯. The distance between these two is just a semitone, which gives the listener a generally unpleasant sensation.

Dissonance doesn't mean that it always sounds bad. In fact most music pieces contain dissonances, as they can be used as cues expressing something amiss. The listener's ear can also be trained to accept dissonances through repetition. In general, the bigger the interval between the two dissonant notes, the easier it is on the listener's ear: a C and a C♯ are always dissonant, but the dissonance is more evident if the notes are played from the same octave and not on two different ones.

C.P.E. Bach, in his *Essay on the True Art of Playing Keyboard Instruments* [20], remarks on the affective power of dissonances, although in a more general way: "*... dissonances are played loudly and consonances softly, since the former rouse our emotions and the latter quiet them*".

Meyer [21] observes that the affect-arousing role of dissonances is evident in the practise of composers as well as in the writings of theorists and critics, remarking how the affective response is not only dependent on the presence of dissonances per se, but also upon conventional association. This means that depending on the conventions of the musical style dissonances might be more or less accepted by the listener and so can arouse different affective reactions. A study on listening preferences on infants conducted by Trainor and Heinmiller [22] shows how even these listeners, which have no knowledge of the musical scale structure, have an affective preference for consonance. Considering that our generator doesn't emulate any musical style, but creates minimalistic, unstructured music, we believe the effect of dissonances would follow this instinctive affective reaction.

Already in our first study we noticed that these features, originally devised to extract mood information, were enough to generate different moods. But we also realised that we could strengthen the impression by introducing dissonances in the music: for Exuberance and Contentment we use a diatonic scale, while for Anxious and Depression an altered one. We believe this is an important feature that cannot be ignored when wanting to show more precise moods in music.

Dissonance feature is valence depending. In our study we just used two scales: a C major scale (C D E F G A B) for positive and a E♭ Harmonic Minor scale minus the third grade (E♭ F [G♭] Ab B♭ B D) for negative valence. Music built on a minor scales is generally considered more sombre than when made in a major key. This is not technically correct in our system because it would require a grade of organisation and harmony that would make plain which is the root note. The notes of the harmonic minor scale are the same as the natural minor except that the seventh degree is raised by one semitone, making an augmented second between the sixth and seventh degrees. For our unstructured music this means that we have a whole-and-a-half interval between B and D and two half intervals (D-E♭ and B♭-B). The removal of the third grade (G♭) makes even more difficult to the listener's ear to identify the key, effectively making the dissonances sound as such.

4   Experiment Design

As described in the previous section, we produced a generator intended to be parameterised by two control axes: arousal and valence. Although this construction is based on theoretical motivations and existing work on the relationship between musical parameters and perceived mood, it does not necessarily follow that these axes *actually* represent arousal and valence. To understand what kind of generative space our music generator actually produces, we designed a study to characterise how the two control axes of our generator influence listeners' perceptions.

Contrary to our previous pilot study [23], we employed a mix of closed-ended questions to validate the axes (e.g. a number of mood expressing words and a Likert scale for valence and arousal), we decided to provide completely open-ended questions to the participants, so as to eliminate as much bias as possible from their answers, and understand the effects of our generator's control parameters in an open-ended way.

We developed the online survey with HTML and PHP, using a MySQL database to hold the data collected; the participants were presented with a page consisting of a music clip and five blank boxes where they were asked to write emotional words that they thought the music expressed.

After each five responses we introduced a special page where the participants could review their answers, listen to the previous five clips again and see some of the most recent answers from other users for the same clips. We created this page to give feedback to the users and to make the survey, hopefully, more interesting for them by giving them the opportunity to confront their answers with the ones other users provided.

The experiment has no pre-defined end: the user is able to continue answering until he/she wants, and can close the online survey at any time.

4.1 Music Clip Generation

We generated 100 clips of 30 seconds of music using our music generator, each of these expressing a randomly chosen point in the bi-dimensional mood space we described in Sect. 2.3.

The music clips have been generated by linearly connecting the features and the respective axis, even though we are conscious that the relationships are probably more complex; in fact we hope the data collected through this study will help us better define these.

The maximum and minimum bounds we gave to the various musical features were:

- **Tempo:** 100–136
- **Intensity:**

	Synth1	Synth2	Synth3(Bass)	Drum machine
Minimum values	69	56	35	60
Maximum values	98	119	83	128

- **Rhythm strength:** -20 % to +20 % intensity to *Synth 3* and *Drum machine*.
- **Timbre:** three different settings for the synthesisers: the lowest is selected when the valence is less or equal of 33, the middle between 33 and 66 and the higher above 66 (valence goes from 0 to 100 in our system).
- **Steadiness:** three settings dependent on the valence axis as the Timbre: *steady*, *medium_steady* and *unsteady*. On the *steady* rhythm all the notes fall on the beat of the measure, on the *medium steady* rhythm all instruments play notes on the beat, while the drum machine plays off-beat. Finally for

the *unsteady* rhythm only Synth 1 (which is the higher pitched instrument, and the one more resembling a lead voice) plays on the beat while all the other instruments play offbeat. Note that if all the instruments played on the offbeat the listener would have no way of telling the beat from the offbeat, effectively perceiving a steady rhythm.

– **Dissonances:** as discussed in Sect. 3.1, we use a C major scale (C D E F G A B) for positive and an E♭ harmonic minor scale minus the third grade (E♭ F [G♭] Ab B♭ B D) for negative valence.

5   Results and Analysis

We collected a total of 2020 free-text labels from 192 distinct users. We can consider patterns in these labels to constitute an open-ended, nonparametric characterisation of how users perceive the music's mood as we vary the control parameters intended to represent arousal and valence. The obvious question is then: are there any patterns, and do they provide any insight into the effects of these control parameters? With free-text labels, it is not entirely implausible that there could end up being no easily discernible patterns in the data. However there turn out to be some strongly localisable responses, particularly among the labels volunteered relatively frequently. Although listeners could in principle respond with any English word or phrase, some words recur often, e.g. "mysterious" was volunteered 34 times.

In order to characterise the control parameters using these labels from the users themselves, for each label we calculate the average (mean) arousal and valence of the clips for which that label was volunteered. The goal of doing so is to localise the label somewhere in the two-dimensional control space. We would like to say things such as: the label "rushed" appears on average in the high-arousal, high-valence part of the space, while the label "relaxed" is given on average to low-arousal, low-valence clips.

Of course, if a given label was only volunteered a few times, an average is not very reliable. Therefore we choose the 20 labels which are *best localised*, in the sense that we have enough data to more reliably determine their average location in the control space. To determine how well localised a label is, we rank labels by the standard error of their mean location on the arousal/valence axes (standard errors summed over both axes). The standard error of a mean, $se = \frac{stddev}{\sqrt{n}}$, will in general be lower for labels with lower sample standard deviations, and for labels which appear more times in the data set.[1]

Before ranking labels by standard error, we perform two preprocessing steps on the data. First, we stem the words using the Snowball stemmer,[2] in order to aggregate minor part-of-speech variations of labels—for example, *relaxed* and

---

[1] Since we make no assumption about the distribution of data, we can't use the standard error as a basis for a confidence interval. Nonetheless, it is useful as a proxy for how well we can localise a label in the arousal/valence space, relative to other labels in our data set.

[2] http://snowball.tartarus.org/.

relaxing are both mapped to the stem *relax*. In addition, we exclude labels that appear fewer than 5 times in the data set even after stemming, because the sample standard deviation is an unreliable measure for extremely small n.

Figure 2 plots the 20 best-localised label stems, at the average location of the (arousal, valence) parameter settings that elicited that label as a response. The standard errors of the mean are plotted as indicative error bars. This plot alone is surprisingly informative as a characterisation of the control parameters' effect on perception of musical moods. Especially considering that users volunteered free-text labels rather than selecting categories, the trends in the axes are rather striking.

We can make a few qualitative observations on the basis of these 20 well-localised labels. In a general sense, the "arousal" and "valence" theory that drove the development of our control axes does not seem to precisely align, in this setting, with the effect of the axes to which we've nominally given those labels, though arousal is closer than valence.

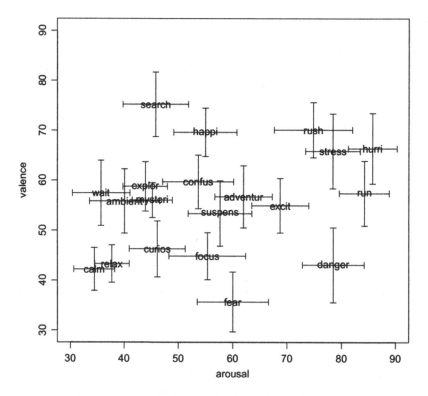

Fig. 2. Free-text, crowdsourced characterization of moods across the generator's two-dimensional control space. Plotted labels are the 20 best-localised labels (post-stemming), plotted at the average location for which they were volunteered as labels. Error bars represent the standard error of the mean.

Arousal maps to something like a calm vs. stress axis (which is, in fact, the definition of arousal). Low-arousal words include (unstemmed): curious, waiting, calm, relaxing, ambient. High-arousal words include: rushed, stressed, hurried, run, dangerous. Valence seems to be largely dominated by arousal, but modifies it in a way that has strong interaction effects.

Looking at high-valence clips, when coupled with a high arousal setting, they elicit labels that accentuate a feeling of being rushed: rushed, stressed, hurried. So, raising valence, rather than being perceived as positive valence, instead emphasises a kind of speed in the context of high arousal, with even a somewhat negative sentiment. Low-valence, high-arousal clips are most often labelled as "danger" instead.

With a mid-level arousal setting, valence does seem to act as a relatively straightforward valence setting: high-valence clips are characterised by "happy", and low-valence clips by "fear". As arousal drops, however, the effect of the "valence" setting becomes particularly inconsistent with the intent that it be a knob used to vary perceived valence. The nominally low-valence clips, when coupled with low arousal, elicit quite *positive* labels: calm, relax. As "valence" increases while arousal stays low, the main effect is to get somewhat more active: from "calm" to "wait" and "explore" at mid-valence, to "search" at high valence settings.

6   Conclusion and Future Work

The goal of this study was an open-ended characterisation of the perceived affects produced by a music generator parameterised by a two-dimensional valence/ arousal control axis. We crowdsourced labels for clips in randomly selected parts of the control space, and looked for labels that are *well-localized*, i.e. where they are volunteered by users most often for specific parts of the control space. Although the generator was designed with a valence/arousal control axis, the purpose of this study was simply to characterise what perceived effect in listeners our two-dimensional control axis actually has, without regard (in the study design or in communication to study participants) for where these two axes came from or what they were supposed to represent.

We designed this experiment as to avoid as much bias from our part as possible by having the participants answer to completely open-ended questions. Overall, we collected a total of 2020 free-text labels from 192 distinct users. We found some interesting results from this study that seem to show how we can express moods through the manipulation of our musical features which can be recognised from the listener relatively correctly in our mood space.

The results are very promising regarding the recognition of the arousal axis, which seems to map very well to the answers provided by the participants. The valence axis, on the other hand, behaves as intended only on medium arousal values, becoming more confused—and exhibiting interesting interplay with the arousal axis—when approaching the extremes of the arousal axis (both positive and negative). This result is in line with previous studies that show valence is harder to characterize [24], although we notice that in our final data sample the emotion words that express positive/negative affect are fewer in number than the ones expressing arousal, suggesting more study of the interaction between the two axes may be useful. We also notice a slight bias towards more positive valence and towards higher arousal. This is unexpected, but might be symptom of an intrinsic bias caused by the music produced by the generator (the sounds and unstructured nature of the music).

An interesting avenue for future work is to investigate the degree to which cultural background of respondents may influence the labels volunteered. Although we describe the study as open-ended in an attempt to be unbiased, the presence of certain frequent words such as *explore* is intriguing; they can be seen as somewhat game-related, whereas this study did not involve games at all (though they are a future application of ours). This may be simply due to the shared background and therefore shared vocabulary and shared attention to salient features of respondents in this study. We plan to conduct a study with respondents from different cultural backgrounds to investigate this issue.

On the application side, we plan to connect this generator with the experience-driven Super Mario level generator described by Shaker *et al.* [25], in order to explore whether we can observe a significant difference in the players' emotional responses through the use of music that reinforces or diverges from the intended emotions elicited by the level generator. Finally we will continue our work in applying this research on expressing narrative clues through music [26].

References

1. Yannakakis, G.N., Togelius, J.: Experience-driven procedural content generation. IEEE Trans. Affect. Comput. **2**(3), 147–161 (2011)
2. Wooller, R., Brown, A.R., Miranda, E., Diederich, J., Berry, R.: A framework for comparison of process in algorithmic music systems. In: Generative Arts Practice 2005 – A Creativity & Cognition Symposium (2005)
3. Birchfield, D.: Generative model for the creation of musical emotion, meaning, and form. In: Proceedings of the 2003 ACM SIGMM Workshop on Experiential Telepresence, pp. 99–104 (2003)
4. Eladhari, M., Nieuwdorp, R., Fridenfalk, M.: The soundtrack of your mind: mind music-adaptive audio for game characters. In: Proceedings of Advances in Computer Entertainment Technology (2006)
5. Livingstone, S.R., Brown, A.R.: Dynamic response: Real-time adaptation for music emotion. In: Proceedings of the 2nd Australasian Conference on Interactive Entertainment, pp. 105–111 (2005)
6. Lazarus, R.S.: Emotion and Adaptation. Oxford University Press, New York (1991)
7. Brewin, C.R.: Cognitive change processes in psychotherapy. Psychol. Rev. **96**(3), 379 (1989)
8. Lerner, J.S., Keltner, D.: Beyond valence: toward a model of emotion-specific influences on judgement and choice. Cogn. Emot. **14**(4), 473–493 (2000)
9. Martin, B.A.: The influence of gender on mood effects in advertising. Psychol. Mark. **20**(3), 249–273 (2003)
10. Batson, C.D., Shaw, L.L., Oleson, K.C.: Differentiating affect, mood, and emotion: Toward functionally based conceptual distinctions (1992)

11. Beedie, C., Terry, P., Lane, A.: Distinctions between emotion and mood. Cogn. Emot. **19**(6), 847–878 (2005)
12. Katayose, H., Imai, M., Inokuchi, S.: Sentiment extraction in music. In: Proceedings of the 9th International Conference on Pattern Recognition, pp. 1083–1087 (1988)
13. Russell, J.A.: A circumplex model of affect. J. Pers. Soc. Psychol. **39**(6), 1161–1178 (1980)
14. Thayer, R.E.: The Biopsychology of Mood and Arousal. Oxford University Press, New York (1989)
15. Kreutz, G., Ott, U., Teichmann, D., Osawa, P., Vaitl, D.: Using music to induce emotions: influences of musical preference and absorption. Psychol. Music **36**(1), 101–126 (2008)
16. Lindström, E., Juslin, P.N., Bresin, R., Williamon, A.: "Expressivity comes from within your soul": a questionnaire study of music students' perspectives on expressivity. Res. Stud. Music Educ. **20**(1), 23–47 (2003)
17. Liu, D., Lu, L., Zhang, H.J.: Automatic mood detection from acoustic music data. In: Proceedings of the International Symposium on Music Information Retrieval, pp. 81–7 (2003)
18. Scirea, M.: Mood dependent music generator. In: Reidsma, D., Katayose, H., Nijholt, A. (eds.) ACE 2013. LNCS, vol. 8253, pp. 626–629. Springer, Heidelberg (2013)
19. Aucouturier, J.J., Pachet, F., Sandler, M.: "the way it sounds": timbre models for analysis and retrieval of music signals. IEEE Trans. Multimedia **7**(6), 1028–1035 (2005)
20. Bach, C.P.E., Mitchell, W.J., John, W.: Essay on the True Art of Playing Keyboard Instruments. WW Norton, New York (1949)
21. Meyer, L.B.: Emotion and Meaning in Music. University of Chicago Press, Chicago (2008)
22. Trainor, L.J., Heinmiller, B.M.: The development of evaluative responses to music: infants prefer to listen to consonance over dissonance. Infant Behav. Dev. **21**(1), 77–88 (1998)
23. Scirea, M., Cheong, Y.G., Bae, B.C.: Mood expression in real-time computer generated music using pure data. In: Proceedings of the International Conference on Music Perception and Cognition (2014)
24. Livingstone, S.R., Brown, A.R., Muhlberger, R.: Influencing the perceived emotions of music with intent. In: Proceedings of the Third International Conference on Generative Systems in the Electronic Arts (2005)
25. Shaker, N., Yannakakis, G.N., Togelius, J.: Towards automatic personalized content generation for platform games. In: Proceedings of the 2010 Conference on Artificial Intelligence and Interactive Digital Entertainment (2010)
26. Scirea, M., Cheong, Y.G., Bae, B.C., Nelson, M.: Evaluating musical foreshadowing of videogame narrative experiences. In: Proceedings of Audio Mostly (2014)

Schemographe: Application for a New Representation Technique and Methodology of Analysis in Tonal Harmony

Anna Shvets[1][✉] and Myriam Desainte-Catherine[2]

[1] Maria Curie-Sklodowska University in Lublin,
Plac Marii Curie 5, 20-031 Lublin, Poland
annashvets11@gmail.com
[2] Laboratoire Bordelaise de Recherche en Informatique, Université Bordeaux 1,
351 cours de la libération, Talence, France
myriam.desainte-catherine@labri.fr

Abstract. A recent development of music theory focuses basically on neo-riemannian angle of harmonic analysis with the use of Tonnetz as a space for harmonic change representation. However the Tonnetz does not cover the functional relations between accords within tonality and is feebly suitable to capture the features of neo-tonal postmodern music based on a new use of tonal functionality. This work presents an alternative method for music harmony progressions representation and analysis which uses two levels of representation. The first level is represented as a system of horizontal and vertical triads of graphs where each graph is an exo-frame filled out by information of specified degree of the scale. The graph pattern in this system represents the specified segment of harmonic progression taken from harmonic analysis of the musical composition. The pattern is then schematized for the second level of representation which examines its structural resemblance to the other schemas received similarly from the segments of harmonic progression. In order to facilitate the understanding of a new methodology and encourage its use in tonal harmony analysis an Android application for tablets called *Schemographe* has been created. The application presents the possibilities of the system on the two described levels of representation on example of three vocal pieces by neo-tonal postmodern composer Valentin Silvestrov.

1 Motivation

The range of recent music theories, such as transformational theory [1] music geometry approach [2], k-nets [3], simplicial complexes [4], hyper-spheres [5], reflected the transition characteristic for information society from substantial, object-oriented analysis to the processual analysis, based on attempts to find general rules of music matter behaviour regarding its movement within the Tonnetz network. The lacks of the Tonnetz representation system were indicated by Meeùs [6], who tried to fill these lacks with his own theory on harmony vectors. Both of these systems, however, use tonality representation as informational

© Springer International Publishing Switzerland 2015
C. Johnson et al. (Eds.): EvoMUSART 2015, LNCS 9027, pp. 212–223, 2015.
DOI: 10.1007/978-3-319-16498-4_19

unit, missing the relation of degrees inside a given tonality. In order to elaborate a new system for tonal harmony analysis let us combine the successful part of Tonnetz – graph theory – with a degree as its informational unit.

2   Graph System Formation

The passing progression can be treated as a mathematical object with possibility of variation of each of the elements. The possible iteration within the same structure of the passing progression represents a proto-frame which being filled out transforms to an exo-frame. The exo-frame expressed graphically results in a set of graph units in which the top and the bottom vertices contain the data about seventh chords and their inversions (the beginning and the end of the passing progression), and three middle edges contain the data about triad chords (all possible passing chords between seventh chords of the top and in the bottom vertices).

The range of exo-frames for passing progressions possible between:

1. the seventh chord in a root position and its first inversion;
2. the first and the second inversions of the seventh chord;
3. the second and the third inversions of the seventh chord

built from each degree of the diatonic scale and presented as a horizontal triad are further organized vertically. The placement of the one horizontal triad below the other will be determined by common passing chords, forming a vertical triad. The relations between seventh chords within the vertical triad is guided by the interval of a third rule, which allows to connect each top vertex of the graph to each bottom vertex through common edge. Considering, that there are 3 passing chords inside the edges and 3 seventh chords inside the bottom vertices, each of three seventh chords inside the top vertices hives 9 possible connections, therefore 27 progressions from one vertical triad. Multiplying these 27 progressions from a single vertical triad to the 6 unique vertical triads within the system of all 7 scale degrees, we receive 162 unique progressions.

The application of this system in music analysis however, requires more flexibility in sense of each chord construction. Thus, using the structure elaborated with passing progressions we'll ignore the part concerning chord construction specification, but leave the order of degrees placement.

3   Description of the Graph System

The graph system is a matrix of all possible connections between degrees of the diatonic scale and consists of two main components – structure and colors, used for different purposes. The general structure of the system, constructed under relation of a third in horizontal and diagonal senses, allows the connection between individual graph structures using common precedences, which are:

1. Edges in vertical triads;
2. Vertices in horizontal triads;
3. Diagonal proximity of the elements of both – vertices and edges.

The common precedences create the modes of connection of the graph units:

1. Vertical mode;
2. Horizontal mode;
3. Diagonal mode;
4. Exchange mode.

The exchange mode is not created by common precedences but follows the general rule of the third interval proximity of the elements in vertical, diagonal and horizontal senses. The colors are used to mark the vertices and the edges of the graph regarding whether the chords of the given progression belong to the specified tonality (green color) or extends it. In case of extension of the diatonic set of chords the following differentiation between colors will be made:

1. Blue color is used for flat degrees (like $III^\flat$, $VII^\flat$ or $II^\flat$ in major tonality);
2. Orange color is used for chords containing a sharp note (for ex. major triad of the III degree in major tonality with the V sharp degree in its structure or major subdominant in minor tonality containing the VI sharp degree);
3. Violet color is used for natural group of dominant (for ex. minor dominant in minor and major or major triad of the VII degree in minor tonality);

The described regularities of a color use are inherent only to the graph representation. The color palette used for presentation of discovered harmonic structure as schemas is discussed in the next section.

When the frame instance represented as pattern in the graph system is formed, it needs to be schematized in order to be compared to the other frame instances. For this purposes we propose the second level of representation consisting of graphic shapes and colors.

4   Second Level of Representation

The color palette application on the second level of representation signifies the functional affiliation of each degree of the diatonic scale. The color groups are formed according to the function affiliation: tonic chord is represented by black color, subdominant chord – by violet and dominant chord – by green colors. Inside the color group of a subdominant function the dark blue color is used to mark the II degree and the rose color is used for the VI degree. Inside the color group of a dominant function there are the cyan color for the III degree and the lime color for the VII degree. In the both groups the same rule is guarded – attribute more dark colors (dark blue, cyan) to the degrees on a distance of a third below the main function degree ($II - S, III - D$) and more light colors (rose, lime) to the degrees on a distance of a third above the main function degree ($S - VI, D - VII$). Such color distribution between functions was presented earlier for the possibility of the $3D$ models use in music harmony [7] and regarding its perception influence was successfully tested in the pedagogical experiments [8].

The shapes used on the second level of representation comprehend such elements as horizontal brackets aimed in up and down directions, vertical sticks and horizontal lines. The horizontal brackets are used for the horizontal triad formalization where aimed in up direction bracket signifies the bottom vertex of the graph (or graphs, if the other bottom vertices of the same horizontal triad are used to represent harmonic progression); aimed in down direction bracket signifies the top vertex (or vertices). The sticks are used to mark the edges of the graph, or, in other words, the degrees inside each horizontal triad (excluding the degrees represented by vertices). The figure below shows a horizontal triad of the first level (graph system) with its schematized representation on the second level (Fig. 1):

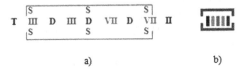

a)   b)

Fig. 1. Schematization of the horizontal triad: (a) horizontal triad of the first level; (b) schema structure of the second level.

If the harmonic progression in a graph representation uses the elements of the other horizontal triads of graphs within the same vertical triad, the corresponding brackets (with an appropriate color of the degree function) are added above the top or below the bottom main graph bracket in schema structure accordingly. The sticks representing edges are always placed within the main brackets. As the system of graphs allows different configuration of the elements, sometimes the diagonal displacement may be considered as more appropriate than displacement within the specified horizontal triad, thus the vertex may never appear. In this case the diagonal lines are used to mark such mode of connection (Fig. 2). In the used example the tonic degree never appears on the sound level, but being the common diagonal precedence between the *III* and the *VI* degrees in the graph system it is marked with a dotted line. The schema representation on the second level follows the same representation strategy.

5   The Use of the Graph System and Derived Schema Structures in Analysis on Example of Music by Valentin Silvestrov

The use of the graph system with derived schema structures in harmony analysis gives birth to a new method which may be called structural harmony approach in analysis. The aim of structural harmony approach consists of reduction and

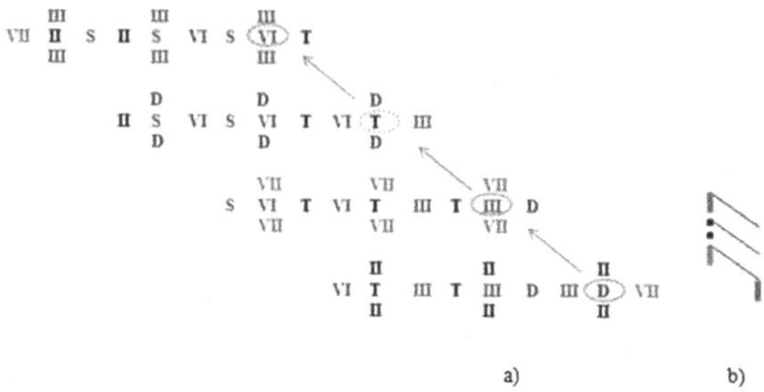

Fig. 2. Schematization of the diagonal mode of connection: (a) graph representation on the first level; (b) schema structure of the second level.

segmentation of harmonic progressions taken from the analysis of a whole composition in order to find similar harmonic structures and lows of their alternation and transformation. That kind of analysis may be especially useful for postmodern music analysis, which is mostly neo-tonal (or modal). The use of specific postmodern harmonic combinations or their specific alternation and/or transformation represented in a graph structure define the motivation for structural harmonic analysis effectuation.

For this structural harmony analysis implementation five chamber compositions from the same album of the vocal cycle *Silent songs* (1987) by Ukrainian postmodern composer Valentin Silvestrov: *Aching spirit, There were storms and bad weather, La belle dame sans merci, A melancholy time* and *Goodbye world* were chosen. The selection of the composer was done under composer's statements about one of the goal of his creation process, which according to the artist consists in finding the alternative harmonic resources of the classical harmony which were not used by romantics [9]. Considering the lack of space in the paper we will present and describe only the structures of the second level of representation. The first level with detailed process of the patterns formation on the first level of representation (graph system) is available in *Schemographe* application, the functionality of which is discussed in the next section. The order of the pieces placement is not important, because the pieces were put into an album afterwords, according to the composer's statement [9]. Therefore the pieces will be placed from simpler structure to the more complex while the following analysis.

There were storm and bad weather. The piece *There were storms and bad weather* is written in one tonality (c-moll), thus all the structures (Fig. 3) represent the dynamic of the degrees use in that specified tonality. It is the second piece within the album, but regarding its harmonic construction the piece may be considered as the most simple, therefore it will be analysed at first place. Nine schema structures shows the strict logic of harmonic development which logically may be expressed as follows:

$$Intro\ A\ B\ A\ B_1\ A_1\ B_2\ A_2\ A_3$$

Fig. 3. Schema structures of the second level of representation of the *There were storms and bad weather* piece.

where the letter A stands for structures with subdominant brackets (representation of the subdominant horizontal triad) and the letter B – for structures with diagonal mode of connection beginning with dominant function (two times V and one time VII degree). The *Intro* structure differs structurally and functionally from all the other structures[1], being placed inside the tonic brackets (tonic horizontal triad) with additional subdominant bracket and two degrees (V and VI) as edges. The role of this intro is similar to the first motif in Bach's preludes – it contains the main resources which will be used while piece development: the subdominant and tonic degrees are further used in the structures A and the rest V and VI degrees will appear in the structures B.

The dynamic of the degrees appearance as edges in the A structures is very clear: the III degree after its first appearance and repetition in the next A structure is replaced by tonic degree in the third and fourth A structures. In the last fifth A structure the degree inherent to the subdominant function – the II degree – is added. The II degree appears for the first time during all the process of harmonic development and may be treated as augmentation of the subdominant gravity in the end as opposition to the augmented tonic gravity at the beginning of the piece.

The B structures represent the varied harmonic progressions: firstly $D - VI$, then $d - III - VI$, and then $D^{\rightarrow}(VII)^2 - III$. These varied structures can be presented as a matrix (Table 1). Only the first element is varying, representing different forms of the dominant function and going away in these changes from harmonic dominant to its natural minor versions – d and then natural VII (presented with its dominant).

Goodbye world. The piece *Goodbye world* is also written in one tonality (d-moll), therefore, as in previous piece, the received range of schemas (Fig. 4) represents the dynamic of functional development within one tonality. The piece is the last in the album, but shows many similarities in the logic of schemas construction and ordering with previously analysed the simplest piece of the album. The *Goodbye world* piece, however lacks two structures – at the very beginning

---

[1] Certain structural resemblance may be seen in the A_3 structure, presenting invention of the *Intro* structure. However, the subdominant environment instead of tonic decides for A_3 structure to be in the A group of structures.

[2] On the second level of representation the degree still appear even if it is presented only by its dominant. In such a way the problem of elliptic chains representation is solved.

Table 1. Matrix of the harmonic structures variation

D	0	VI
d	III	VI
D →(VII)	III	0

and at the very end of the piece, comparing to the *There were storms and bad weather*, and has the smallest range of schemas of the entire album.

Fig. 4. Schema structures of the second level of representation of the *Goodbye world* piece.

We may present the range of schemas logically, using alphabetic representation:

$$A\ B\ A\ C\ A_1\ D\ A_2$$

where the group of structures A stands for structures which use horizontal triads of the tonic and VI degrees simultaneously. The B structure corresponds to the brackets of the III degree; the C structure – to the VII degree brackets and the D structure – to the VI degree brackets. The A structure contains the representation of all the main functions with domination of the dominant function as it is presented by two accords – its fundamental V degree representation and one substitution – the VII degree. The following B structure shows the inverted logic of domination with augmented role of the subdominant function which is now presented by its fundamental degree (the IV degree) and one of its substitution – the II degree; the dominant function, instead, is represented by its feeble substitution – the III degree, just like the subdominant was in the A structure before. The repeated farther A structure finishes this stage of development, creating a kind of a simple ternary form with two previous schemas.

The C structure is similar compositionally to the B structure: the subdominant function presented with two accords (IV and VI degrees) is enclosed along with tonic function inside the VII degree brackets. The C structure introduces a new stage of development with transformed by insertion of the subdominant chord A structure. The D structure plays the same role of a contrast that the B structure played earlier in opposition to the not transformed A structures. However if the B structure contained augmented subdominant function, the D structure contains all possible representations of the dominant function. Therefore the group of structures where the subdominant function was enclosed between dominant function at the beginning of the piece, ended by reversed opposition, where the structure with dominant function is contoured by subdominant function.

A melancholy time. The piece *A melancholy time* begins in d-moll and ends in g-moll (subdominant tonality in d-moll) with preceding modulation to Es-dur (*IIb* degree in d-moll). The piece appears as the fourth within the album order and contains more harmonic structures than two previous pieces of the album, it also contains modulations to the other tonalities. However, the number of transformations is smaller than in two other pieces left for analysis. Therefore it will be analysed on the third place. The schema structures of the entire piece are presented on Fig. 5.

Fig. 5. Schema structures of the second level of representation of the *A melancholy time* piece.

The range of schemas may be presented logically with the use of alphabetic representation:

$$A\ B\ C\ C_1\ D\ C\ C_2\ D\ C\ A_1$$

where the A structure stands for structure containing a pair of the *II* and *V* degrees and A_1 structure – for structure containing the same pair with added *VII* degree; the B structure represents the structure enclosed in the subdominant degree brackets; the group of C structures presents the set of the same degrees, placed inside the *III* degree bracket; the D structure stands for the similar set of degrees as the C group of structures, placed inside the tonic degree bracket.

The resources for harmonic development of the whole piece are gathered in the very first structure, which contains almost all the degrees used while the piece development. The meaning of this structure is the same as the meaning of the *Intro* from the *There were storms and bad weather* piece. A kind of harmonic arc is also visible in the A_1 structure, as neither *II* nor *V* degrees will not appear before the A_1 structure after the A structure. Such arc created by used harmonic resources is also a point of comparison with the harmonic development of the piece *There were storms and bad weather*. The alternation of the C group of structures with D structures yet reveals the alternation principle from the piece *There were storms and bad weather*, but more important is that those structures almost entirely based on subdominant and tonic degrees combination. The *III* degree as feeble representation of the dominant function does not change a strong subdominant domination in the development part of the piece. The B structure plays the role of the initial setup for such subdominant-tonic development, farther leaded by C and D structures.

La belle dame sans merci. The piece *La belle dame sans merci* is written in h–moll and contains two modulation to the tonalities on a distance of a major second up (cis–moll) and down (A–dur), being its *II* doric (cis) and *VII* natural (A) degrees. The piece appears as the third within the album order, and contains

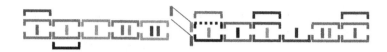

Fig. 6. Schema structures of the second level of representation of the *La belle dame sans merci* piece.

the longest chain of harmonic structures, however its structures are more simply composed than the structures of the first piece of the album, which will be analysed further. The schema structures of the piece are presented on Fig. 6. Twelve schematic harmonic structures of the piece shows more complicated logic of harmonic development than in previous examples which logically may be expressed as follows:

$$A\ A_1\ B\ A_2\ B_1\ C\ A_3\ B_2\ A_4\ A_5\ A_2\ A$$

where the A structures represent the degrees inherent to the subdominant function, the B structures represent the degrees inherent to the dominant function, and the C structure represents diagonal mode of connection starting with dominant and finishing with II degree. The placement of the C structure in the symmetrical middle point of the harmonic structures range coincides with first change of tonality and leads to the resolution in cis–moll, the tonality of the II degree, developed in the A_3 structure. The B_2, A_4 and A_5 structures are in A–dur; the appearance of the main tonality is made with use of the same modulation strategy, as h-moll is the tonality of the II degree for A–dur. The A and A_2 structures in h–moll create structural arcs of the piece in sense of used harmonic progressions. The A_1 structure is an extension of the A structure being its reversed version.

Aching spirit. The piece *Aching spirit* begins in As–dur and ends in its subdominant tonality – Des–dur. This is the piece which begins the album, however it contains the most of harmonic structures transformations, therefore it appears as the most complex piece of the album. The schema structures of the piece are presented on Fig. 7. Eleven harmonic schema structures of the piece show variety of structures transformation. For simplification of the analysis let us group these structures as follows:

$$A\ B\ A_1\ B_1\ A_2$$

were the A group of structures contains the degrees inherent to the subdominant function (II, S, VI), and the B group of structures represents the dominant function. The A, B, B_1, A_2 groups of structures contain two elements and the middle A_1 group of structures is larger and contains three elements. The structural resemblance of the very first and very last elements of the A and A_2 groups of structures respectively force to think about the structural arc in sense of harmony we saw in the *There were storms and bad weather* and *La belle dame sans merci* pieces. However the tonic and dominant degrees of the edges inside the very first structure are replaced by III and VII degrees inside the very last

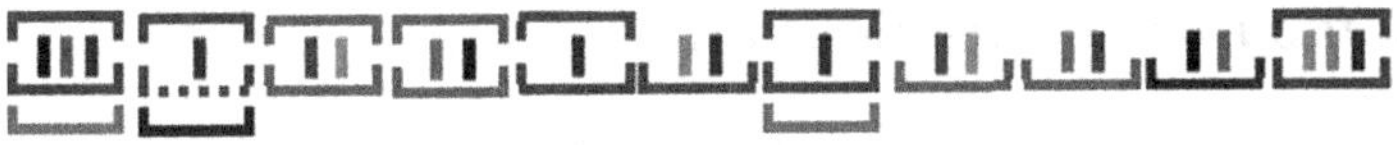

Fig. 7. Schema structures of the second level of representation of the *Aching spirit* piece.

structure. Used in the last structure VII degree appears for the first time in the symmetrical structural center of the piece – second structure of the A_1 group.

The previous analysis may be concluded to the following statements:

1. On the level of the operations with schema structures:
   (a) Harmonic structures are usually placed as simple alternation (*There were storms and bad weather, Goodbye world, A melancholy time*).
   (b) The first structure may play the role of the initialization containing resources for all the following process of harmonic development (*There were storms and bad weather, A melancholy time*).
   (c) The arc embracing whole piece created by similar harmonic structures is used frequently (*There were storms and bad weather, A melancholy time, Aching spirit*).
   (d) There may appear a symmetrical point marked structurally (*La belle dame sans merci, Aching spirit*)

2. On the level of the functional dramaturgy:
   (a) The domination of the subdominant function expressed with the specified group of degrees use (*There were storms and bad weather, Goodbye world*) of by tonal modulation (*A melancholy time, Aching spirit*).
   (b) Alternation of the subdominant and dominant areas (*There were storms and bad weather, Goodbye world, La belle dame sans merci, Aching spirit*).
   (c) The framing of a subdominant function degree by the III degree (*Goodbye world, A melancholy time, La belle dame sans merci*) and vice-versa (*There were storms and bad weather, A melancholy time, La belle dame sans merci*).

3. On the level of the degrees alteration and the elliptic chains application, visible on the first level of representation:
   (a) Preference in the use of natural group of dominant (*There were storms and bad weather, Goodbye world, A melancholy time*);
   (b) Frequent use of the doric IV degree in minor tonality (*Goodbye world, La belle dame sans merci*);
   (c) Flat alteration of the III, VII degrees in major (*Aching spirit*) and II degree in minor (*There were storms and bad weather, Goodbye world, A melancholy time, La belle dame sans merci*) tonalities.
   (d) Sharp alternation of the VI and III degrees in minor (*A melancholy time*) and the III degree in major (*Aching spirit*) tonalities;
   (e) The use of the elliptic chains (*There were storms and bad weather*: $D \rightarrow (VII) - III, D \rightarrow (s) - III/T$, *La belle dame sans merci*: $D \rightarrow (s) - III$, *Aching spirit*: $D \rightarrow (VI) - II$).

6   *Schemographe* Application

The *Schemographe* application was developed at Laboratoire Bordelaise de Recherche en Informatique (October–November 2014) during realization of the Polish Young Researches grant project given by Maria Curie-Sklodowska University. The main goal of the application is to present in detail the structural harmony methodological approach on visual and sound levels simultaneously.

The main view (specified page interface) contains four buttons to the other views. Three buttons named *Piece 1*, *Piece 2*, *Piece 3* give access to three analysed pieces: *There were storms and bad weather*, *La belle dame sans merci* and *Aching spirit* respectively. The button named *Compare schemas* will open the view with harmonic schemas of all three pieces.

When button *Piece 1* is pressed, the next view (Fig. 8a) containing images of harmonic schemas from *There were storms and bad weather* piece and the button *Play entire piece* appear. Each of the elements of this view is interactive and lead to the first level of representation with corresponding music (Fig. 8b), with a difference that images of schemas when pressed shows the formation of the graph pattern reflected by this schema only and the *Play entire piece* button shows all patterns formed in time with appropriate piece of music played simultaneously. The other two buttons of the main view – *Piece 1* and *Piece 2* – lead to the similar views and functionality with *La belle dame sans merci* and *The ailing spirit* pieces representation respectively.

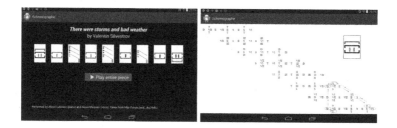

Fig. 8. Application views screenshots. (a) *Piece 1* view; (b) First schema animation.

7   Summary

The presented method allows to capture functional logic of the whole piece in a concise and visible manner. The structures received on the second level of representation are ordered on a time-line, which makes possible to follow the harmonic dramaturgy as a process and as an instance simultaneously. The pattern based representation within a graph system of the first level is familiar from the Tonnetz representation, however the use of colors representing alteration of the specified degree, saving the general logic of the degrees movement, makes the system unique in this sense. The abstraction of the higher logical level along with the possibilities of the details display shows the system as a perfect tool for tonal music analysis and regarding its clear strategies of graphic representation, it makes possible the implementation of the method on the level of a program interface, as we showed with *Schemographe* application. Farther process of the system implementation may include the automatic pattern building and schematization on the second level in a software for automatic harmonic analysis with a possibility of an expert system in tonal harmony creation, which will be able to simulate different tonal and neo-tonal compositional styles.

References

1. Lewin, D.: Generalized Musical Intervals and Transformations. Yale University Press, New Haven (1987)
2. Tymoczko, D.: A Geometry of Music. Oxford Univeristy Press, New York (2011)
3. Lewin, D.: Klumpenhouwer networks and some isographies that involve them. Music Theory Spectr. **12**(1), 83–120 (1990). (Spring)
4. Bigo, L., Andreatta, M., Giavitto, J.-L., Michel, O., Spicher, A.: Computation and visualization of musical structures in chord-based simplicial complexes. In: Yust, J., Wild, J., Burgoyne, J.A. (eds.) MCM 2013. LNCS, vol. 7937, pp. 38–51. Springer, Heidelberg (2013)
5. Baroin, G.: Applications de la thorie des graphes des objets musicaux. Modlisations, visualisations en hyperspace. Ph.D. thesis, Université de Toulouse (2011)
6. Meeùs, N.: Vecteurs harmoniques. Musurgia **X**(3–4), 7–34 (2003)
7. Shvets, A.: Application of 3D in visualization of knowledge in music harmony. Digital Turn in Humanities: Internet-New Media-Culture 2.0. (in Polish) E-naukowiec: Lublin, 2013, pp. 127–137 (2013)
8. Pistone, P., Shvets, A.: Investigation of the activity based teaching method in e-learning musical harmony course. In: Cappellini, V. (ed.) Proceeding of EVA Florence 2014, 7–8 May 2014, pp. 107–112. Firenze University Press, Florence (2014)
9. Shvets, A.: Certains aspects des tendances modernes du dveloppement de l'art (2011). Musicologie.org

Biological Content Generation: Evolving Game Terrains Through Living Organisms

Wim van Eck[1,2(✉)] and Maarten H. Lamers[1]

[1] Media Technology Research Group, Leiden Institute of Advanced Computer
Science, Leiden University, Leiden, The Netherlands
{w.j.o.m.van.eck,m.h.lamers}@liacs.leidenuniv.nl
[2] Royal Academy of Art, The Hague, The Netherlands

Abstract. This study explores the concept of evolving game terrains
through intermediation of living biological organisms and presents a
proof of concept realization thereof. We explore how fungal and bacterial
cultures can be used to generate an evolving game terrain in real-time.
By visually capturing growing cultures inside a Petri-dish, heightmaps
are generated that form the basis of naturally evolving terrains. Possible consequences and benefits of this approach are discussed, as are
its effects on the visual appearance of simulated terrains. A novel and
convenient method for visually capturing growing microorganisms is presented, with a technical description for translating captured footage to
virtual terrains. This work is experimental in nature and is an initial
venture into the novel domain of organically growing virtual terrains.

Keywords: Bio-digital hybrid systems · Living organisms · Virtual terrain · Computer games · Procedural content generation · Fungi · Bacteria

1 Introduction

Generally, game terrains are manually designed with the aid of procedural content generation or completely procedurally generated at the start of the game
[1]. Game terrains which procedurally evolve while the game is being played are
rarely seen, likely since this has a too high impact on the computer's resources. In
an earlier study [2] in which we discuss the potential of biological systems within
digital games for the game player, game designer, or bio-digital integrated organism, we posed the possibility of generating an evolving game terrain in real-time,
based on the growth of a live biological system.

Applying biologically inspired algorithms in the development and design of
computer games is common. Perlin noise [3], developed to generate fractal patterns as found in nature, is heavily used in the generation of game terrains.
Instead of simulating such natural patterns, we opt the possibility to apply naturally generated patterns directly. This study explores the concept of evolving
game terrains through intermediation of living biological organisms and presents
a proof of concept realization thereof.

© Springer International Publishing Switzerland 2015
C. Johnson et al. (Eds.): EvoMUSART 2015, LNCS 9027, pp. 224–235, 2015.
DOI: 10.1007/978-3-319-16498-4_20

We have several reasons to investigate this approach. Firstly we want to see if the natural growth of the organism is reflected in the generated terrain. Will the shape of the terrain and its growth look and feel natural? Secondly, the player experience might be different; exploring a terrain with the knowledge that it is derived in real-time from a living organism might give a different player experience from knowing it was digitally generated. With respect to in-game opponent characters, it was shown [4] that players who falsely believed they played online games against human-controlled opponents experienced more enjoyment, presence and flow in doing so, as opposed to subjects aware of the opponent's true non-biological control. A similar "awareness-effect" could be hypothesized for biologically grown game terrains. Thirdly, our approach has the potential advantage that the terrain keeps evolving even when the computer is powered off. This adds a potentially interesting element of real-time behaviour to the terrain. Community simulation games such as *Harvest Moon* (Nintendo, 2001), in which the game continues even when the player is not actively playing may benefit from this. Fourthly there is an element of unpredictability; it is difficult to predict the development of the living organism and therefore the outcome of the terrain. Lastly, since our research in general investigates the possible advantages of integrating live biological systems within digital games we are also merely curious for the outcome of such an approach.

Prior studies or applications that develop game terrains through the observation and possible interaction with living organisms do not exist to the best of our knowledge. In *Lumberjacked* [5] movement of leafs in real trees influences the behaviour of tree-avatars in a basic hack 'n' slash-type game. Although virtual trees are typically part of game environments, in this particular game they act as opponents within a static environment. In *Metazoa Ludens* [6] the real (physical) floor on which a hamster walks deforms according to in-game virtual states. Although this game revolves around a biological organism and includes a physically changing environment, the environment is not evolved but parametrically changed and not as the direct result of the organisms behaviour. An example of a computer game which uses an external factor (although not biological) for generating game levels is *Vib Ribbon* (NanaOn-Sha, 1999). This platform game in which the player must avoid obstacles on the rhythm of music gives the option to insert an audio CD of choice which is then analyzed and used to generate the obstacles in the game.

Living organisms within games have however already been successfully utilized in other ways. Developers and players can benefit from behaviour generation [5,7], apply crowdsourcing mechanics in which players perform experiments on actual living biological matter [8], conduct animal welfare studies [6,9] or create physical contextualization [10]. Although not used in a gaming context yet, also the natural sensing and processing capabilities of living organisms can be used as part of larger digital systems [11–13].

In the remainder of this article, we first take a closer look at how game terrains are created using traditional PCG techniques. Then, we explore how a living organism can be used to generate an evolving game terrain, which organisms are most suited for our purpose and which are the advantages/disadvantages of such a hybrid biological-digital approach. With a concluding discussion of our results, we aim to broaden the scope of content generation for gaming - even though our work is highly experimental. Additional resources of this study can be found on our project webpage [14].

2   Game Terrains Through Procedural Generation

Procedural content generation in computer games has been used already since *Beneath Apple Manor* (Don Worth, 1978), where rooms of a dungeon are procedurally generated each time you start the game. In this case procedural generation is mostly used to add replay value; every time you play the game the environment is slightly different. Also modern games such as *Minecraft* (Mojang, 2009) procedurally generate an environment each time you start the game. It is less common however to have a generated environment which keeps on developing while the game is being played. During the development of *Fable* (Big Blue Box, 2004), designer Peter Molyneux announced that it would feature a constantly evolving world in which you could for example plant an acorn and then watch it grow into an oak tree over the course of the game. This feature was indeed coded by the developers, but since this option alone took 15 % of the total processor time it was discarded. The feature did not return in later *Fable* games which ran on more powerful hardware.

Naturally, many different types of game terrains exist. Some aim at natural realism, whereas others appear more abstract. A common element of terrains are differing heights. Within 3D animation packages and game engines these height differences are usually generated through a heightmap, often generated through noise patterns. Ken Perlin developed Perlin noise with the intention to simulate natural phenomena with fractal features such as landscapes, waves and clouds. A single slice of Perlin noise results in evenly distributed height elevations, which do not particularly resemble a realistic landscape (Fig. 1). By stacking multiple slices of Perlin noise, with each stack subsequently half the scale and half the intensity of the underlying slice, fractal features are formed resulting in a much more realistic landscape (Fig. 2).

3   Generating Terrains Through Living Organisms

As stated in the introduction we investigate the possibilities of generating an evolving game terrain based on a living organism. Eventually this game terrain should be generated in real-time, while the organism is actually growing. However, for this study we focus on the feasibility of such an idea using pre-captured data. This makes testing much more practical since waiting repeatedly for the organism to grow is quite time consuming. We choose to generate our virtual terrains based on time-lapse images of an organism. By doing so we focus on the organism's growth which might exhibit natural growth phenomena such as fractals, symmetries and spirals; these phenomena are actually often simulated when

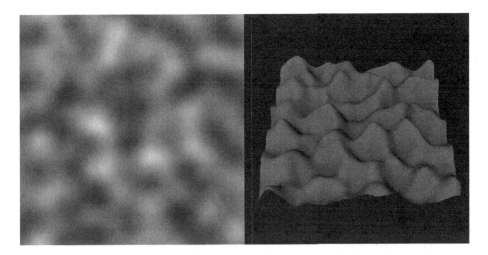

Fig. 1. Perlin noise pattern represented as greyscale image (left) and the resulting terrain (right)

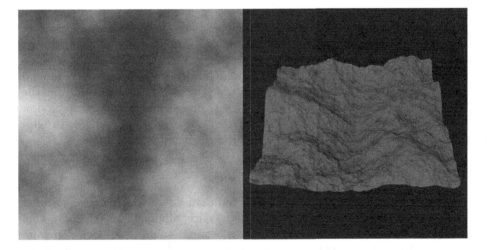

Fig. 2. Seven layers of stacked Perlin noise patterns (left) and the resulting terrain (right)

procedurally generating landscape terrains for gaming. Although it is technically possible, we discarded the idea of using sound or bioelectrical activity produced by organisms, since they yield one-dimensional information which is less suitable for generating a 3-dimensional terrain.

3.1 Fungi and Bacteria

When choosing a living organism there are certain factors that are important to our intended use: growth pattern, growth speed, how easily it can be grown, availability of the organism and ease of imaging. While for example snail shells, pinecones, seed heads of flowers, Romanesco broccoli and tree branches display growth patterns such as spirals, symmetries and fractals, it is difficult to image these since they cannot be easily contained on a fixed spot while growing. Fungi and bacteria however are easily grown in Petri-dishes, and can display afore-mentioned growth patterns. Growth patterns of bacteria such as *Bacillus subtilis* can resemble the structures of mountain ranges as seen on satellite imagery in a remarkable way.

Moreover, bacteria and fungi are very easy to obtain; Petri-dishes that are prepared in a non-sterile environment are likely contaminated with various cultures. The authors of this article have no background in biology and there-fore cannot identify specific (micro)organisms appearing in the dish. Knowing the specific species however is not essential for our purpose. If desired, visually interesting fungi and bacteria can be cultivated by transferring them into a new Petri-dish using a swab.

We grow our cultures in Petri-dishes on self-made agar of which the ingredi-ents (agar, honey, marmite, milk powder and activated carbon) offer a nutritious base. The activated carbon is added to colour it black, providing better visual contrast with the cultures.

The Petri-dishes are prepared and kept in a non-sterile (domestic) environ-ment. No cultures are purposefully introduced, but are contaminated during preparation, handling and exposure to the environment. In our experience the first colonies appear after roughly two days, followed by steady growth of around 6 days. These times can fluctuate depending on the ambient temperature and the types of bacteria and fungi. Higher or lower temperatures will speed up or slow down the growth, while 37 °C is generally regarded as an optimal growth tem-perature. After this growth period the cultures generally stabilize.

3.2   Visually Capturing the Organism

The visual captures of our fungi and bacteria must fulfil the following criteria; stable lighting, fixed exposure, fixed white balance, minimal imaging noise, high resolution and the setup should not move between shots. Any deviation from these requirements introduces visual artifacts that influence the outcome of the generated terrain. Since we only want the growth of the culture itself to shape our terrain, all other visual artifacts are unwanted.

Stable photography proves to be challenging; the transparent plastic lid of Petri-dishes degrades the image quality and condensate forms on the lid, introducing visual artifacts. Removing the lid results in rapidly dried-out agar, introducing new visual artifacts and limiting organic growth. We counter these problems by not using a lid on the dishes and placing them upside-down on a consumer flatbed scanner (Fig. 3). A CCD based scanner is preferred over a CIS based scanner since the latter does not scan beyond the surface of the glass plate. The Petri-dishes are filled with agar 2 mm from the top so the cultures are near enough the glass plate to be in focus. The 21 by 29,7 cm sized flatbed scanner can scan 6 Petri-dishes simultaneously at a resolution of 1200 dpi with

Fig. 3. Epson Perfection V370 Photo flatbed scanner with 5 upside-down Petri-dishes and one upright Petri-dish showing colony growth

full color depth. This results in scans of roughly 9000 by 13000 pixels. Cropping a single Petri-dish from the scan results in 4200 by 4200 pixel images. Higher resolution scans are possible but not required for our purpose. A single scan takes 3 min. We manually underexpose the scanner slightly to prevent artifacts caused by overexposure. Scans are made with intervals of 5 min, yielding a high enough

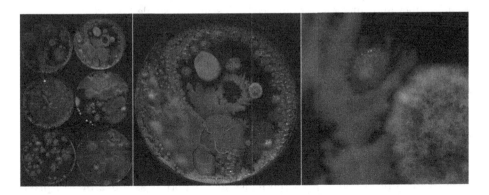

Fig. 4. A single color scan of 6 Petri-dishes with cultures (left), a cropped section showing a single Petri-dish (middle), and a 512 by 512 pixel crop showing details of growing cultures (right)

frequency to determine the optimum interval (a multiple of 5 min) post-hoc. We start scanning a day after the agar was poured into the Petri-dishes, allowing the agar to cool down to the ambient temperature. We stop scanning when the growth of the colonies appears to have stopped or when the agar dries out.

The resulting scans are of sufficient resolution, free of artifacts, and evenly illuminated (Fig. 4). Unfortunately, the light emitted from the scan head is reflected by glossy surfaces, resulting in unwanted bright artifacts on glossy bacteria. While not all bacteria have glossy surfaces it would be preferable to work only with fungi. We noticed that agar mixed with honey and instant coffee powder reduced the amount of bacterial colonies, but a sterile setup is required to entirely avoid them. We choose to continue working with both fungi and bacteria, retaining a simple and more affordable DIY setup. The bacteria furthermore exhibit growth patterns which we do not want to exclude.

3.3 Translating Captured Images into a Virtual Terrain

There are numerous ways to translate our captured data into a virtual terrain. This study does not aim to find the best technical way to accomplish this, since what is best is at least partially determined by requirements from the intended game. Instead we explore a single method, hoping to trigger others to continue upon this work.

This study serves as a proof-of-concept, and generated terrains need not yet be visualized within a game engine in real-time, but can be generated after the visual capturing is completed. Although we did create a real-time setup using the Unity game engine, we choose to use 3D animation package Maxon Cinema 4D to render still images and movies, making it easier to document our results. To retain compatibility with current game creation workflows we choose to use our captures as aforementioned heightmaps. Since the bright coloured cultures contrasts well with the black agar these captures are actually very suited for such usage. A heightmap resolution of 512 by 512 pixels is common within popular game engines and sufficient for our needs. A scan of a single Petri-dish measures 4200 by 4200 pixels, so we can either downscale a section of a scan or use a 512 by 512 pixel crop. Working with pre-captured images offers the advantage of knowing on which area of the Petri-dish the cultures formed and how they are shaped. In case of a real-time setup one could contaminate a specific area of the Petri-dish to ensure that a certain culture will grow on that area.

Although our experiment makes captures with an interval of 5 min we decide to have the terrain update only once an hour (every 12 frames), since the difference between each capture is quite small. This results in 191 captures, visualizing 190 h, or 7 days and 22 h of growth. We select an area featuring both fungi and glossy bacteria, and convert the images to grayscale (256 levels). We crop a 2048 by 2048 pixel region from the image and export it as a 512 by 512 pixel PNG-format sequence. We can directly load the image-sequence as an animated height-map into the displacement channel of Cinema 4D.

The direct mapping of grayscale values to terrain height results in sudden peaks on areas where the light of the scanner was reflected. Also, it is notable that

Fig. 5. Grayscale 512 by 512 pixel image showing fungi and bacterial cultures (left), and generated terrain using the image directly as a heightmap (right)

the terrain height does not increase monotonously, but both rising and lowering of terrain height occurs over time. We also notice that the terrain undulates strongly with high spatial frequency, a phenomenon referred to as "terrain noise" in broader terrain-developing communities (Fig. 5). This makes the terrain not easily accessible for ground-traveling in-game characters. Reducing the level of vertical displacement results in a terrain that varies lesser in height.

To achieve a more accessible terrain, one could apply some form of post-processing on the heightmap, effectively smoothing the terrain and thereby reducing terrain noise. Many methods to achieve this can be considered. One such method is multiscale stacking of heightmaps, a technique commonly applied to Perlin noise heightmaps. A more simple approach would be to smooth the heightmap using a low-width blurring filter (Fig. 6). An additional advantage of the latter approach is that the resulting heightmap corresponds more closely to the original one, whereas multiscale stacking leads to increased structural changes, and therefore smaller resemblance to the organisms' structures. It should be noted that large peaks and troughs caused by unwanted artifacts in the capturing process cannot be fully eliminated by blurring.

Our example experiment does not use colour information of the captured images. It would be possible to use colour information to assign terrain features such as grass, rocks, trees, snow, foliage, and flowers, or to assign more game-specific features, such as portals or special locations.

To achieve a more recognizable terrain, common shaders can be applied. For example, slope-angle information can be used to accumulate virtual snow on peaks and horizontal planes. Another trivial solution is the assignment of terrain types (e.g. water, grass, rock, snow) to predefined height ranges (Fig. 7). More examples, including scans, terrains, and time-lapse videos can be found on the project webpage [14].

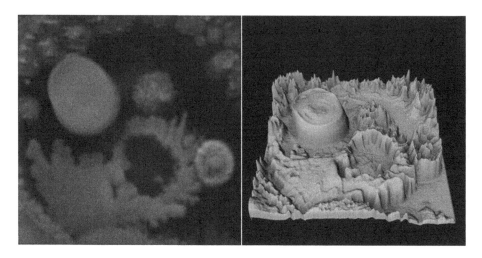

Fig. 6. 4-pixel radius blurred image from Fig. 5 (left), and the corresponding terrain (right)

4   Discussion

As shown in this study, it is indeed possible to generate digital game terrains based on the growth of fungi and bacteria, but what are the actual advantages and disadvantages of such an approach? The introduction questions whether the natural growth of organisms is reflected in the generated terrain, and whether the shape of the terrain and its growth look and feel natural. We fully recognize

Fig. 7. Generated terrain with slope-angle based accumulation of virtual snow (left), and assignment of terrain types to height ranges (right)

Fig. 8. Generated terrain as seen from a first-person view

that such qualities cannot be directly measured, expressed or proven to exist. Although a user-study could be employed to shed light on the users' experiences when confronted with biologically "grown" terrains, this falls beyond the scope of this initial proof-of-concept study and remains to be further investigated. Moreover, this proof-of-concept study was unavoidably undertaken in the form of a case study, whereby a specific case was investigated. Nonetheless, we trust that the thoughts and experiences derived from this case study transfer to the broader spectrum of biological terrain generation. Overall the appearance of terrains generated by our method looks natural. To a geologically untrained observer, they appear as possible results of geological processes.

Natural growth of the organisms is indeed reflected in the change of terrains over time, possibly since our method translates captures of the organism almost directly into heightmaps. Although this can be seen clearly from a bird's-eye perspective (Fig. 7), a ground-travelling player would probably lack overview to perceive the organism's change over time (Fig. 8). In our opinion the growth of the terrain has a quite natural look when changes are seen in a rapid succession. This would be harder to notice however when the terrain evolves in real-time and hourly updates show only small changes. Even with a less clear overview of the terrain and its growth, the player experience might be positively influenced by awareness that the terrain is generated by a live organism (c.f. [4]).

To create a more accessible and common terrain we choose to slightly blur the captures, introducing minor post-processing. It is possible to view such blurring, and effectively smoothing of the terrain, as the virtual analogy of naturally occurring erosion. Naturally, it is possible to use unprocessed captured images to create deviating alien worlds, underwater landscapes, or environments free of atmospheric erosion such as planetary landscapes.

The evolving aspect of terrains could in principle be problematic since each new capture might change the terrain considerably and instantly, possibly hindering and disorienting the player. In fact, a player could suddenly be positioned underneath the terrain. A higher update rate would certainly reduce this problem, but not eliminate it. As a solution the terrain could gradually morph from the prior to a new state after each capture.

It is interesting to note that within the setup explored here, a single Petri-dish can accommodate 37 unique 512 by 512 pixel (common sized) evolving heightmaps simultaneously. Given that our simple setup develops 6 Petri-dishes simultaneously on a single flatbed scanner, a likewise very simple approach could stream 222 unique terrains to different game clients simultaneously in real time. Such a system would avoid players having to grow and capture their own organisms.

Although not yet explored in this study, live interaction between player and organism could be a promising addition. A player could stimulate, delay or stop growth at a certain area using light, temperature, nutrition or toxics (e.g. alcohol or antibiotics). Such terrain-altering concepts could even be integrated into gameplay mechanics. For example, it might be a goal within the game to "grow" a path towards a certain area, or attacks on the terrain could be achieved by dropping drips of alcohol on the organism. Such interaction would however require an alternate capturing method than the upside-down Petri-dish capturing employed in this proof-of-concept case study.

An unexpected byproduct of our research is the capturing method that we devised by utilizing a consumer flatbed scanner, dark-colored agar, and upside-down growing cultures. Surprisingly, this cost-friendly DIY approach to imaging bacterial and fungal cultures enables very high quality capturing of six Petri-dishes simultaneously. One could imagine also other research to benefit from this simple approach.

Acknowledgments. Preliminary results of this study were presented at the symposium "What's Next for Procedural Content?" at IT University of Copenhagen, November 2014. We thank the participants for their useful feedback and comments.

References

1. Hendrixk, M., Meijer, S., Van Der Velden, J., Iosup, A.: Procedural content generation for games: a survey. ACM Trans. Multimed. Comput. Commun. Appl. (TOMCCAP) **9**(1), 1:1–1:22 (2013)
2. Lamers, M.H., van Eck, W.: Why simulate? hybrid biological-digital games. In: Di Chio, C., et al. (eds.) EvoApplications 2012. LNCS, vol. 7248, pp. 214–223. Springer, Heidelberg (2012)
3. Perlin, K.: An image synthesizer. ACM siggraph Comput. Graph. **19**(3), 287–296 (1985)
4. Weibel, D., Wissmath, B., Habegger, S., Steiner, Y., Groner, R.: Playing online games against computer- vs. human-controlled opponents: effects on presence, flow, and enjoyment. Comput. Hum. Behav. **24**(5), 2274–2291 (2008)

5. Young, D.: Lumberjacked (2005). http://rhizome.org/artbase/artwork/35526/
6. Tan, R.K.C., et al.: MetazoaLudens: mixed reality interactions and play for small pets and humans. Leonardo **41**(3), 308–309 (2008)
7. van Eck, W., Lamers, M.H.: Animal controlled computer games: playing pac-man against real crickets. In: Harper, R., Rauterberg, M., Combetto, M. (eds.) ICEC 2006. LNCS, vol. 4161, pp. 31–36. Springer, Heidelberg (2006)
8. Riedel-Kruse, I.H., Chung, A.M., Dura, B., Hamilton, A.L., Lee, B.C.: Design, engineering and utility of biotic games. Lab Chip **11**, 14–22 (2011)
9. Alfrink, K., van Peer, I., Lagerweij, H., Driessen, C., Bracke, M.: Playing with pigs (2012). http://www.playingwithpigs.nl/
10. Vermeulen, A.: Biomodd (2007). http://www.biomodd.net/
11. van Eck, W., Lamers, M.H.: Hybrid biological-digital systems in artistic and entertainment computing. Leonardo **46**(2), 151–158 (2013)
12. Rinaldo, K.: Augmented fish reality (2004). http://kenrinaldo.com/
13. Hertz, G.: Cockroach controlled mobile robot (2004). http://www.conceptlab.com/roachbot/
14. van Eck, W., Lamers, M.H.: Hybrid biological digital games blog. http://biodigitalgames.com/

Interpretability of Music Classification as a Criterion for Evolutionary Multi-objective Feature Selection

Igor Vatolkin[1]([⊠]), Günter Rudolph[1], and Claus Weihs[2]

[1] Department of Computer Science, TU Dortmund, Dortmund, Germany
{igor.vatolkin,guenter.rudolph}@tu-dortmund.de
[2] Faculty of Statistics, TU Dortmund, Dortmund, Germany
claus.weihs@tu-dortmund.de

Abstract. The development of numerous audio signal characteristics led to an increase of classification performance for automatic categorisation of music audio recordings. Unfortunately, models built with such low-level descriptors lack of interpretability. Musicologists and listeners can not learn musically meaningful properties of genres, styles, composers, or personal preferences. On the other side, there are new algorithms for the mining of interpretable features from music data: instruments, moods and melodic properties, tags and meta data from the social web, etc. In this paper, we propose an approach how evolutionary multi-objective feature selection can be applied for a systematic maximisation of interpretability without a limitation to the usage of only interpretable features. We introduce a simple hypervolume based measure for the evaluation of trade-off between classification performance and interpretability and discuss how the results of our study may help to search for particularly relevant high-level descriptors in future.

Keywords: Interpretable music classification · Evolutionary multi-objective optimisation · Feature selection

1 Introduction and Previous Work

Supervised classification of music is one of the most prominent research areas in Music Information Retrieval (MIR). Examples of related tasks are recognition of harmonic properties, such as key and mode, extraction of instrumentation, identification of composers and artists, detection of cover songs, optical music recognition, and so on. In general, supervised classification consists of the following steps: (a) feature extraction, (b) feature preprocessing (e.g., normalisation and removal of outliers), (c) training of classification models with the help of labelled data for the learning of dependencies between the distribution of features and the corresponding labels, and (d) finally the application of these models to categorise unlabelled data represented with feature vectors.

The **evaluation and tuning** of a classification algorithm chain is usually done w.r.t. one or several performance criteria, such as classification error, accuracy, recall, specificity, generalisation ability, etc. Another common optimisation

© Springer International Publishing Switzerland 2015
C. Johnson et al. (Eds.): EvoMUSART 2015, LNCS 9027, pp. 236–248, 2015.
DOI: 10.1007/978-3-319-16498-4_21

goal is to reduce demands on resources (runtime and indexing space for the storage of features), applying, e.g., statistical methods like principal component analysis for the reduction of the number of features.

The **interpretability of classification models** is very seldom addressed in most of MIR studies, although it plays an important role, in particular, for classification scenarios related to a music listener or a musicologist. More comprehensible classification models provide new possibilities for computer aided music analysis of musical genres, styles, or personal preferences. Classification models built with high-level, semantic features help to understand important properties of user-defined categories, for example, learning whether a listener prefers slow music with female vocals and guitar, or music composed in a Greek scale with organ and percussions.

Furthermore, the extracted high-level information can be integrated into **automatic composition systems** for the creation of new music with properties important for a listener. An overview of evolutionary inspired composition systems is provided in [18]. Consider two counter-examples using low-level audio features only. A chroma vector describes strengths of halftones in the spectrum and may help to create classification models if harmonic properties are relevant. Features in phase domain correlate with the strength of percussive components in music and distinguish very well between classic and pop [17]. However, these low-level features can be hardly integrated into a rule-based composition system, in contrast to related high-level properties of harmony (key, number of inharmonic tones, etc.) and instrumentation (amount of percussions). It is also possible to first learn interpretable fuzzy rules which describe some music style [9] and to use them later for the generation of new music.

An obvious way to significantly increase the interpretability of classification models is to use only **high-level features with relation to music theory**: properties of instrumentation, applied digital effects, melody, harmony, moods, tempo, structure, and rhythm instead of low-level audio signal characteristics. Many high-level features can be robustly extracted from the score; examples of such features are provided in [10,15]. However, the classification of audio recordings has several strong advantages: the score is not always available, only audio may capture the style of the performer and digitally applied effects, and the popularity of music pieces does not restrict the extraction of features.

The estimation of **high-level features from low-level ones** was proposed more than a decade ago [4,20]. In a more recent study on genre recognition, test listeners selected most appropriate semantic descriptors ("classicality, grooviness, roughness") for pre-clustered audio tracks [24]. The extension of this approach with more descriptors can be also done with the help of the social web using systems for automatic tag prediction [8] or results of mood recognition systems [11]. Other works introduced different ways of aggregation of low-level features which can be seen as a "mid-level" representation: e.g., statistics of pitch and harmony [3], or description of the temporal progress of underlying features with so called structural complexity of chroma, rhythm, and timbre [14] and later structural complexity of feature groups with a higher interpretability (chords, harmony, instruments, and tempo and rhythm) [23].

The classification with only high-level features may lead to a pitfall: there is no guarantee that the features available at hand would be among the most relevant for a concrete classification task. Several studies on musical genre recognition proposed successful **combinations of different feature groups**: low-level features and descriptors of instrumentation [25], audio and symbolic features [13], low-level and chord features [2], audio and harmonic features [1], audio, symbolic, cultural, and lyric features [16]. In [21], low-level features and melodic properties were applied for emotion recognition. For all these studies, with only a few exceptions characterised by marginal decrease of accuracy, combinations of feature groups led to an increase of classification performance. Interestingly, to our knowledge, none of the related studies introduced interpretability as an optimisation criterion.

Thus, the **novel contribution** of our work is to start with a large set of low-level and high-level features and to apply multi-objective optimisation for the simultaneous minimisation of the classification error and the maximisation of the interpretability measured as relative amount of interpretable features. Further, we introduce a simple hypervolume based measure to validate the trade-off between classification error and interpretability. In the remainder of the paper, we first describe methods and provide a formal definition of feature selection task within the scope of this work. Then, the results of experiments are discussed with regard to several aspects: trade-off between interpretability and error, analysis of extreme non-dominated solutions, and comparison to another data set from the previous work on interpretable classification. Further, we discuss how the identification of relevant low-level features may induce the search for new relevant high-level descriptors. In the concluding section we briefly reconsider the findings of the study and discuss promising research ideas for the future.

2   Evolutionary Multi-objective Optimisation for More Interpretability

Evolutionary Algorithms (EAs) are very well suited for feature selection and multi-objective optimisation for several reasons. The number of evaluations necessary for a sufficient improvement of performance is usually significantly lower compared to other wrapper feature selection approaches [12]. Because the number of possible feature sets with an increasing number of available features becomes very high (for F features there exist $2^F - 1$ non-empty possible feature subsets), mutation helps to overcome local optima. Further, the evolution of a population of solutions helps to identify compromise feature subsets which approximate the Pareto-front best (see below Definition 3). For an overview of studies on evolutionary multi-objective feature selection, see [19].

Both optimisation criteria in this study are the **balanced relative classification error** m_{BRE} and the **share of high-level features** m_{HL} relative to the overall number of features F:

$$m_{BRE} = \frac{1}{2} \left(\frac{FN}{TP + FN} + \frac{FP}{TN + FP} \right), \tag{1}$$

$$m_{HL} = \frac{F_{HL}}{F}. \tag{2}$$

TP is here the number of true positives (excerpts of songs which belong to a category to predict and are correctly classified), TN true negatives (excerpts which do not belong to a category and are correctly classified), FP false positives (excerpts which do not belong to a category but are classified as belonging to it), FN false negatives (excerpts which belong to a category and are classified as not belonging to it), and F_{HL} is the number of selected high-level features.

The **feature selection task** is defined as follows:

Definition 1. *Given the set of selected features denoted with a binary vector q, the goal is to find an optimal feature set denoted with q^*, so that*

$$q^* = \arg\min_{q}[m_{BRE}\,(y,\hat{y},\mathcal{F}(q))\,,1 - m_{HL}\,(\mathcal{F}(q))], \tag{3}$$

where $\mathcal{F}(q)$ is the set of features denoted with q, y are the correct labels, and $\hat{y}$ the predicted ones. For binary classification applied in this study, $y,\hat{y} \in \{0;1\}$.

Feature subsets are compared by means of **Pareto-dominance**, i.e.:

Definition 2. $\mathcal{F}(q_a) \prec \mathcal{F}(q_b)$ *(feature subset denoted with q_a strongly dominates the subset denoted with q_b), iff all three following constraints hold:*

- $m_{BRE}\,(\mathcal{F}(q_a)) \leq m_{BRE}\,(\mathcal{F}(q_b))$
- $m_{HL}\,(\mathcal{F}(q_a)) \geq m_{HL}\,(\mathcal{F}(q_b))$
- $m_{BRE}\,(\mathcal{F}(q_a)) < m_{BRE}\,(\mathcal{F}(q_b))$ *OR* $m_{HL}\,(\mathcal{F}(q_a)) > m_{HL}\,(\mathcal{F}(q_b))$

Because in most cases not all feature subsets are comparable, the main task of multi-objective optimisation is to find the **Pareto-front** with the "best" set of trade-off solutions:

Definition 3. *The feature subset $\mathcal{F}(q_a)$ belongs to the Pareto-optimal set iff:*

- $\nexists \mathcal{F}(q_b) : \mathcal{F}(q_b) \prec \mathcal{F}(q_a)$.

Then, the point $[m_{BRE}\,(\mathcal{F}(q_a))\,;m_{HL}\,(\mathcal{F}(q_a))]$ in the objective space belongs to the Pareto-front.

As there is no guarantee that the Pareto-front will be found in a single or several optimisation runs (in particular if the number of solutions in the Pareto-front is higher than the population size of an EA), we describe best found compromise solutions as the **non-dominated front**. For a general introduction to evolutionary multi-objective optimisation we refer to [7].

For the evaluation of feature subsets with respect to the closeness to Pareto-front as well as to the diversity of solutions, the **hypervolume** or $\mathcal{S}$-metric was proposed in [26]:

$$\mathcal{S}(q_1, ..., q_N) = vol\left(\bigcup_{i=1}^{N} [q_i, \mathbf{r}]\right), \tag{4}$$

where $q_1, ..., q_N$ are binary vectors representing feature subsets from the non-dominated front, r is the reference point in the objective space usually positioned at the coordinates of the worst possible solution (here $m_{BRE} = 1$ and $m_{HL} = 0$), and $vol\,(\cdot)$ denotes the joint volume of hypercubes spanned between solutions of the non-dominated front and the reference point.

As an optimisation strategy we apply an $\mathcal{S}$-metric selection evolutionary multi-objective algorithm (**SMS-EMOA**) [5], a $(\mu + 1)$-EA which selects individuals based on dominated hypervolume, so that also solutions which are non comparable in terms of Pareto-dominance can be evaluated.

Initial feature subsets are drawn with equal probability belonging to only one of three groups: (a) low-level features, (b) high-level features, and (c) both low-level and high-level ones. The first reason for this initialisation is that in the preliminary study even a strong mutation rate could not help to find feature sets built with only high-level features after the optimisation, because of a large number of features and a limited number of evaluations. Another advantage is that subsets with the highest and lowest interpretability are available already at the very beginning of the optimisation process: for categorisation tasks which can be characterised very well with high-level features, weak solutions with a too large share of low-level ones are eliminated faster, and for tasks which can not be explained well with available high-level features, the solutions with only low-level ones may boost the performance w.r.t. classification error.

3   Experiments

3.1   Setup

The **setup of our experiments** is based on [23], where main binary categorisation tasks were to identify each of 3 genres and 3 styles using either low-level or high-level audio descriptors. Only small sets of 10 positive and 10 negative music pieces were used for the training of classification models to better match real-world situation where a listener would prefer to select only few tracks for the definition of a personal category. The models were optimised by means of multi-objective evolutionary feature selection using set of other 120 tracks for fitness estimation (m_{BRE} and m_{HL}), and were finally evaluated with a track-independent test set TS120 of 120 music pieces not used for training and optimisation, however randomly selected from the same albums.

Compared to previous work, we do not just compare interpretable features against low-level ones, but allow both kinds searching for best trade-off subsets of features which contain as many high-level features as possible and produce as small classification error as possible. In particular, we suggest that even in cases where high-level features perform better than low-level ones, addition of some low-level characteristics may reduce the classification error. Further, we use more music categories (6 genres and 8 styles) and provide a more credible assessment of the generalisation ability of our approach validating optimised feature subsets on a new album- and artist-independent set TAS120 of 120 music pieces with the same distribution across genres as TS120. Song lists with corresponding categories are provided on https://ls11-www.cs.uni-dortmund.de/rudolph/mi#music_test_database.

Table 1 lists **groups of audio features**, at overall 636 low-level and 566 high-level ones. Column "No." provides numbers of individual feature dimensions after the estimation of mean and standard deviation of short-framed features for texture windows of 4 s with 2 s overlap (excerpts from music tracks). The high-level group "Various features" contains characteristics defined by musicologists in [22].

Table 1. Groups of features for music classification.

Group	Examples	No.
LOW-LEVEL AUDIO FEATURES		
Cepstral domain	Mel frequency cepstral coefficients	202
Chroma and harmony	Fundamental frequency, chroma vector	202
ERB and Bark domains	Bark scale magnitudes	106
Phase domain	Angles and distances	4
Rhythm	Characteristics of fluctuation patterns	24
Spectral domain	Spectral centroid, bandwidth, tristimulus	58
Tempo and correlation	Periodicity peak	6
Time domain	Linear prediction coefficients, zerocrossing rate	34
HIGH-LEVEL AUDIO FEATURES		
Chord statistics	Number of recognised chords in 10s	5
Chroma and harmony	Key, consonance, strengths of pitch intervals	258
Instruments	Share of guitar, piano, strings, wind instruments	32
Moods	Aggressive, earnest, energetic, sentimental	64
Structural complexity	Complexity of chords, harmony, instruments	70
Tempo, rhythm, and structure	Beats per minute, rhythmic clarity	9
Various features	Activation level, vocal descriptors	128

Four classification algorithms are used for the training of the models: decision tree C4.5, random forest, naive Bayes, and support vector machines with a linear kernel. SMS-EMOA population size was equal to 50, the number of evaluations was limited to 3,000, and each experiment was repeated 10 times. The initial expected number of features was set to 20 % of the complete set and the asymmetric mutation parameter γ [6] to 64. The two latter parameters were adjusted after a preliminary study. Please note that the optimal tuning of parameters was beyond the scope of this study and other settings may lead to better results, in particular, depending on the concrete categorisation task.

3.2 Discussion of Results

Table 2 presents the **main results** of the study, and non-dominated fronts are plotted in the Appendix, Figs. 1 and 2. Thin lines and smaller signs mark non-dominated fronts for each classifier (circles: C4.5, rectangles: random forest, diamonds: naive Bayes, triangles: SVM), thick lines and larger signs overall non-dominated fronts. Note that the fronts contain a rather small number of solutions because they were constructed for the artist-independent data set TAS120; fronts found for the optimisation set contain more solutions which are less generalisable. It can be clearly observed that performances of individual classifiers and high-level features have a strong variance between categorisation tasks.

Table 2. Results of experiments. For details see the text.

Category (6 genres/ 8 styles)	TAS120						TS120
	S_α	m_{BRE} (q_L)	m_{HL} (q_L)	$|q_L|$	m_{BRE} (q_R)	$|q_R|$	m_{BRE} (q_L)
Classic	0.00089	0.0128	0.8515	101	0.0276	105	0.0091
Electronic	0.00566	0.1070	0.5636	110	0.1610	124	0.0988
Jazz	0.00695	0.0929	0.7714	105	0.1400	109	0.0504
Pop	0.00149	0.1240	0.8707	116	0.1575	99	0.1214
Rap	0.00123	0.0504	0.8182	99	0.0642	104	0.0580
R'n'B	0.00040	0.1297	0.9750	120	0.1458	99	0.1300
AdultContemporary	0.00299	0.1952	0.6555	119	0.2417	89	0.1053
AlbumRock	0.01452	0.1785	0.4359	117	0.2316	89	0.1010
AlternativePopRock	0.00038	0.1859	0.9900	100	0.2251	96	0.0954
ClubDance	0.00035	0.1384	0.9444	108	0.1760	94	0.1317
HeavyMetal	0.00002	0.1210	0.9358	109	0.1213	86	0.0756
ProgRock	0.01757	0.1763	0.5367	177	0.2309	117	0.0834
SoftRock	0.00148	0.1480	0.9196	112	0.1862	108	0.1089
Urban	0.00861	0.1290	0.6283	113	0.2061	111	0.0783

First, we verify whether the **multi-objective optimisation makes sense** at all. For instance, if the smallest m_{BRE} can be achieved with high-level features only, it is not necessary to extend them with low-level features. As a consequence, in this extreme case the best high-level feature subset would dominate all other solutions. To measure this effect, we estimate the hypervolume which is exclusively dominated by an *ideal* (fictive) feature subset q_{ID} positioned at the individual best values of m_{BRE} and m_{HL} from all non-dominated solutions $q_1, ..., q_N$:

$$\mathcal{S}_\alpha = \mathcal{S}(q_{ID}) - \mathcal{S}(q_1, ..., q_N). \tag{5}$$

If a non-dominated front contains a single solution with $m_{HL} = 1$, then $\mathcal{S}_\alpha = 0$. Larger $\mathcal{S}_\alpha$ values correspond to larger non-dominated fronts, meaning that the combination of both feature groups leads to an increase of classification performance. From $\mathcal{S}_\alpha$ values listed in the 2nd column of Table 2, it can be observed that for none of the tested categories the best performance can be achieved with high-level features only. Categories HeavyMetal, ClubDance, AlternativePopRock, and R'n'B can be explained at best with high-level features, and ProgRock, AlbumRock, and Urban contain many trade-off feature subsets.

Columns 3–7 ($m_{BRE}(q_L),...,|q_R|$) describe the **characteristics of extremal non-dominated feature subsets.** q_L denotes subsets with the smallest m_{HL} and smallest m_{BRE} and q_R subsets with the largest m_{HL} (equal to 1 for all tasks) and largest m_{BRE}. We can see that, e.g., m_{BRE} for ProgRock falls from 0.2309 to 0.1763 if low-level descriptors are allowed, and for HeavyMetal (an opposite case), the error changes only marginally from 0.1213 to 0.1210. The m_{BRE}-best subset for ProgRock contains 177 features, among them $1 - 0.5367 = 46.33\,\%$ low-level, in absolute values 82 low-level and 95 high-level ones. Similarly, the HeavyMetal model with the smallest m_{BRE} contains 7 low-level and 102 high-level descriptors. Numbers of features in extreme solutions vary between 86 and 177 (see columns 5 and 7), being significantly lower than numbers of features at the beginning of the optimisation with an expected number of $0.2 \cdot 1202 = 240.4$ features, see Sect. 3.1.

Finally, we provide the **comparison with the album-dependent test set** TS120. Column 8 ($m_{BRE}(q_L)$) contains smallest m_{BRE} achieved with mixed sets of features when the classification models are validated on the track-independent but album- and artist-dependent set TS120 as used in [23] instead of album- and artist-independent validation set TAS120. As it can be suggested, in almost all cases an increase of performance can be observed, the largest effect of "overfitting" towards artists/albums in per cent is observed for ProgRock: $m_{BRE} = 0.0834$ using TS120 (47.31 % of $m_{BRE} = 0.1763$ for TAS120). Only for Rap and R'n'B m_{BRE} is slightly lower for TAS120.

3.3   Relevant Low-Level Features for the Identification of Relevant High-Level Descriptors

As stated in Sect. 3.2, there was no category among the tested ones for which only high-level features helped to build a classification model with the smallest classification error. On the other side, music genres, styles, and personal preferences can be typically well explained with some meaningful properties, like instrumentation or harmonic characteristics. The results of our study just showed that some of the relevant high-level descriptors were not among the 566 features. Thus, a possibility for improvement is to extract and integrate other high-level characteristics. For this goal, we can first try to **identify the most relevant low-level features** which often reduced m_{BRE} in our study. In the second step, among many possible new candidates for high-level features (moods, tags, instruments, etc.)–the ground truth for learning can be generated with the help of music experts or web statistics–we may concentrate on the optimisation of the robust extraction of only those ones which strongly correlate with the most relevant low-level features. While the exhaustive implementation of the second step is beyond the scope of this study, we briefly sketch here a possible way for the estimation of the relevance of low-level features.

Table 3 lists four most "relevant" low-level features indicated by the **relevance rank** $\mathcal{R}$. As an example, we show how $\mathcal{R}$ (the 5th column in the Table 3) is estimated for the mean of the 4th delta MFCC. In the 2nd column, abbreviations of four categories are listed, for which this feature appears in all feature subsets from non-dominated fronts, i.e. contributing to best trade-off solutions. In the 3rd column, we list numbers of *different* low-level features which belong to all non-dominated subsets of each category. Note that we do not count absolute values of such occurrences, because several non-dominated feature subsets may be built by mutation from the same EA individual: this does not necessarily mean that a feature which appears very frequently in a non-dominated front is in general relevant.

Table 3. Most relevant low-level features. LPC: linear prediction coefficient; MFCC: mel frequency cepstral coefficient. For further description see the text.

Name	Categories	No. features	$\mathcal{E}_N$	$\mathcal{R}$
Mean(4th delta MFCC)	Elec, Jazz, Rap, Soft	92, 44, 47, 19	0.0141	71.1671
Stddev(7th LPC)	Adul, Prog, Soft, Urba	49, 108, 19, 68	0.0266	37.6261
Mean(2nd tristimulus value)	Clas, Elec, Albu, Prog	27, 92, 146, 108	0.1522	6.5682
Stddev(12th delta MFCC)	Elec, Pop, Albu, Prog	92, 30, 146, 108	0.1692	5.9113

Now, consider some feature F_i. For simplicity and for intentional reduction of the above mentioned impact of related feature subsets sharing the same features, we assume that each feature has an equal probability to appear among 92 features which occur in non-dominated subsets of the category Electronic. Then, a probability of being among the 92 is $\frac{92}{636}$ (636 is the number of low-level features). Assuming that experiments for different categories are independent, the probability that feature F_i would be among non-dominated subsets for all four categories Electronic, Jazz, Rap, and SoftRock is $\frac{92}{636} \cdot \frac{44}{636} \cdot \frac{47}{636} \cdot \frac{19}{636} = 2.2093\text{E-}5$. Because $i \in \{1, ..., 636\}$, the expected number $\mathcal{E}_N$ of such features which appear in non-dominated feature subsets of these four categories is equal to $2.2093\text{E-}5 \cdot 636 = 0.0141$. This number is significantly smaller than 1. The 4th delta MFCC feature occurrence rank $\mathcal{R} = \frac{1}{0.0141} = 71.1671$ means that the real occurrence of this feature in all non-dominated feature subsets of four categories is 71.1671 times higher than the expected occurrence.

4   Conclusions and Outlook

In this work, we have introduced and applied evolutionary multi-objective feature selection for the creation of more interpretable music classification models.

The results showed that a large set of state-of-the-art high-level descriptors could not lead alone to the best classification performance, but it is also not necessary to simply combine all available groups of features as done in several recent studies. A majority of low-level audio signal characteristics can be omitted to build feature subsets with smallest classification errors. After the measurement of trade-off between error and interpretability, we proposed an idea how the most important low-level features can be used in future for the optimised extraction of relevant high-level descriptors.

This work can be seen as an initial step towards a systematic maximisation of interpretability in music audio classification. Therefore, we are aware that our method and various aspects of the experimental design can be improved. The parameters of EAs can be optimised, e.g., by adjustment of mutation with self-adaptation. For a better evaluation and reproducibility we plan to run the experiments using a larger and publicly available music data set–a particular problem here is that almost all publicly available data sets either contain no audio, only short audio snippets, or provide only a limited set of low-level and high-level descriptors, and it is not possible to extract own features. As discussed in Sect. 3.3, another promising possibility to increase the interpretability is to optimise the extraction of relevant high-level characteristics, keeping both efficiency and robustness in mind. Last but not least, we suggest that features with aggregated high-level information are particularly suitable to also build simple and comprehensible classification models (e.g., decision trees with a small number of levels, or interpretable fuzzy rules) without a significant decrease of classification performance.

Appendix

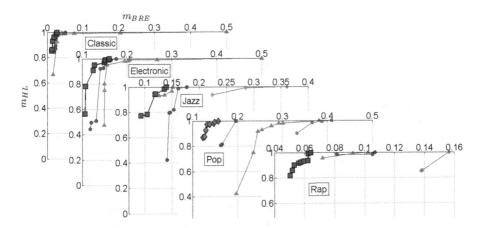

Fig. 1. Non-dominated fronts of feature subsets - Part I. Circles: C4.5, rectangles: random forest, diamonds: naive Bayes, triangles: support vector machines.

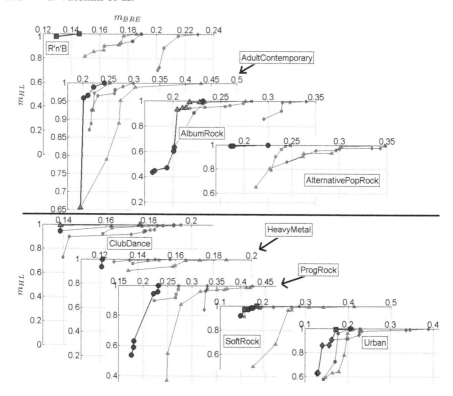

Fig. 2. Non-dominated fronts of feature subsets - Part II.

References

1. Anglade, A., Benetos, E., Mauch, M., Dixon, S.: Improving music genre classification using automatically induced harmony rules. J. New Music Res. **39**(4), 349–361 (2010)
2. Arabi A.F., Lu, G.: Enhanced polyphonic music genre classification using high level features. In: Proceedings of the IEEE International Conference on Signal and Image Processing Applications (ICSIPA), pp. 101–106 (2009)
3. Van Balen, J., Bountouridis, D., Wiering, F., Veltkamp, R.: Cognition-inspired descriptors for scalable cover song retrieval. In: Proceedings of 15th International Society for Music Information Retrieval Conference, pp. 379–384 (2014)
4. Berenzweig, A., Ellis, D.P.W., Lawrence, S.: Anchor space for classification and similarity measurement of music. In: Proceedings of the IEEE International Conference on Multimedia and Expo, pp. 29–32 (2003)
5. Beume, N., Naujoks, B., Emmerich, M.: SMS-EMOA: multiobjective selection based on dominated hypervolume. Eur. J. Sci. Res. **181**(3), 1653–1669 (2007)
6. Bischl, B., Vatolkin, I., Preuss, M.: Selecting small audio feature sets in music classification by means of asymmetric mutation. In: Schaefer, R., Cotta, C., Kołodziej, J., Rudolph, G. (eds.) PPSN XI. LNCS, vol. 6238, pp. 314–323. Springer, Heidelberg (2010)
7. Deb, K.: Multi-objective Optimization Using Evolutionary Algorithms. Wiley, Chichester (2001)

8. Ellis, K., Coviello, E., Chan, A., Lanckriet, G.: A bag of systems representation for music auto-tagging. IEEE Trans. Audio Speech Lang. Process. **21**(12), 2554–2569 (2013)
9. Fernández, F., Chávez, F.: Fuzzy rule based system ensemble for music genre classification. In: Machado, P., Romero, J., Carballal, A. (eds.) EvoMUSART 2012. LNCS, vol. 7247, pp. 84–95. Springer, Heidelberg (2012)
10. Herlands, W., Der, R., Greenberg, Y., Levin, S.: A machine learning approach to musically meaningful homogeneous style classification. In: Proceedings of the 28th AAAI Conference on Artificial Intelligence (AAAI), pp. 276–282 (2014)
11. Kostek, B., Plewa, M.: Parametrisation and correlation analysis applied to music mood classification. Int. J. Comput. Intell. Stud. **2**(1), 4–25 (2013)
12. Kudo, M., Sklansky, J.: Comparison of algorithms that select features for pattern classifiers. Pattern Recogn. **33**(1), 25–41 (2000)
13. Lidy, L., Rauber, A., Pertusa, A., Iñesta, J.M.: Improving genre classification by combination of audio and symbolic descriptors using a transcription system. In: Proceedings of the 8th International Conference on Music Information Retrieval (ISMIR), pp. 61–66 (2007)
14. Mauch, M., Levy, M.: Structural change on multiple time scales as a correlate of musical complexity. In: Proceedings 12th International Society for Music Information Retrieval Conference (ISMIR), pp. 489–494 (2011)
15. McKay, C.: Automatic Music Classification with jMIR. Ph.D. thesis, Department of Music Research, Schulich School of Music, McGill University (2010)
16. McKay, C., Burgoyne, J.A., Hockman, J., Smith, J.B.L., Vigliensoni, G., Fujinaga, I.: Evaluating the genre classification performance of lyrical features relative to audio, symbolic and cultural features. In: Proceedings of the 11th International Society for Music Information Retrieval Conference (ISMIR), pp. 213–218 (2010)
17. Mierswa, I., Morik, K.: Automatic feature extraction for classifying audio data. Mach. Learn. J. **58**(2–3), 127–149 (2005)
18. Miranda, E.R., Biles, J.A.: Evolutionary Computer Music. Springer, London (2007)
19. Mukhopadhyay, A., Maulik, U., Bandyopadhyay, S., Coello Coello, C.A.: A survey of multiobjective evolutionary algorithms for data mining: Part I. IEEE Trans. Evol. Comput. **18**(1), 4–19 (2014)
20. Pachet, F., Zils, A.: Evolving automatically high-level music descriptors from acoustic signals. In: Wiil, U.K. (ed.) CMMR 2003. LNCS, vol. 2771, pp. 42–53. Springer, Heidelberg (2004)
21. Panda, R., Rocha, B., Paiva, R.P.: Dimensional music emotion recognition: combining standard and melodic audio features. In: Proceedings of the 10th International Symposium on Computer Music Multidisciplinary Research (CMMR), pp. 583–593 (2013)
22. Rötter, G., Vatolkin, I., Weihs, C.: Computational prediction of high-level descriptors of music personal categories. In: Lausen, B., van den Poel, D., Ultsch, A. (eds.) Algorithms from and for Nature and Life, pp. 529–537. Springer, Heidelberg (2013)
23. Vatolkin, I.: Improving Supervised Music Classification by Means of Multi-Objective Evolutionary Feature Selection. Ph.D. thesis, TU Dortmund (2013)
24. Zanoni, M., Ciminieri, D., Sarti, A. Tubaro, S.: Searching for dominant high-level features for music information retrieval. In: Proceedings of the 20th European Signal Processing Conference (EUSIPCO), pp. 2025–2029 (2012)

25. Zhu, J., Xue, X., Lu, H.: Musical genre classification by instrumental features. In: Proceedings of the 2004 International Computer Music Conference (ICMC), pp. 580–583 (2004)
26. Zitzler, E., Thiele, L.: Multiobjective optimization using evolutionary algorithms - a comparative case study. In: Eiben, A.E., Bäck, T., Schoenauer, M., Schwefel, H.-P. (eds.) PPSN 1998. LNCS, vol. 1498, pp. 292–304. Springer, Heidelberg (1998)

On the Stylistic Evolution of a Society of Virtual Melody Composers

Valerio Velardo[1]($\boxtimes$) and Mauro Vallati[2]

[1] School of Music, Humanities and Media,
University of Huddersfield, Huddersfield, UK
`velardovalerio@gmail.com`
[2] School of Computing and Engineering,
University of Huddersfield, Huddersfield, UK

Abstract. In the field of computational creativity, the area of automatic music generation deals with techniques that are able to automatically compose human-enjoyable music. Although investigations in the
area started recently, numerous techniques based on artificial intelligence
have been proposed. Some of them produce pleasant results, but none is
able to effectively evolve the style of the musical pieces generated.
   In this paper, we fill this gap by proposing an evolutionary memetic
system that composes melodies, exploiting a society of virtual composers.
An extensive validation, performed by using both quantitative and qualitative analyses, confirms that the system is able to evolve its compositional style over time.

Keywords: Stylistic evolution · Melody generation · Memetic approach ·
Computational creativity

1 Introduction

Automatic generation of music is a new exciting area of computational creativity.
Many techniques to generate music have been developed, which draw upon several approaches of artificial intelligence, such as evolutionary algorithms, machine
learning and expert systems [1]. Even though some of these methods produce
music which can be deemed as pleasant by human listeners, none of them is actually capable to convincingly evolve its compositional style. The main problem is
that systems are usually based on a single agent, whose compositional process
is predetermined by the programmer, and cannot be changed. To avoid that
pitfall, a number of systems characterised by a society of software agents, which
exchange information have been implemented. Pachet [2] designed a system in
which a society of agents play rhythms together, creating new variations of rhythmic passages, according to transformation rules. Gimenes et al. [3] expanded the
initial idea of Pachet, proposing a society of software agents, which generate
rhythmic passages, following an evolutionary process based on memetics. However, both methods described are focused only on rhythm, so that their outputs

© Springer International Publishing Switzerland 2015
C. Johnson et al. (Eds.): EvoMUSART 2015, LNCS 9027, pp. 249–260, 2015.
DOI: 10.1007/978-3-319-16498-4_22

cannot be defined as music. Miranda [4] solved the issue designing a society of composers, which interact with one another and develop a shared repertoire of melodies. The system is effective, but the agents do not evolve the way they produce melodies.

In this paper, we introduce an evolutionary memetic system, which generates melodies and is capable of evolving its compositional style over time. To obtain that, we developed a mixed approach, which simulates both the psychological and the social levels of human composers [5]. The system is the result of a number of virtual composers connected together, which generate melodies, exchange them with their fellow composers, and evolve their compositional style, thanks to the influence of other agents.

The method has been extensively validated using quantitative analysis and music experts. Results suggest that the system effectively evolve its own compositional style. This not only is the first case of stylistic evolution we are aware of, but it also demonstrates that computers are potentially capable of evolving the style of the creative artifacts they generate. In this regard, the system is one of the first computational techniques characterised by a primitive form of transformational creativity [6], i.e., the ability to generate artifacts that completely transcend a given conceptual space. Moreover, some of the findings that emerge from the experiments can be easily extended to the real-world musical environment. This is the case of *musical attractors*, which are specific stylistic configurations shaped by cultural and cognitive constraints, likely to be positively assessed by human listeners.

The remaining paper is organised as follows. First, we provide the musical background and describe the system. Then, we discuss the experimental setup, report results and interpret them. Finally, we give conclusions.

2   Musical Background

This section provides introductory information about memes, musical memes (i.e., *musemes*), and musical style; necessary to understand the system.

Memes and musemes. Memes are cultural replicators that spread from person to person within a society [7]. Examples of these are ideas, fashion and technologies. Each meme carries a unit of cultural information, that can be passed from person to person by the means of writing, speech, gestures and rituals. Memes can be regarded as sociocultural analogues to genes [8]. Indeed, just like genetic information undergoes a continuous process of evolution, so memetic information does. In particular, the memetic evolutionary process is characterised by three distinct steps: variation, replication and selection [9]. Random variation introduces novelty within a meme pool. Replication allows a single element to be copied and spread within a population. Selection guarantees that only the fittest memes survive within a specific cultural environment. Since music is a subset of human culture, it is possible to extend the concept of meme to the musical domain. As Jan suggests [10], a musical meme or museme is:

a replicated pattern in some syntactic/digital elements of music - principally pitch and, to a lesser extent, rhythm - transmitted between individuals by imitation as part of a neo-Darwinian process of cultural transmission and evolution.

For the purpose of this paper, we consider melodic musemes as small monophonic phrases containing 5–9 notes. The length of musemes has been chosen accordingly to short-term memory constraints [11]. Musemes are stored within the brain and are actively used for processing/composing music [12]. Considering the finite memory capacity of human brain, a continuous fight for survival happens among musemes. Each person unconsciously selects musemes, based on a personal musical fitness function, influenced both by musical universals [13], and by the musical environment she happens to live in.

Musical style. Musical style is a very loose concept, which has no single agreed definition among academics. Indeed, there are many - sometimes contradictory - theoretical definitions of musical style. For Fabbri [14], musical style is the recurring presence of specific musical events, which is typical of a composer, a place, or a period of time. This definition does not explain how/why stylistic change happens, as well as how/why a composer internalises specific musical events. Meyer solves the issue, by proposing an interdisciplinary definition of style, at the intersection of information theory, cognitive science and music theory [15]. For Meyer, style emerges from the replication of specific musical patterns chosen from a potentially infinite repertoire of musical constructs. The choice of specific patterns over others results from the combination of composer temperament, cognitive constraints and cultural constraints Stylistic change happens thanks to the tension between composer temperament and the cultural environment, which leads to instability, and therefore to the invention of new compositional strategies. Even though the definition proposed by Meyer is powerful, it is difficult to implement into a computational system, in order to extract useful stylistic information from musical pieces. For this reason, numerous operational definitions of musical style have been developed by researchers interested in classifying pieces, based on their style [16–20]. These definitions consider style as a synthetic metric, which is the combined result of a number of musical features, such as pitch distribution, types of intervals and rhythmic structure.

3   Framework

The system we propose in this paper simulates the compositional process of human composers at two different levels, i.e., psychological and social [5]. The former encompasses all those processes and musical elements that univocally identify the generation process of a single composer. Compositional rules, style and aesthetic judgement are all instances of the psychological level, which differ from musician to musician. The social level considers a composer as a node within a network of composers. This level analyses the way composers change their psychological elements while interacting with each other, thanks to a constant

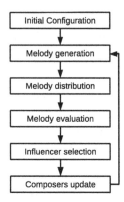

Fig. 1. Steps followed by the system to generate melodies and to evolve its own compositional style.

exchange of musical information. The psychological level of the system models how composers generate music, while the social level simulates how composers influence and are influenced by the musical environment.

To implement the psychological level, the systems relies on a mixed top-down bottom-up approach, that was proposed in [5]. The top-down element provides a coherent hierarchical musical structure for a melody, which is then filled by a bottom-up technique. To emulate the behaviour of a human composer, virtual composers are characterised by three elements: *musical content, musical grammar* and *evaluation function*. Musical content is provided under the form of a set of musemes, generated using Markov Chains, trained on 5000 German folksongs of the Essen database. The musical grammar is based on a generative grammar, which is responsible for the development of the musical structure, as well as for the variation of musemes. The evaluation function assesses the quality of a melody according to a linear combination of three musical parameters: *pitch range, rhythmic homogeneity* and *step ratio*. Pitch range indicates the difference between the highest and the lowest pitch of a melody. Rhythmic homogeneity measures the overall rhythmic coherence of a melody on a note-by-note basis. Step ratio returns the percentage of steps within a melody. The process of generation of a melody consists of four steps: initiating musical content, generating musical structure, filling the structure, evaluating a melody. After the generation of a symbolic hierarchical structure, a number of musemes are chosen to fill the backbone. These musical phrases can either be left unchanged or modified, depending on the structure. If the quality of the melody is not satisfying, according to the evaluation function, the algorithm goes back to step two and generates a new structure.

All elements of a virtual composer can potentially be modified over time, thus its style can evolve. Indeed, the values of the parameters of the musical grammar and the evaluation function can change, as well as the raw musical content of a composer. In order to model musical evolution as it happens in the real world, a network of virtual composers is necessary. To implement the social level, we use a multi-agent system. A number of virtual composers are tied together, and build up a fully connected network. Each composer can be affected by all other composers of the network. The mutual influence of nodes is guaranteed by a continuous exchange of melodies among elements. Indeed, agents "listen" to melodies created by other agents, and are usually influenced by the music of the composer they think is best. The social level is implemented through a multi-step algorithm (Fig. 1). The specific steps are: configuration of composers, generation of melodies, melodies distribution, evaluation of melodies, choice of influencer, update of composers' style.

During the initial configuration, the value of some parameters of the musical grammar and the evaluation function of a composer are randomly seeded. For the evaluation function, the weights of all three parameters of the function (i.e., pitch range, rhythmic homogeneity, step ratio) are randomly chosen. The same happens for the value of three parameters of the musical grammar called *pitch change ratio*, *duration change ratio* and *delete ratio*. These parameters are responsible for the variation of a museme during the bottom-up filling process. Specifically, they indicate the probability that a note contained in a museme can change pitch/duration or can be deleted, when modifying a museme. Furthermore, a set of 500 musemes is generated for each composer, using Markov chains. These musical phrases are the actual musical content composers will use to fill the musical structure of their melodies.

After configuration is completed, each composer generates a melody according to the mixed top-down bottom-up approach described above. Melodies are then distributed across the network, and "heard" by composers. This means that the values of pitch range, rhythmic homogeneity and step ratio are retrieved from each melody. During the evaluation phase, each composer judges all melodies according to its specific configuration of the evaluation function, and stores the melody with the best score. Afterwards, agents choose another agent as a source of influence. The likelihood of the composer of the best melody to be chosen is by far higher than that of other agents. This procedure guarantees that composers are generally influenced by those nodes, whose music they like best.

The final step of the algorithm is the update phase. This process involves both musical content and musical grammar. Each composer randomly picks a museme from the melody it likes best, and substitutes it to one of its own musemes. This ensures a steady change in the musical content, while respecting memory constraints of human composers. In order to guarantee a clear influence in the compositional process, the musical grammar is modified as well. One parameter is randomly chosen among pitch change ratio, duration change ratio and delete ratio. The value of the chosen parameter is changed, and gets closer to the value of the same parameter of the influencer. After completion of the first iteration, the algorithm goes back to step two, in which all composers generate new melodies.

4   Methods

Experiments with different network size have been conducted, to investigate how the number of virtual composers affects stylistic evolution. Precisely, we tested the system with 10, 30 and 100 composers. For each size of the network, 100 experiments were run. The initial configuration of the parameters of the musical grammar and the evaluation function for each composer was derived randomly. When updating the compositional grammar, the value of parameters can be modified up to 30 % of their current value, in order to avoid radical changes in compositional style, which are uncommon in the real world.

All experiments aimed to measure the average stylistic evolution of the system over time. However, evaluating stylistic evolution of a composer is a challenging task, since in the first place, there is no agreement on the definition of musical style among scholars. To avoid this issue, we considered two approaches: a quantitative-based analysis, and an expert-based analysis. The latter relies on judgement of music experts, while the former processes large amount of musical data. In particular, we used quantitative-based analysis to track style from three different perspectives, i.e., the evolution of melodic output, musical content and musical grammar.

Style is considered as an emergent quality of a melody, which can be reduced to a handful of musical features. To track the stylistic evolution of melodies over time, we introduce the *melodic style phase space*, which is a 3-dimensional space, whose axes are pitch range, rhythmic homogeneity and step ratio. Specifically, pitch range carries timbral information, rhythmic homogeneity is a synthetic measure for the duration of notes at a local level, and step ratio provides a synthetic information about the intervallic content of a melody. A single point within the melodic style phase space corresponds to a specific melodic style, and conversely, a specific melodic style corresponds to a single point within this space. Of course, musical style cannot be reduced to three musical features. However, working with only three features facilitates the visual representation of stylistic evolution, otherwise impossible, as well as it provides an effective method to reduce/manage the complexity of musical style. To have a dynamic view of the stylistic evolution of the melodies over time, we introduce the *melodic style event space*. In this space, all axes are the same as those of the phase space, except for the pitch range, which is replaced by the number of iterations of the algorithm. The same spaces - event and phase - are used for visualising the evolution of musemes. While melodic spaces consider the actual melodies produced by composers, museme spaces consider musemes stored by composers.

In order to be informed about the evolution of the musical grammar, we introduce the *grammar phase space* and the *grammar event space*. These spaces reflects the internal state of the system, by considering those parameters of the grammar that change over time: pitch change ratio, duration change ratio and delete ratio. For the grammar event space, a combined parameter called *change ratio* is used, calculating the mean of pitch change ratio and duration change ratio, so that an axis can be available to the parameter number of iterations; without losing too much information about the musical grammar. Figure 2 shows the typical evolution of melodic style, musemes and grammar, through the aforementioned spaces, in our experiments. For all types of spaces, the actual metrics we track are obtained considering the average values of all musical features, calculated over the entire population of composers at the end of each iteration. Consequently, a trajectory within any of the event spaces expresses the average value of the system considered as a whole, and each point represents a picture of the system at a specific point in time.

5   Results

A relevant aspect that emerges from the experiments is the limited impact of differently sized networks of composers. The system with 10, 30 and 100 composers behave the same way.

A quantitative analysis of the style of the melodies generated by the system reveals that there is a continuous coherent change in style after each iteration. A typical example of melodic evolution can be seen in Fig. 2. No large jumps have been noticed within the melodic phase space and within the melodic event space. Melodies seems to change a little at each iteration, causing style to evolve slowly over time. Over 60 % of the experiments have the style of melodies converging towards a precise point of the melodic style phase space. However, before converging melodies visit small regions of the phase space. Different runs of the algorithm always visit different regions of the phase space, even though overlaps are frequent. Also, some regions of the phase space are clearly preferred over others, while others have never been visited. This is the case of regions that lie at the extremes of the domain of the musical features considered.

A similar result is obtained by analysing the style of musemes stored by composers. Stylistic evolution of musemes is a slow coherent process, which never shows large jumps (Fig. 2). Less than 40 % of the experiments converge towards a single point in the museme style phase space. Another major difference with the case of melodies, is that musemes usually anticipate the points of the phase space, that are visited by melodies after a number of iterations. Musemes visit small regions of the phase space, as melodies do. Also, no two different runs of the system visit the same regions of the phase space, and some subspaces such as the extreme of the axes have never been visited.

Results are different with regards to the evolution of the musical grammar. As can be seen in Fig. 2, the configuration of the features of the grammar tends to change conspicuously over time, until it converges towards a precise point of the space. Large jumps are always present during initial iterations. These tends to get smaller over time, until the system falls in a certain configuration. After the system converges towards a point in the space, it stays stable for the remaining iterations. Different runs of the algorithm explore different regions of the phase space, and again there are some subspaces which are never visited.

A general question that encompasses many runs of the algorithm at once is: do melodies/grammar/musemes converge always in the same points of their respective phase spaces? The answer is no, since there seem to be preferred regions of the phase space, where the system is attracted into. As it is shown in Fig. 3, the region of attraction for the grammar phase space is bigger than that for the museme style phase space.

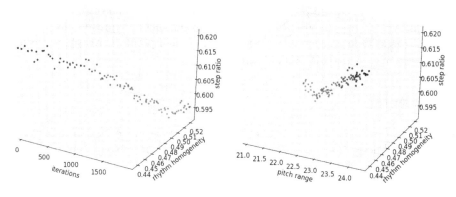

Melodic style event space (left) and phase space (right).

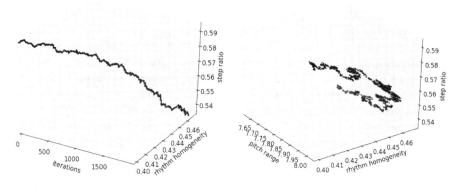

Musemes style event space (left) and phase space (right).

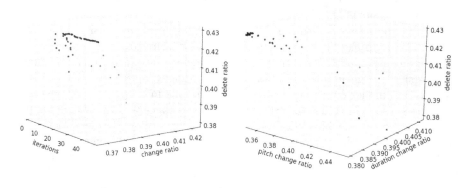

Grammar event space (left) and phase space (right).

Fig. 2. An example of stylistic evolution for melodies, musemes and grammar; obtained from an experiment with 30 composers.

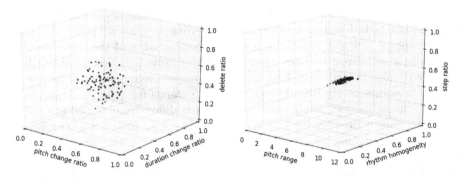

Fig. 3. Regions of convergence for grammar (left) and musemes (right), obtained by plotting the last configuration of the system for 100 experiments with 30 composers.

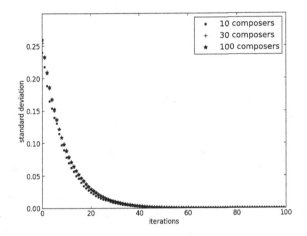

Fig. 4. The mean of the standard deviations of all nine musical features used to build the style phase spaces, for experiments with 10, 30 and 100 composers.

Since all the metrics we are using are based on the mean of values calculated over the entire population of composers, we have no information about possible local variations of the values for single agents. To have an idea of the dispersion from the average, we calculated the mean of the standard deviations of all nine musical features used to build all three style phase spaces. Figure 4 clearly shows that the standard deviation tends to approach zero after 50 iterations. Moreover, there is no clear difference between the systems with 10, 30 and 100 composers, since they always drop to zero following the same curve.

To assess whether or not the system evolves its compositional style, we also used an expert-based analytic approach. Four music experts (i.e., two composers, one music theorist and one musicologist) assessed ten pairs of melodies produced by the system during ten different runs.[1] Each pair of melodies consists of a

---

[1] One of the pairs of melodies is available at http://goo.gl/9nHVKl.

melody randomly chosen between those generated at the beginning of a run, and another picked among those composed during the last iteration of a run. Music experts had to evaluate both the aesthetic quality of the melodies and the stylistic difference between members of the same pair. To do that, they used two scales ranged from 1 to 5, where 1 respectively means "no aesthetic value"/"absolute no stylistic difference", and 5 stands for "very high aesthetic values"/"melodies completely different". Stylistic difference obtained a score of 3.25, while aesthetic scored 2.78. Experts said that some melodies are musically interesting, presenting an overall good directionality with nice distributions of pitches and rhythms; while others sound uncreative or even "dull". We used Fleiss Kappa to evaluate inter-rater reliability among experts. Indeed, if experts agree on an assessment, it is likely that their evaluation might be valid. We obtained Fleiss Kappa [21] values of 0.26 for stylistic difference and of 0.32 for aesthetic quality. According to the classical interpretation of Fleiss Kappa, both values indicate a fair agreements among raters [22].

6   Discussion

Both quantitative-based and expert-based analyses confirm that the proposed system is likely to produce a change in the style of the melodies. The specific term to define this process is evolution, since the change is blindly guided by a process of memetic selection, which happens both at the level of the grammar and the musical contents. The system encapsulates the most important aspects needed to have an evolutionary process, i.e., a population of composers which replicate, vary and select a number of musical patterns, while modifying their grammars accordingly to the musical content they like. Indeed, for stylistic evolution to happen, it is necessary to have at least a group of agents which exchange musical information with one another. This process can be regarded as a musical analogue to the biological case. Just as in nature for genetic evolution to occur, a huge number of animals is needed to carry, share, reproduce and select genetic information; so for musical style to evolve, a group of interconnected composers is needed to allow selection and replication of musical ideas. To obtain the same type of evolution with computer generators, the same basic elements are needed.

We would like to emphasise the importance of a complex social structure, with regards to the evolution of musical style. If the compositional goal is to create a melody which has the same melodic style of our system at a specific time, then one can use a single composer with all parameters configured specifically to obtain that precise melodic style. But, if the compositional goal is to simulate a steady stylistic evolutionary process, that does not solely randomly explore areas of the style spaces, there is no way traditional search/evolutionary algorithms can succeed. All nuances given by non-linear interactions of many agents, whose grammars and musical contents are slightly different from one another, cannot be reproduced by a single agent. Indeed, the value of a many-composers approach lies in the musical journey, not in the single stages. The social level of the system adds an extra layer of complexity that cannot be reduced.

As experimental analysis suggests, the systems tends to converge rapidly. The plot of the standard deviation highlights that after 50 iterations all composers have only small differences in all their parameters. The fast convergence rate as well the fact that there is no difference in the way the system with different numbers of composers behaves, are probably due to the fully connected network used to model the musical environment. To provide unpredictability and instability, which are necessary elements of creativity, a scale-free network is needed.

However, since all experiments of the system converge within specific regions of the three phase spaces, it is probable that those regions are attractors for the system. In other words, not all regions of the phase spaces are equally likely to be visited. Even considering all the simplifications made to develop the system, we can extend this idea to the real world, since the system is based on sound cognitive elements. Our hypothesis is that the real-world musical style phase space is divided into a number of attractors These regions are privileged portions of the phase space, whose shape depends on a number of cognitive and social factors such as musical universals, exposure to music, and cognitive constraints.

The system we proposed has two main limitations. First, only three parameters of the musical grammar change over time. As a consequence, composers can hardly completely revolutionise their musical style, since they are severely constrained by many other parameters that do not evolve. However, if many parameters could be modified, then the musical results of the system would be completely unpredictable, and it would be really difficult to trace the contribution of one parameter to a specific compositional behaviour. Also, the complexity of the system would increase a lot, making the system less manageable. Second, the evaluation function is simple and its parameters are stationary. This implies that composers cannot have sophisticated aesthetic judgement on melodies they "listen to". However, a complex evaluation function for simulating the aesthetic preferences of human composers, would be extremely difficult to develop.

7   Conclusion

Automatic melodic generation is a challenging task, and a large number of approaches that are able to produce human-enjoyable melodies have been proposed. However, no system has been capable of evolving its compositional style until now. In this paper, we presented such a system. The method we introduced relies on a memetic evolutionary approach, whose backbone is a multi-agent society of composers organised into a network. Composers evolve their musical grammar and the musical contents they use to generate music, by constantly exchanging musical information. Both quantitative analysis and music experts confirm that the system is able to effectively evolve its own compositional style over time. As a consequence, the paper has also indirectly demonstrated that computers can show at least a low degree of transformational creativity.

Future work includes the improvement of the evaluation function of composers, the exploitation of a scale-free network for simulating the society, and the generation of small polyphonic pieces rather than simple monophonic lines.

References

1. Fernández, J.D., Vico, F.J.: AI methods in algorithmic composition: a comprehensive survey. J. Artif. Intell. Res. (JAIR) **48**, 513–582 (2013)
2. Pachet, F.: Rhythms as emerging structures. In: Proceedings of 2000 International Computer Music Conference, Berlin, ICMA (2000)
3. Gimenes, M., Miranda, E.R., Johnson, C.: A memetic approach to the evolution of rhythms in a society of software agents. In: Proceedings of the 10th Brazilian Symposium on Computer Music (SBCM), vol. 16 (2005)
4. Miranda, E.R.: On the evolution of music in a society of self-taught digital creatures. Digit. Creativity **14**(1), 29–42 (2003)
5. Velardo, V., Vallati, M.: Automatic melody composition and evolution: a cognitive-based approach. In: Proceedings of the Conference on Interdisciplinary Musicology (CIM) (2014)
6. Boden, M.A.: The Creative Mind: Myths and Mechanisms. Psychology Press, New York (2004)
7. Dawkins, R.: The Selfish Gene. Oxford University Press, Oxford (1976)
8. Graham, G.: Genes: A Philosophical Inquiry. Psychology Press, New York (2002)
9. Dennett, D.C., Mittwoch, U.: Darwin's dangerous idea: evolution and the meanings of life. Ann. Hum. Genet. **60**(3), 267–267 (1996)
10. Jan, S.B.: The Memetics of Music: A Neo-Darwinian View of Musical Structure and Culture. Ashgate, Aldershot (2007)
11. Miller, G.A.: The magical number seven, plus or minus two: some limits on our capacity for processing information. Psychol. Rev. **63**, 81 (1956)
12. Jan, S.: Music, memory, and memes in the light of calvinian neuroscience. Music Theor. Online **17**(2), 3–50 (2011)
13. Brown, S., Jordania, J.: Universals in the world's musics. Psychol. Music **41**, 229–248 (2013)
14. Fabbri, F.: Browsing music spaces: categories and the musical mind. In: Proceedings of the IASPM Conference (1999)
15. Meyer, L.B.: Style and Music: Theory, History, and Ideology. University of Chicago Press, Chicago (1989)
16. Cope, D.: Computers and Musical Style. Oxford University Press, Oxford (1991)
17. Dannenberg, R.B., Thom, B., Watson, D.: A machine learning approach to musical style recognition. In: Proceedings of the ICMC (1997)
18. Lartillot, O., Dubnov, S., Assayag, G., Bejerano, G.: Automatic modeling of musical style. In: Proceedings of the 2001 International Computer Music Conference, pp. 447–454 (2001)
19. Hontanilla, M., Pérez-Sancho, C., Iñesta, J.M.: Modeling musical style with language models for composer recognition. In: Sanches, J.M., Micó, L., Cardoso, J.S. (eds.) IbPRIA 2013. LNCS, vol. 7887, pp. 740–748. Springer, Heidelberg (2013)
20. de León, P.J.P., Iñesta, J.M.: Musical style classification from symbolic data: a two-styles case study. In: Wiil, U.K. (ed.) CMMR 2003. LNCS, vol. 2771, pp. 167–178. Springer, Heidelberg (2004)
21. Fleiss, J.L.: Measuring nominal scale agreement among many raters. Psychol. Bull. **76**(5), 378 (1971)
22. Landis, J.R., Koch, G.G.: The measurement of observer agreement for categorical data. Biometrics **33**, 159–174 (1977)

DrawCompileEvolve: Sparking Interactive Evolutionary Art with Human Creations

Jinhong Zhang[1], Rasmus Taarnby[1],
Antonios Liapis[2]([✉]), and Sebastian Risi[1]

[1] Center for Computer Games Research,
IT University of Copenhagen, Copenhagen, Denmark
{jinh,reta,sebr}@itu.dk
[2] Institute of Digital Games, University of Malta, Msida, Malta
antonios.liapis@um.edu.mt

Abstract. This paper presents *DrawCompileEvolve*, a web-based drawing tool which allows users to draw simple primitive shapes, group them together or define patterns in their groupings (e.g. symmetry, repetition). The user's vector drawing is then compiled into an *indirectly* encoded genetic representation, which can be evolved interactively, allowing the user to change the image's colors, patterns and ultimately transform it. The human artist has direct control while drawing the initial seed of an evolutionary run and indirect control while interactively evolving it, thus making DrawCompileEvolve a mixed-initiative art tool. Early results in this paper show the potential of DrawCompileEvolve to jump-start evolutionary art with meaningful drawings as well as the power of the underlying genetic representation to transform the user's initial drawing into a different, yet potentially meaningful, artistic rendering.

1 Introduction

In evolutionary art and music, interactive evolutionary computation is often the method of choice for exploring the search spaces of such highly subjective domains [1–7]. Human users are uniquely capable of detecting visual or aural patterns and associating them with real-world stimuli. Moreover, the individual tastes of each human user can drive evolution to focus on different areas of the search space that are uniquely valuable to the current user. The particular imagination, preference and real-world experience of a human user can guide search in interesting, unexpected and meaningful ways.

Often, the genetic representation in evolutionary art and music allows for a vast expressive range and therefore an expansive search space. In order for human users to navigate such space, extensive interaction with the system may be necessary, leading to user fatigue [8]. Moreover, when a human explores the search space without a purpose or a tether, their lack of aim or context makes the evaluation of artifacts less meaningful.

This paper introduces *DrawCompileEvolve*, a web-based drawing tool which allows human users to seed the initial population of their evolutionary search

© Springer International Publishing Switzerland 2015
C. Johnson et al. (Eds.): EvoMUSART 2015, LNCS 9027, pp. 261–273, 2015.
DOI: 10.1007/978-3-319-16498-4_23

with their own drawings. DrawCompileEvolve allows users to draw certain primitive shapes on a canvas, and define regularities between them such as symmetry and repetition; these primitives and patterns are compiled into an indirect representation called *computational pattern-producing network* (CPPN; [9]) and can be subsequently evolved interactively building on the Picbreeder art application [1]. Importantly, because the compiled CPPNs directly embody the annotated regularities, the produced offspring shows meaningful variations (e.g. symmetrically defined body parts exhibit a coordinated change in size). The expressive range of a CPPN, its ability to effectively encode repetition, symmetry and elaboration [9], and the locality in its search (compared to e.g. genetic programming) makes it uniquely suited for the presented mixed-initiative art tool.

By starting the interactive evolution of images from a semantically meaningful or aesthetically preferable area of the search space, DrawCompileEvolve allows for more control over the evolutionary process. Moreover, as early results in this study show, users of DrawCompileEvolve are more likely to use interactive evolution to transform their initial drawings to other types of meaningful imagistic representations.

2   Background

DrawCompileEvolve compiles vector graphics into CPPN-encoded images via a method described in Sect. 5; resulting CPPN images are interactively evolved via CPPN-NEAT, using the Picbreeder evolutionary art tool. Details on CPPNs and Picbreeder are provided in Sect. 2.1, while interactive evolution is discussed in Sect. 2.2.

2.1   CPPN-NEAT

A compositional pattern producing network (CPPN) is, in essence, an artificial neural network (ANN) with a wider variety of activation functions [9]. The activation functions of a CPPN include Gaussian and sine functions, which produce patterns such as symmetry and repetition. This allows a CPPN to recreate and describe underlying structures found in nature as a result of an evolutionary process but without the need of simulating this process [1,9]. The patterns in the CPPN's outputs are affected by the inputs of the network, by the activation functions of its nodes and by the weights of connections between these nodes. The pattern-producing capability of CPPNs has been exploited to create images [1], three-dimensional models [2], artificial flowers [3], spaceships [4], particle effects [5], musical accompaniments [6] and drum tracks [7]. CPPNs can be evolved via *neuroevolution of augmenting topologies* (NEAT), which traditionally starts from minimal topology networks and adds nodes and links [10]. As NEAT adds new nodes on top of existing pattern-producing nodes, it is very likely that the underlying patterns of smaller networks (e.g. symmetry) will be retained in the larger networks of their offspring. In this paper, instead of starting from a minimal topology, the initial CPPNs (which encode images) are created based on the user's vector drawing.

Among the different implementations of CPPN-NEAT, DrawCompileEvolve makes heavy use of Picbreeder [1]. Picbreeder is an online service where users can collaboratively evolve images and describes itself as a "Collaborative Interactive Art Evolution" program. The two-dimensional images in Picbreeder and in this paper are created by providing the coordinates of each pixel in the image as input to the CPPN and extracting the color of that pixel from the CPPN's output. The program displays the images of the current generation to the user, who can guide evolution by selecting one or more images; those images breed to create the next generation. Users can start "from scratch" with a minimal topology network, or can start from another user's saved creation.

2.2   Interactive Evolution

Interactive evolutionary computation (IEC) uses human feedback to evaluate content; essentially, with IEC human users decide which individuals breed and which ones die. As surveyed by Takagi [8], IEC has been applied to several domains including games, industrial design and data mining. Evolutionary art and music often hinges on human evaluation of content due to the subjective nature of aesthetics and beauty. However, constant requirement for feedback and the cognitive overload of evaluating a broad range of content can result in *user fatigue*. Several steps have been taken to lessen user fatigue by IEC methods, such as limiting the rating levels of fitness, predicting fitness from user rankings [11], or showing a subset of the evolving population to the user.

Another potential solution to the problem of user fatigue is seeding the initial population of IEC with meaningful, high-quality individuals. By ensuring that the starting point of evolution is tailored to the problem at hand, the user needs to spend less time exploring the space of possible solutions; the initial seed largely defines the area of the search space that should be explored. More importantly, however, using a personalized initial seed which is appealing or meaningful to the current human user of IEC enriches the interaction. As Takagi puts it: "IEC users evaluate individuals according to the distance between the target in their psychological spaces and the actual system outputs, and the EC searches the global optimum in a feature parameter space according to the psychological distance" [8]: an initial seed that resonates either semantically (e.g. a depiction of a loved one) or aesthetically (e.g. a desired color palette) with the user ensures that the system output will have a high value in the user's psychological space.

Several attempts at seeding interactive evolution have been made: superficially, choosing the right genotypical representation is a form of seeding as well. Seeding IEC can be achieved by starting from previous users' creations, e.g. in saved, previously evolved images of Picbreeder [1]. Endless Forms allows users to upload any three-dimensional model, the shape of which is then transformed by CPPNs but yet recognizable due to its input matching the uploaded model closely [12]. Similarly, MaestroGenesis indirectly seeds evolution by using a human-authored sound file as a scaffold to generate musical accompaniments through IEC [6]. Finally, Sentient World seeds evolution by using back-propagation to generate game terrain that matches a low-level sketch drawn by the user [13].

3   DrawCompileEvolve System Architecture

DrawCompileEvolve is a web-based tool which allows users to create shapes
via a traditional draw interface, then evolve their vector drawings as rasterized
images encoded by CPPNs. The tool is available at http://rasmustaarnby.dk/
drawcompileevolve. The individual components of the tool will be described in
the next sections.

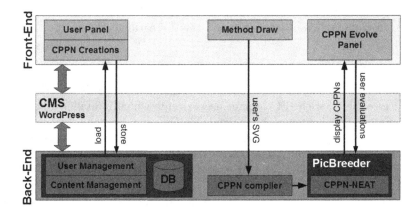

Fig. 1. System architecture of DrawCompileEvolve.

The overall structure and the relation between the different parts of the
program are depicted in Fig. 1. The system consists of three layers: frontend, content management system (CMS) and backend. The frontend handles the drawing
interface and displays the user's profile and the other users' creations. The CMS
system *WordPress* acts as a separation layer between the frontend and the backend, leaving the Picbreeder backend intact while retaining full access to the
database. The backend is divided into the database which holds all website content, user information and data about the different CPPN creations, and the
Picbreeder applet which is responsible for compiling the user created shapes (in
scalable vector graphics format) into a CPPN, evolving the CPPN and rendering
the images into viewable JPG format.

4   Drawing Interface

A core motivation of DrawCompileEvolve is allowing users, regardless of technical proficiency, to create CPPN-encoded images. This is achieved via an online
web application, which lets users log in and draw images directly in the browser;
the images are then automatically transferred into an evolvable genotypic representation by the CPPN-Compiler (explained in the next section) and saved on
the server. The browser-based drawing tool MethodDraw (http://codevisually.
com/method-draw/) was extended towards this end, allowing users to define

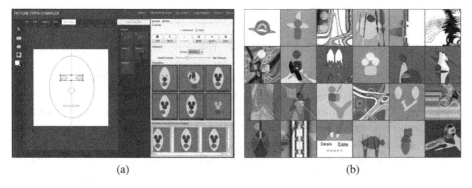

(a)   (b)

Fig. 2. User Interface of DrawCompileEvolve. (a) In the drawing interface the user can draw a SVG image on the canvas (left) and can compile and evolve it as a CPPN image (right) via the Picbreeder applet. (b) In the gallery interface the user can rate another user's CPPN image, see the original SVG image and evolve it further.

regularities between different primitive shapes. For example, Fig. 2a shows how symmetries are designated and drawn via the automatic duplication of shapes along the y-axis (which can either be turned on or off). Additionally, the scalable vector graphic (SVG) output of MethodDraw was altered to comply with the standards of the CPPN-Compiler. Finally, the interface of MethodDraw was simplified and some features omitted, leaving only those features which are supported by the compiler; this design choice non-intrusively limits the users to only use shapes that can be meaningfully expressed via the genotypic representation.

At any point while drawing, the user can press the compile button on the web interface and send their current drawing (in SVG format) to the server back-end, where it is compiled into a CPPN. The compiled CPPN then seeds the initial population of images displayed back to the user via the Picbreeder applet on the front-end (Fig. 2a). The user can evolve the images further by selecting one or more individuals to breed through the same interactive evolution method as in the original Picbreeder program [1].

In addition to the online drawing board, several features to support and motivate user interaction were implemented. The web application allows users to login to their personal account, to tag and give titles to their creations as well as to browse and rate the CPPN creations of other users (Fig. 2b). Furthermore, by selecting an already saved CPPN image, any user can carry on evolving it and finally save it as another image. This gives users the opportunity to collaborate on evolving new images and CPPN structures.

5   CPPN-Compiler

In the original Picbreeder, users typically start from randomly initialized populations (or elaborate on designs evolved by other users), in which case the CPPNs have randomized weights and a few randomly created hidden nodes. The NEAT algorithm then adds complexity over generations by adding new nodes and connections through mutations.

Instead of starting with random CPPNs, the approach presented in this paper enables users to jump-start evolutionary art by automatically converting their SVG drawings into CPPNs. The basic idea behind this *CPPN-Compiler* is that complex patterns with regularities can be represented by a few basic building blocks [14]. The current version of DrawCompileEvolve allows a set of primitive shapes to be converted to CPPN patterns, as well as arrange those in groupings such as symmetrical or repetitive patterns.

Importantly, defining these regularities allows coordinated and meaningful mutations on the generated structures. For example, because the compiled CPPN representation instills the fact that the two user-defined eyes in Fig. 2a should be symmetric, one mutation can decrease the size of *both* eyes simultaneously. In effect, the CPPN-Compiler together with the DrawCompileEvolve tool allow the gradual transformation of the user's initial drawing into different artistic renderings.

5.1   Compiling Shape Primitives

The current version of the compiler allows the user to draw ellipses, rhombi, rectangles, triangles, and trapezoids. These shapes are then automatically converted into a CPPN representation, which is explained next:

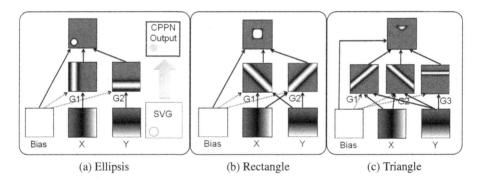

(a) Ellipsis   (b) Rectangle   (c) Triangle

Fig. 3. Example shape primitives and their CPPN representations.

- **Ellipsis:** Constructing a CPPN that encodes a single ellipsis is achieved by using two nodes assigned with Gaussian activation functions ($G1$, $G2$) connected as shown in Fig. 3a. The ellipsis' radii along the x and y axis are determined by the weights from the x-input to $G1$ and the y-input to $G2$ respectively. The position of an ellipsis is determined by the weight of the bias to $G1$ (horizontal movement) and $G2$ (vertical movement).
- **Rhombus:** A rhombus is constructed in the same way as an ellipsis, but using a different weight value on the connection between the bias and the output node.

- **Rectangle:** Constructing a rectangle is achieved via two nodes assigned with Gaussian activation functions ($G1$, $G2$) connected as shown in Fig. 3b: unlike the rhombus, the x-input is also connected to $G2$ and the y-input to $G1$. The rectangle's width is determined by the weights from both x and y inputs to $G1$ and its height from both x and y inputs to $G2$. Positioning the rectangle is somewhat more involved, and requires that the x and y CPPN inputs are normalized in accordance to the rectangle's original dimensions and the size of the final image. Rotation has not yet been implemented for rectangles.
- **Triangle:** A triangle is constructed in a similar fashion as a rectangle, with the addition of a third Gaussian node ($G3$). For triangles with a rotation of $0°$ or $180°$, the triangle's width is defined by the weights of links from x-input to $G1$ and $G2$ and its height by links from y-input to $G1$ and $G2$. $G1$ and $G2$ construct something akin to a rhombus, while the triangle is shaped via the connection between x-input and $G3$ (Fig. 3c). Position of the triangle is defined by the links from the bias node to $G1$ and $G2$; when triangles are rotated at other angles (not $0°$ or $180°$), position is also affected by the weight of the connection between bias and $G3$.
- **Trapezoid:** A trapezoid is constructed similar to a triangle by changing the weights of several connections, in order for $G3$ to "intersect" the patterns of $G1$ and $G2$ in a way that forms a trapezoid (at the correct angle and position) rather than a triangle.

5.2   Compiling Regularities

A user can assign a specific set of patterns on some of the shape primitives (the ellipsis and the rhombus at the time of writing). The current interface allows primitives to be reflected along the vertical axis at the middle of the canvas (symmetry); alternatively the user can create multiple instances of a selected shape along the vertical axis (repetition), and optionally create a symmetrical array or have variation in the multiple instances.

- **Symmetry:** An important regularity in natural systems from human faces to animal bodies is symmetry. Symmetry along the y-axis can be compiled into a CPPN by applying an absolute function to the x coordinate before feeding it into $G1$.
- **Repetition:** Repetition of an ellipsis or rhombus can be compiled into a CPPN via a sine function. In the current version of DrawCompileEvolve, repetition along the y-axis can be encoded by applying a sine function on the y coordinate before it is input to $G2$ when drawing ellipses or rhombi. The frequency of the sine function determines how many copies of the primitive are shown on the canvas, and the distance between repeated primitives; the weight of the bias to the sine function determines the placement along the y axis of the sequence of primitives.
- **Repetition with symmetry:** The CPPN representation naturally allows the combination of repetition and symmetry by combining an absolute function (symmetry) and a sine function (repetition) in a manner depicted in Fig. 4a.

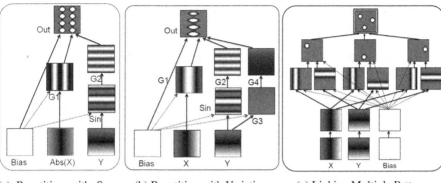

(a) Repetition with Symmetry   (b) Repetition with Variation   (c) Linking Multiple Patterns

Fig. 4. Compiling regularities into CPPN representations.

- **Repetition with variation:** Repetition with variation is another fundamental regularity evident throughout nature (e.g. human fingers and toes, fern leaves, etc.). Repetition is compiled in the CPPN via the sine function; variation is introduced with the addition of two Gaussian nodes: $G3$ (using the y coordinate and the bias as inputs) and $G4$ (using the output of $G3$ as input). The weight of the connection between the bias node and $G3$ controls the variation of the output pattern, e.g. from small to large and vice versa.
- **Linking primitives:** Linking multiple primitives allows the user to group multiple pattern encodings into a single network. As the primitives initially share the weights from the same input nodes, mutations on the connections from the original input nodes may affect multiple primitives simultaneously [14]. As shown in Fig. 4c, linking multiple primitives requires that the creation of a copy of all input nodes (via an identity function), and the patterns' sizes and positions are normalized (in a similar way as individual ellipses of Fig. 3a) before they are combined in the final output node.

6 Experiment

The web interface and persistent database of DrawCompileEvolve allows for any number of users to interact with the tool and evolve their own or others' creations. Creations included in this paper are collected primarily from early tests and internal trials. As the tool gains traction, it is expected that much more diverse and unexpected creations will be collected, and more branching from such images will occur by a growing community of users. As the web-based tool can be updated on-the-fly, future versions will likely include additions discussed in Sect. 8 to improve the quality of results.

Experimental Parameters: Because CPPN-NEAT differs from original NEAT only in its set of activation functions, it uses the same parameters [10]. Offspring had a 20 % chance of link weight mutation, 10 % chance of link addition, and 7 % chance of node addition. The available CPPN activation functions were sigmoid, Gaussian, absolute value, cosine, and sine, all with equal probability of being added.

The compiled CPPNs (in their current state) have one brightness output. Because hue and saturation are set to fixed values (-2.0, -0.5), a different brightness value will produce different RGB colors. Currently, the color values of the original image are disregarded and instead chosen so that overlapping shapes have different colors, making them discernible.

7   Results

Figure 5 shows an indicative set of drawn SVG images which are compiled into CPPNs and displayed back to the user. The compiler seems to more or less faithfully represent the original shapes' position, rotation and outline, and maintains symmetry (e.g. the third image in Fig. 5). The corners of triangles and rectangles appear softer in the CPPN image, which is not surprising given the smooth activation functions used (e.g. Gaussian and sine functions). Additionally, the proportions of shapes in the CPPN encoded images can sometimes vary slightly from the original image. These discrepancies are due to the CPPN's non-linear mapping from input to output values (which could potentially be compensated for in the future).

Acting as a seed for interactive evolution, the CPPN versions of user drawings can quickly generate interesting alternatives to the original drawing via interactive evolution. For instance, within five generations the duck in Fig. 6 is transformed into a chicken. There is an interesting underlying reason for the transformational power of DrawCompileEvolve: unlike Picbreeder creations evolved "from scratch", users of DrawCompileEvolve ascribe specific semantic attributes to the otherwise abstract shapes they are drawing. In the case of Fig. 6, the light gray triangle is a beak while the darker triangle is a foot (despite both shapes being of the same shape and size). After five generations, some of the

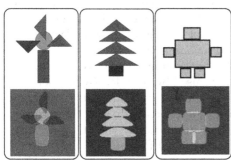

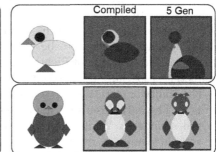

Fig. 5. Indicative user-created SVG images and corresponding CPPN images.

Fig. 6. Starting from a user's drawing, a chicken is evolved from a duck, and an ant from a penguin in five generations.

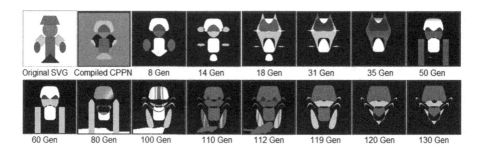

Fig. 7. When symmetry is maintained, one life-like artifact is transformed into another.

shapes have new semantic attributes: the beak is still there, but the foot has been converted into a wing. This transformation leads to diagrammatic lateral thinking, enhancing the users' creativity as they evolve their creations [15].

Interactive evolution can fundamentally change the user's image by moving, transforming and recoloring existing shapes and by adding new shapes and background elements. While the user is in control of the process, it was observed that users tend to prefer to evolve the more radically different images among those presented in Picbreeder. Some additional criteria for user selection were often (a) whether the evolved image represented real-world objects (e.g. a chicken or a face) and (b) whether it retained the semantic attributes of the original image (e.g. whether the evolved image of Fig. 6 still had a beak, or represented an animal).

While CPPNs can evolve into more complex and colorful images, some of the patterns were more persistent across generations of interactive evolution than others. Specifically, the symmetry compiled into the CPPN via the "symmetry" option of the drawing interface (see Fig. 2a) was maintained even after more than 100 generations (e.g. in Fig. 7). Although less pronounced, repetition (including repetition with symmetry as in Fig. 8 and repetition with variation as in Fig. 9) often persisted for many generations. There are likely two reasons for the persistence of these two features (as opposed to the individual ellipses in cases such as Fig. 6). It is likely that the CPPN-Compiler itself biases this behavior by directly connecting the absolute function (for symmetry) and the sine functions (for repetition) to the input nodes, thereby reducing the likelihood of node additions through NEAT which would disrupt symmetry. A secondary reason is that symmetry is likely to be preferred among asymmetrical alternatives in the interactive evolution of Picbreeder, due to the human cognitive bias towards symmetry—especially the vertical symmetry used by the CPPN-Compiler.

The ability of vertical symmetry to create life-like visual artifacts is evidenced in Fig. 7. The initial user drawing represented a human body with the necessary vertical symmetry. While the legs promptly disappear by the 8th generation, the vertical symmetry remains and eventually the CPPN image evolves into the face of a cat at generations 31–35. Further evolution retains vertical symmetry (although generations 80–112 include an asymmetrical feature at the bottom) and the CPPN image transforms into a gasmask head (at generation 60) and eventually into a spider at generation 130.

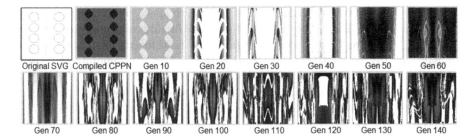

Fig. 8. Repetition with symmetry (especially symmetry) is maintained from the user's drawing (first image) and throughout IEC after more than 100 generations.

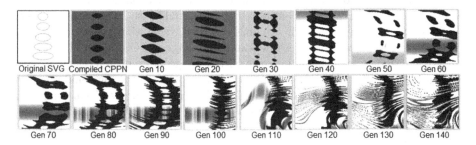

Fig. 9. Repetition with variation is maintained from the user's drawing (first image) and for 30 generations of IEC, before the images diverge to less obvious repetitive patterns.

8   Discussion and Future Work

This study presented the first steps towards creating a mixed-initiative tool that allows users to automatically convert their vector drawings into evolvable representations, which can then be transformed through interactive evolution. There are several extensions to DrawCompileEvolve that would increase its expressivity and its ability to seed interactive evolution with desirable artifacts. Firstly, the CPPN-compiler could be enhanced to represent symmetry, repetition and related patterns along any axis (vertical, horizontal or diagonal). Due to the normalization of input when positioning rectangles, triangles and trapezoids within the CPPN-Compiler, groupings of Sect. 5.2 cannot work with those primitives; future work should address this limitation. Moreover, the accuracy of the compiler when dealing with multiple patterns and shapes could be enhanced, as linking primitives is less likely to represent the grouped shapes precisely. Finally, an important addition to DrawCompileEvolve is the carryover of color from SVG image to CPPN image: allowing the user to specify the color of each shape in the CPPN-Compiler would greatly enhance the user's creative control over the initial artifacts of the Picbreeder applet.

Additionally, in the future it will be important to more closely compare the artifacts evolved through a seeded approach with artifacts that are evolved from scratch. Seeding the initial population with meaningful images creates an evolutionary bias towards certain parts of the search space. While results in this paper show that it is possible to transform one life-like artifact into another (Fig. 7), an important question is how far these transformation can go and if a longer running interaction with DrawCompileEvolve can generate the same breadth of image motifs as a system like Picbreeder [1].

Beyond two-dimensional drawings and evolutionary art, however, the principle of compiling user input into CPPNs can be applied to a variety of domains. Using the same drawing tool and treating the image as a heightmap, game terrain can be drawn by a human designer and (interactively) evolved by a computational designer in a similar manner to Sentient World [13]. The user can draw elliptical lakes (transformed into areas of very low altitude on the 3D terrain) or a repetitive pattern of mountains (transformed from rhombi into high altitude points of the 3D terrain); potentially, the user could also "paint" more than height values on the map, such as climate ranges, vegetation types or temperature maps. Other variants of DrawCompileEvolve can be used for the mixed-initiative design of agent behaviors: the CPPN image can represent the mapping between a range of sensors of a robot controller (input) and its angle and velocity (output). Since such a mapping is less intuitive than a purely visual imagistic representation, the users can observe the resulting simulated robot behaviors in real-time, providing insights into the effects of different changes in the mapping in a similar fashion to BrainCrafter [16].

9   Conclusion

This paper presented DrawCompileEvolve, a mixed-initiative drawing tool which allows users to seed interactive evolution with primitives and patterns that they find desirable. The drawing interface allows users to define a meaningful, visually appealing and personalized inspiration piece; this inspiration piece can then be further refined or transformed via the Picbreeder interactive evolutionary interface. Transforming vector art to CPPN images is accomplished via a CPPN-Compiler [14], which has been significantly refined and enhanced within DrawCompileEvolve. Early results have demonstrated the expressivity of CPPNs when directly controlled by human artists, as well as the power of interactive evolution to transform one semantically meaningful image, provided by the human user, into another equally meaningful image created by the algorithm.

Acknowledgments. We would like to thank the users of DrawCompileEvolve for their contributions. The research was supported, in part, by the FP7 ICT project C2Learn (project no: 318480) and by the FP7 Marie Curie CIG project AutoGameDesign (project no: 630665).

References

1. Secretan, J., Beato, N., D'Ambrosio, D.B., Rodriguez, A., Campbell, A., Folsom-Kovarik, J.T., Stanley, K.O.: Picbreeder: a case study in collaborative evolutionary exploration of design space. Evol. Comput. **19**, 373–403 (2011)

2. Clune, J., Lipson, H.: Evolving three-dimensional objects with a generative encoding inspired by developmental biology. In: Proceedings of the European Conference on Artificial Life (2011)
3. Risi, S., Lehman, J., D'Ambrosio, D., Hall, R., Stanley, K.O.: Introducing a marketplace for evolved content in the petalz social video game. In: Proceedings of the AAAI Conference on Artificial Intelligence and Interactive Digital Entertainment (2012)
4. Liapis, A., Yannakakis, G.N., Togelius, J.: Adapting models of visual aesthetics for personalized content creation. IEEE Trans. Comput. Intell. AI Games **4**(3), 213–228 (2012)
5. Hastings, E., Guha, R., Stanley, K.O.: NEAT particles: design, representation, and animation of particle system effects. In: Proceedings of the IEEE Symposium on Computational Intelligence and Games (2007)
6. Hoover, A., Szerlip, P., Stanley, K.O.: Generating musical accompaniment through functional scaffolding. In: Proccedings of the Sound and Music Computing Conference (2011)
7. Hoover, A., Rosario, M.P., Stanley, K.O.: Scaffolding for interactively evolving novel drum tracks for existing songs. In: Proceedings of the European Workshop on Evolutionary and Biologically Inspired Music, Sound, Art and Design (2008)
8. Takagi, H.: Interactive evolutionary computation: fusion of the capabilities of EC optimization and human evaluation. Proc. IEEE **89**(9), 1275–1296 (2001)
9. Stanley, K.O.: Compositional pattern producing networks: a novel abstraction of development. Genet. Program. Evolvable Mach. **8**(2), 131–162 (2007)
10. Stanley, K.O., Miikkulainen, R.: Evolving neural networks through augmenting topologies. Evol. Comput. **10**(2), 99–127 (2002)
11. Liapis, A., Martínez, H.P., Togelius, J., Yannakakis, G.N.: Adaptive game level creation through rank-based interactive evolution. In: Proceedings of the IEEE Conference on Computational Intelligence and Games (CIG) (2013)
12. Clune, J., Chen, A., Lipson, H.: Upload any object and evolve it: injecting complex geometric patterns into CPPNs for further evolution. In: Proceedings of the IEEE Congress on Evolutionary Computation (2013)
13. Liapis, A., Yannakakis, G.N., Togelius, J.: Sentient world: human-based procedural cartography. In: Machado, P., McDermott, J., Carballal, A. (eds.) EvoMUSART 2013. LNCS, vol. 7834, pp. 180–191. Springer, Heidelberg (2013)
14. Risi, S.: A compiler for CPPNs: transforming phenotypic descriptions into genotypic representations. In: Proceedings of the AAAI Fall Symposium Series (2013)
15. Yannakakis, G.N., Liapis, A., Alexopoulos, C.: Mixed-initiative co-creativity. In: Proceedings of the 9th Conference on the Foundations of Digital Games (2014)
16. Risi, S., Zhang, J., Taarnby, R., Greve, P., Piskur, J., Liapis, A., Togelius, J.: The case for a mixed-initiative collaborative neuroevolution approach. In: Proceedings of the ALIFE Workshop on Artificial Life and the Web (2014)

Author Index

Printed in the United States
By Bookmasters